TAKING STOCK OF BONHOEFFER

For DGH

*wie eine Burg, in die nach Gefahr und Verwirrung
der Geist zurückkehrt,
in der er Zuflucht, Zuspruch und Stärkung findet,
ist dem Freunde der Freund.*

*Like a fortress, where the spirit returns
after confusion and danger,
finding refuge, comfort, and strength,
such is the friend to the friend.*

Dietrich Bonhoeffer, 1945
(DBW 8, p. 588; DBWE 8, p. 529)

Taking Stock of Bonhoeffer
Studies in Biblical Interpretation and Ethics

STEPHEN J. PLANT
Trinity Hall, Cambridge, UK

ASHGATE

Published by
Ashgate Publishing Limited
Wey Court East
Union Road
Farnham
Surrey, GU9 7PT
England

Ashgate Publishing Company
110 Cherry Street
Suite 3-1
Burlington, VT 05401-3818
USA

www.ashgate.com

British Library Cataloguing in Publication Data
A catalogue record for this book is available from the British Library.

The Library of Congress has cataloged the printed edition as follows:
Library of Congress data has been applied for.

ISBN 9781409441052 (hbk)
ISBN 9781409441069 (pbk)
ISBN 9781409441076 (ebk – PDF)
ISBN 9781409471196 (ebk – ePUB)

Printed in the United Kingdom by Henry Ling Limited,
at the Dorset Press, Dorchester, DT1 1HD

Contents

Preface

With the exception of Chapter 1, which is published here for the first time, the essays collected in this volume have all been published before. These essays represent over two decades of my engagement with Bonhoeffer's life and writings: I wrote the first as a research student in 1988 and the last was published in 2013.

I first read Bonhoeffer for an undergraduate essay in 1985. Knowing a little of Bonhoeffer's reputation I invested in a copy of his *Letters and Papers from Prison*. The day before my essay was due in I had an appointment to have injections in preparation for a trip to the Indian subcontinent (a trip, I did not know at the time, that Bonhoeffer longed to make in the days before air travel made it possible for a student to do in his Christmas vacation). At the Tropical Diseases Clinic I reached the beautiful and startlingly creative letters written by Bonhoeffer in July 1944. I was, at this point, in the second year of a degree in theology; but I date my theological awakening from this moment. Something in Bonhoeffer's letters took hold of all my attention and I missed my name being called. After rescheduling my appointment I read on well into the night and finished the book at a single sitting.

Nonetheless, Bonhoeffer was not my first choice of topic when I came to frame a proposal for doctoral research in 1987. I worked on Gregory of Nyssa for half a year before changing to Bonhoeffer. At that time, to the best of my knowledge, I was one of only two students undertaking Bonhoeffer research in the UK (the other was the late Jörg Rades at St Andrew's, from whom I learned a great deal). Bonhoeffer was damned by association at that time with the radical theologies of the 1960s and was regarded by many as theological 'fast-food', his writings not substantial enough as objects of serious study. The revival of interest in his work is in large part a result of the publication between 1986 and 1999 of the 17-volume *Dietrich Bonhoeffer Werke* by Chr. Kaiser Verlag and, from 1996, of the 16-volume *Dietrich Bonhoeffer Works in English*. But it is also and more simply because, while other theologians and theological fashions have come and gone, Bonhoeffer's theology has continued to speak urgent and important truths to the Church and the world.

Because these essays span over two decades, changes in my writing style, my understanding of Bonhoeffer and my personal theological perspective are observable in them. Yet, as I considered collecting them together, I was struck by common focal points, particularly Bonhoeffer's use of the Bible and his commitment to making connections between theology and ethics. In my doctoral studies I tried – unsuccessfully in the main – to write about both these subjects and they have continued to occupy me since that first reading at the clinic in Birmingham, to the present moment. The essays differ further with respect to the varied audiences for whom they were written, from the simple bold brush-strokes suited to a national broadsheet newspaper, to the much more technical and painstaking writing suitable for a German academic volume. Through them all, I can see the extent to which I have been Bonhoeffer's theological apprentice.

The most obvious question facing a writer collecting such diverse texts is the extent to which they should be revised; the answer that has seemed most sensible in this case is: 'as little as possible'! I have, therefore, limited myself to changes of two kinds in re-presenting these essays. Firstly, I have updated all references to and all translations of Bonhoeffer's writings to either the DBW or the DBWE or to both. This is not only because the new editions in German and English are of the finest quality taken as a whole, but because it makes sense to help readers chase up references in the most recent editions.

The second type of change I have made is to take out, for the sake of clarity, any references that made sense in the context in which the essay first appeared but will not make sense in this new context. Otherwise I have left the essays exactly as they first appeared, with all their blemishes.

Over the years I have worked on these essays I have incurred more intellectual and personal debts than I can properly acknowledge, but I want to single two out. In June 1989, shortly before the 'changes' that would end with the unification of Germany, I visited the late Dr Martin Kuske in Teterow, a pretty little town in Mecklenberg-Western Pomerania. Dr Kuske was the author of an important monograph on Bonhoeffer's understanding and use of the Old Testament that opened several avenues of enquiry for me. Dr Kuske was a busy man but parted with his day off to spend it with me – though at the time my German was poor and his English even poorer. Together we went to Güstrow, some 20 miles away, where we visited the Ernst Barlach centre and the Güstrower Dom. This was my first encounter with the work of Ernst Barlach (1870–1938) and it left a permanent mark on my imagination. Barlach, like Bonhoeffer, fell foul of Nazi ideology when his work was condemned as degenerate in 1937; 381 pieces of his work were compulsorily removed from German galleries and museums and many were destroyed. A number churches also removed war memorials by Barlach. Among the pieces I saw with Martin Kuske was the *Lesender Klosterschüler*, carved from wood in 1930. This calmingly symmetrical carving is of a novice reading a book alone (might it be the Bible?) with complete attention and composure. In 1932 Barlach cast in bronze *Lesende Mönche* (now in the Chicago Art Institute) in which two monks read and discuss a book together. As Bonhoeffer knew, reading the Bible alone and reading it together are both essential parts of the Christian life. This, taken together with my memory of the wisdom and generosity of Martin Kuske, explains the choice of cover for this book.

Without doubt the individual who has taught me most about Bonhoeffer is Clifford J. Green. I got to know him first in Heidelberg in the summer of 1990 when he was working on the manuscripts of Bonhoeffer's *Ethics* for the new volume 6 in the *Dietrich Bonhoeffer Werke*. While he really worked on the manuscripts I tried hard to appear to work on them while in fact struggling to read a word of

Bonhoeffer's distinctive handwriting. At the end of the day we would drink gins and tonic – something else Clifford introduced me to. He is a remarkable scholar whose selfless work to make Bonhoeffer's writings available in texts of the very highest quality in both German and English has done so much to make possible the work of others on Bonhoeffer's theology.

In connection with this particular volume I am grateful to Sarah Lloyd at Ashgate for her encouragement and to Nicola J. Wilkes, who helped prepare essays in different formats for republication in a single format. Work on this book was completed during a term's research leave from Trinity Hall, Cambridge and I am grateful to the Master and Fellows of the College for permission to take my leave and to the Revd Roger Greeves for acting as Dean while I was away. While preparing the manuscript for this book the remarkable Dennis Avery died. Amongst many generous benefactions to international charities, educational institutions, research and the arts, Dennis endowed the Runcie Fellowship, of which I am the current holder at Trinity Hall, Cambridge. Dennis Avery's generosity therefore literally made this book possible. On a more personal note I thank my wife Kirsty Smith and our children Caleb and Leah who give me ground beneath my feet.

This book is dedicated to my friend David Horrell, Professor of New Testament Studies at the University of Exeter. We were next-door neighbours when we were both Cambridge research students and frequently talked about the Bible and ethics over our morning '*café pause*'. Our conversations have continued on these topics and many others for more than a quarter of a century and I am glad now to take this opportunity to thank him for his friendship.

Stephen J. Plant

Acknowledgements

All the chapters published in this volume appear with permission of the original publishers. I am grateful to my publishers and former publishers for their cooperation.

1. Previously unpublished.
2. 'Faith, political duty and one man's costly grace', news article in *The Times* marking the centenary of Bonhoeffer's birth, published 4 February 2006.
3. 'How Theologians Decide: German Theologians on the Eve of Nazi Rule', in M. Forward, S. Plant and S. White (eds), *A Great Commission: Christian Hope and Religious Diversity* (Oxford: Peter Lang, 2000), pp. 147–65.
4. '"In the Bible it is God who speaks": Peake and Bonhoeffer on reading Scripture', *Epworth Review* (October 2006): 7–22.
5. '"Jonah" Guilt and Promise', in Bernd Wannenwetsch (ed.), *Who am I?: Bonhoeffer's Theology through His Poetry* (London: T&T Clark, 2009), pp. 198–212.
6. 'The Evangelization of Rulers: Bonhoeffer's Political Theology', in Keith L. Johnson and Timothy Larsen (eds), *Bonhoeffer, Christ and Culture* (Downers Grove, IL: IVP, 2013).
7. 'Ethics and Materialist Hermeneutics', in W.W. Floyd and C. Marsh (eds), *Theology and the Practice of Responsibility* (Valley Forge, PA: Trinity Press International, 1994), pp. 107–15.
8. 'The sacrament of ethical reality: Dietrich Bonhoeffer on ethics for Christian citizens', *Studies in Christian Ethics*, 18/3 (December 2005): 49–69.
9. 'Bonhoeffer's interfaith encounters', *Discernment* [British Council of Churches] (1988): 19–23.
10. 'In the sphere of the familiar: Heidegger and Bonhoeffer', in Peter Frick (ed.), *Bonhoeffer's Intellectual Formation: Theology and Philosophy in His Thought* (Tübingen: Mohr Siebeck, 2008), pp. 301–27.
11. 'Reading Bonhoeffer in Britain', in R.K. Wüstenberg (ed.), *Dietrich Bonhoeffer lessen im internationalen Kontext: Von Südafrika bis Südostasien* (Frankfurt-am-Main: Peter Lang, 2007), pp. 117–33.

Abbreviations

German Primary Literature

Dietrich Bonhoeffer Werke, Bd.1–17, Hrsg. von Eberhard Bethge, Ernst Feil, Christian Gremmels, Wolfgang Huber, Hans Pfeifer, Albrecht Schönherr, Heinz-Eduard Tödt, Ilse Tödt, München 1986–1991, Gütersloh 1992–1999.

DBW 8 – *Widerstand und Ergebung*, Hrsg. von Christian Gremmels, Eberhard Bethge und Renate Bethge in Zussamenarbeit mit Ilse Tödt (Gütersloh, 1998).

DBW 11 – *Ökumene, Universität, Pfarramt 1931–1932*, Hrsg. von Eberhard Amelung und Christoph Strohm (München, 1994).

DBW 13 – *London 1933–1935*, Hrsg. von Hans Goedeking, Martin Heimbucher und Hans-Walter Schleicher (Gütersloh, 1994).

DBW 14 – *Illegale Theologenausbildung: Finkenwalde 1935–1937*, Hrsg. von Otto Dudzus und Jürgen Henkys (Gütersloh, 1996).

English Primary Literature

DBWE Dietrich Bonhoeffer Works, General Editor: Victoria J. Barnett, Executive Director: Clifford J. Green, Minneapolis: Fortress Press, 1996–2014.

DBWE 1 – *Sanctorum Communio*, ed. Clifford J. Green (Minneapolis, 1998).

DBWE 2 – *Act and Being*, ed. Wayne Whitson Floyd, Jr. (Minneapolis, 1996).

DBWE 3 – *Creation and Fall*, ed. John W. de Gruchy (Minneapolis, 2004).

DBWE 4 – *Discipleship*, ed. John D. Godsey and Geffrey B. Kelly (Minneapolis, 2003).

DBWE 5 – *Life Together/Prayerbook of the Bible*, ed. Geffrey B. Kelly (Minneapolis, 2004).

DBWE 6 – *Ethics*, ed. Clifford J. Green (Minneapolis, 2004).

DBWE 7 – *Fiction from Tegel Prison*, ed. Clifford J. Green (Minneapolis, 1999).

DBWE 8 – *Letters and Papers from Prison*, ed. John W. de Gruchy (Minneapolis, 2010).

DBWE 9 – *The Young Bonhoeffer 1918–1927*, ed. Paul Duane Matheny, Clifford J. Green and Marshall D. Johnson (Minneapolis, 2003).

DBWE 10 – *Barcelona, Berlin, New York 1928–1931*, ed. Clifford J. Green (Minneapolis, 2008).

DBWE 11 – *Ecumenical, Academic, and Pastoral Work: 1931–1932*, ed. Michael Lukens with Victoria J. Barnett and Mark S. Brocker (Minneapolis, 2012).

DBWE 12 – *Berlin, 1932–1933*, ed. Larry L. Rasmussen (Minneapolis, 2009).

DBWE 13 – *London, 1933–1935*, ed. Keith W. Clements (Minneapolis, 2007).
DBWE 15 – *Theological Education Underground: 1937–1940*, ed. Victoria J. Barnett (Minneapolis, 2012).
DBWE 16 – *Conspiracy and Imprisonment 1940–1945*, ed. Mark S. Brocker (Minneapolis, 2006).

Secondary Literature

DB-EB – Eberhard Bethge, *Dietrich Bonhoeffer: A Biography*, revised edition, revised and edited by Victoria J. Barnett (Minneapolis, 2000).
All biblical citations are from the New Revised Standard Version (NRSV) Anglicised edition (Oxford, 1998).

Nineteen forty-three, Tegel prison, Berlin.
I picture a face superimposed on a grille:
first widening of a smile, the mooning hairline,
something plump and composed, relentless will.
Time-servers slide; many in their armchairs
rage. Call them opters-out or captives.
Success makes history, I hear him say. *There's
no out. How will another generation live?*
The question echoes on: yardstick of ambition,
our spirit-level. Hanged Flossenbürg camp,
April of forty-five. Dietrich Bonhoeffer,
Like an eavesdropper, I glean smuggled wisdom.
Sometimes, it was piano wire – slower than hemp.
Suffer them in the light of what they suffer.[1]

Micheal O'Siadhail

[1] From 'Perspectives', in Micheal O'Siadhail, *Collected Poems* (Northumberland: Bloodaxe Books, 2013), reprinted here by kind permission of the author and of Bloodaxe Books.

PART I
Historical Context

Chapter 1
Bonhoeffer and Moltke: Politics and Faith in a Time of Crisis

Introduction: Letters from Tegel Prison

I fear this chapter will please no one. Historians will recognise it as the work of an amateur while theologians will find the doctrinal fruits meagerly distributed through the historical dough. Perhaps such dissatisfaction is inevitable when one engages with political theology from the perspective of its role in concrete historical events. This is certainly the case in connection with the role of theology in the two circles of opposition to Nazi misrule with which this chapter is concerned: the Canaris conspiracy and the Kreisau Circle.

On 29 September 1944 Helmuth James Graf von Moltke was moved from Ravensbrück concentration camp to the forbiddingly named *Totenhaus* wing of Tegel prison in Berlin. From here, Moltke wrote his first letter to his wife Freya Gräfin von Moltke, one of only two women members of the Kreisau Circle. The correspondence continued until the morning of 23 January 1945, the day on which Helmuth was hanged. Though the voluminous early correspondence between the Moltkes had been published in 1988,[1] the final letters remained unpublished until after Freya's death in 2010, reflecting the clear historical importance of the former and the highly personal nature of the later letters. In his review of *Abschiedsbriefe Gefängins Tegel*[2] in the *Times Literary Supplement*[3] Christophe Fricker fairly sums up the book's contribution: 'The couple's letters offer insight into their thinking in the face of both imminent National Socialist defeat and the failure of their resistance group.' Yet Fricker opens his review with a puzzling assessment of the letters' value: 'The collection is unique: no other member of the resistance was able to write such a substantial number of letters from prison.'

---

[1]   Helmuth James von Moltke, *Letters to Freya: A Witness against Hitler*, English edn, ed. Beata Ruhm von Oppen (London, 1991).

[2]   Helmuth Caspar von Moltke and Ulrike von Moltke (eds), *Helmuth James und Freya von Moltke Abschiedsbriefe Gefängins Tegel September 1944–January 1945* (München, 2010).

[3]   Christophe Fricker, 'Whether we live or die', *Times Literary Supplement*, 16 September 2011, pp. 8–9.

Fricker's comment is odd because at least one other resister did write a substantial number of letters from prison, and both the letters[4] and their author are well-known. By the time Moltke was being taken to his cell in Tegel prison Dietrich Bonhoeffer had already been held there for well over 19 months. Only a few days later however, on 8 October, Bonhoeffer was taken to the cells in the basement of Gestapo headquarters in Prinz Albrecht Strasse. But between April 1943 and October 1944 Bonhoeffer had sent a weekly letter via the prison censor and many more smuggled by a friendly guard; more than 100 of his letters from Tegel survive and we know a number were lost. After 8 October the Gestapo permitted Bonhoeffer only two further letters and there was no more chance for him to smuggle letters before he was taken from Berlin via several concentration camps en route to his execution at Flossenbürg on 9 April 1945 alongside his fellow conspirators Admiral Canaris and Brigadier Hans Oster.

In Tegel Bonhoeffer was held incommunicado. The prison chaplain, Harold Poelchau, a close friend and collaborator of Moltke's who risked his life to smuggle letters between the Silesian count and countess, was in theory forbidden to visit Bonhoeffer, though in fact he did manage to do so once or twice, commissioning from him the morning and evening prayers Bonhoeffer wrote for fellow prisoners. Yet, though Bonhoeffer and Moltke did not meet during the brief period they both occupied Tegel cells, they had met before Bonhoeffer's arrest. Moltke first reports meeting Dietrich and his brother Klaus in Berlin on 23 January 1942 when they discussed opposing Hitler; they began at 7.00 p.m. and did not part company until well after midnight. On 10 April 1942 Moltke and Bonhoeffer, at short notice, travelled together through neutral Sweden into German occupied Norway. The two men were officially emissaries of German Military Intelligence whose ostensible task was to report on the struggle that had flared up in February between the German army of occupation and the Lutheran Church in Norway. As members of overlapping circles of the resistance their real task, however, was to stiffen the backbone of the opposition, a task in which they were successful – indeed the very effective strike of Norwegian pastors was exactly what Bonhoeffer had unsuccessfully proposed in Germany in 1933. Moltke's letters to Freya during his Scandinavian journey suggest he and Bonhoeffer worked efficiently in tandem, but convey no particular warmth between them. Eberhard Bethge, who met Bonhoeffer following his return to Germany on 18 April, recalls that Bonhoeffer's 'few days with Helmuth von Moltke had made quite an impression on him'. Bethge's recollection is worth quoting as an introduction to the similarities and differences between the two men and the resistance groups of which they were members, which forms the substance of this chapter. Bethge continues that: 'Moltke was a year younger and had founded the Kreisau group. I cannot remember in detail what Bonhoeffer told

---

[4]   For an engaging account of the reception history of Bonhoeffer's letters see Martin E. Marty, *Dietrich Bonhoeffer's Letters and Papers from Prison: A Biography* (Princeton, 2011).

me about their conversations. We did not yet realize the group's special potential.' What Bethge did remember however, was that Bonhoeffer and Moltke:

> 'were not of the same opinion'. They were united in the depth of their Christian convictions and in their judgment of Germany's desperate position ... But Moltke 'rejected ... for his own part the violent removal of Hitler'. And Bonhoeffer, who already knew that the judgment of God cannot be halted, was already pleading the need for assassination.[5]

In order to think theologically about the similarities and differences hinted at by Bethge, something further needs to be said about the two opposition groups of which Bonhoeffer and Moltke were members. This is, at least in German language historical literature, relatively well-travelled territory and we may gather what we need from published sources. The fresh elements in this chapter consist first, in *comparing* the respective political philosophies of the two groups – which has, surprisingly to me, scarcely been done – and in a brief theological commentary on the differences yielded by that comparison. The comparison affords an instructive illustration for contemporary political theologians of the distance that must be travelled between theological theory and political practice.

The Canaris Conspiracy[6]

Wilhelm Franz Canaris[7] had become head of the Abwehr, German Military Intelligence, in 1933: it was a good appointment. A naval officer since 1905, he had shown a flare for intelligence work during the First World War while a lieutenant aboard SMS *Dresden* when he built up a network of informants in Latin America that kept his ship one step ahead of the British Royal Navy for several months. In 1915, after the *Dresden* was scuttled during a battle with the British, he was interned in Chile. His heroic and cunning efforts to escape and then to make his way back to Germany established the glamorous reputation that made him a favourite of Hitler's until his arrest.

After the abdication of Kaiser Wilhelm in 1918 Canaris wore the uniform of a republic very reluctantly. His experience of the Weimar Republic confirmed his opinion that democracy was, at least for Germany, bound to lead to weak government. As with many German officers of his generation, Canaris was drawn, rather, to strong government based on a restoration of the monarchy. Until 1940, when the former Kaiser's grandson Prinz Wilhelm of Prussia was killed in action in France, a monarchist state remained a possibility; indeed when 50,000 mourners

---

[5]　DB-EB, p. 755.

[6]　For an overview of the Canaris group see Roger Manvell and Heinrich Fraenkel, *The Canaris Conspiracy: The Secret Resistance to Hitler in the German Army* (London, 1969).

[7]　For biographical details see Heinz Höhne, *Canaris* (London, 1979).

attended the Prince's funeral, the Nazis banned members of former German royal families from serving in the military to prevent another royal candidate from potentially establishing rival military connections. Canaris was, therefore, a liberal of the right, profoundly opposed to socialism: a patriot but committed to the rule of law. To begin with, Canaris saw Adolf Hitler, as did a majority of Germans, as the saviour of the German people. Canaris was convinced of Hitler's soldierly qualities of honour, duty, self-sacrifice and courage.[8] It took some time before Canaris saw through the brutish, illegal and self-serving elements of Hitler and his party.

Very quickly after 1933 the army became the only force in Germany not fully infiltrated by Nazis, and therefore the only body capable of meaningful opposition. Yet within the army, senior officers with little instinctive sympathy for Hitler were bought off by the policy of rearmament, and with blandishments such as estates. Many took seriously their personal oath of loyalty to the Führer. After the astonishing German victories in Poland, Norway and France a coup became out of the question for an army reared on the myth of the stab in the back as an explanation for German defeat in 1918. Nonetheless, Canaris acted where he could in what he took to be the national interest. Evidence is strong that Canaris played an important role in persuading General Franco to keep Spain out of the war; he certainly found a way to warn France on the eve of German invasion. Canaris was playing a long game. He recruited to the ranks of the Abwehr a number of like-minded men, including Colonel (later Brigadier) Hans Oster, another patriotic monarchist. Canaris also employed Bonhoeffer's brother-in-law Hans von Dohnanyi as a legal adviser. Dohnanyi had shown little interest in politics before the war but had been convinced of the hazards Nazism posed when an unpleasant investigation into his ancestry revealed a Jewish grandparent. As much as anything, he was driven by strong Christian convictions, and was consequently fearful of the prospect of the Bolshevisation of Europe should Germany lose the war which, after the invasion of Russia in 1941, he thought inevitable.

From the outbreak of war members of the Canaris group began systematically collecting evidence of war crimes with a view to mounting prosecutions after the end of hostilities. Yet assassinating Hitler was easier said than done, even with access to military intelligence, because Hitler did not allow armed men in his presence and changed his travel plans daily. In any case, killing Hitler had to be accompanied by an organised seizure of power. After several abortive or unsuccessful attempts, Oster recruited Claus Schenk Graf von Stauffenberg on the principle that if the Generals would not act the Colonels would have to step up to the mark. After the failure of the July 1944 bomb plot vigorous investigation by the Gestapo eventually came across the files kept by Dohnanyi and Oster on war crimes for which there was no innocent explanation. Canaris and Oster were executed on the same gallows as Bonhoeffer at Flossenbürg concentration camp; Dohnanyi was hanged at Sachsenhausen on or around the same day. On 8 March

---

[8]   Höhne, *Canaris*, p. 213.

Dohnanyi smuggled a letter to his wife, Bonhoeffer's sister Christel, which gives a succinct account of his own motives and those of the Canaris group: 'What you have been and are to me and the children could have made me one of the happiest men under God's sun. Still, I believe we were right to worry about the fate of others, which makes one become political.'[9]

In contrast with the Kreisau Circle, which, as we will see, devoted its energies to planning a post-war German constitution, the Canaris group expended its energies, first, in recording war crimes and second, in planning a seizure of power. They envisaged a military takeover that would, over a period of several years, gradually release authority to a civilian administration. This military government would, in contrast with the Nazis, respect the rule of law. They hoped to negotiate a cessation of hostilities with the Allies and a restoration of pre-war German territorial boundaries. Even without the benefit of hindsight one may wonder how realistic this possibility was by July 1944. Only a few months later, at the Yalta conference in February 1945, Churchill, Roosevelt and Stalin would agree to partition Germany into the Allied Occupation Zones that would eventually become the two post-war German states. Even in 1944 that must have been the only solution to which the Allies would have agreed.

Bonhoeffer's Contribution

In one sense, Bonhoeffer's contribution to the Canaris group was limited, certainly so compared with that of Dohnanyi, the moral and intellectual backbone of the group. Bonhoeffer's main practical role was to exploit his ecumenical contacts on behalf of the opposition. Much is made of this among Bonhoeffer scholars, but the reality is that the German pastor did not find a welcome for his viewpoint even amongst his friends. Two overseas trips made by Bonhoeffer in May 1942 illustrate the isolation of Bonhoeffer and the Canaris group. From around 12 to 26 May, Bonhoeffer was in Switzerland. There, several former contacts were curious about how a known opponent of the Nazi regime was now able to travel so freely. Bonhoeffer got wind of these suspicions and wrote to Karl Barth openly to ask if it was true that Barth had found his stay 'unsettling as to its objectives'.[10] Though he initially laughed at the rumour, he felt it necessary to confirm that it had no substance. On 17 May Charlotte von Kirschbaum, Barth's assistant, wrote a mollifying reply: 'What a pickle to be in! Above all, please be assured that we too are laughing at this matter, although with tears in our eyes'.[11] Though it was true that Barth had, as Kirschbaum put it, never mistrusted Bonhoeffer for a second, she continues with a very clear statement that Barth did not support the form of opposition planned by the Canaris group of which Bonhoeffer was a part:

---

[9]   Manvell and Fraenkel, *Conspiracy*, p. 218.
[10]   DBWE 16, p. 277.
[11]   Ibid., p. 279.

For Karl Barth there is in fact something 'unsettling', and that is all the attempts
to recue Germany, by means of further 'national' endeavors, from the immense
predicament into which it has now been swept. This also includes the attempts
that may be undertaken if necessary by the generals.[12]

In a 1968 letter Karl Barth himself recalled, even more explicitly, his discussion of
a possible coup with Bonhoeffer:

I still remember, as if it were yesterday, how the hints that Dietrich Bonhoeffer
personally gave me about the venture [the conspiracy to remove Hitler],
that is, about the conversations preceding it, gave me the impression of
something hopelessly passé ... for all my human sympathy for the fate of the
participants ... a dead end which did not seem to offer any light of promise for
the future.[13]

A few days after his return from Switzerland Bonhoeffer was in Sweden where he
met George Bell, Bishop of Chichester. After his return to Britain, Bell passed on
information about German opposition to the British government: the approach got
short shrift. By this stage Bell was held in low regard by the British government
because of his persistent efforts to keep the prosecution of war within moral
boundaries, but the rebuff was not simply to Bell as a troublesome cleric; it was
to the whole idea of resistance within the German army. By 1942, the prospect of
a military coup struck the British as simply too little too late, and as a self-serving
attempt to save the skin of the officers themselves.

We can be sure that Bonhoeffer's own political views were similar to other
members of the Canaris group. Though he had occasionally flirted with socialist
vocabulary – for example in his Christology lectures – Bonhoeffer did not
share his brother Klaus' Social Democratic sympathies. Until it was disbanded
following the Reich Concordat, Dietrich Bonhoeffer had voted for the Catholic
Centre Party. One of the most explicit political remarks he made during the war
occurs in Bonhoeffer's letter in 1941 to his American friend Paul Lehmann. He
foresaw the post-war dominance of the United States, and an uncertain future for
Britain. American domination would be, he continues, 'one of the best solutions'.
The future of Europe was less certain for Bonhoeffer, but this was clear:

What, for instance, of Germany? Nothing would be worse than to impose upon
her any anglosaxon form of government – as much as I should like it. It simply
would not work ... As far as I know Germany, it will just be impossible, for
instance, to restore complete freedom of speech, of press, of association. That
sort of thing would throw Germany into the same abyss. I think we must try to
find a Germany in which justice, lawfulness, freedom of the churches is being

---

12   Ibid., pp. 280–81.
13   Ibid., p. 286, fn.2.

restored. I hope there will be something like an authoritarian 'Rechtsstaat' as the Germans call it.[14]

Note the rather odd juxtaposition, on the one hand, of an authoritarian *Rechtsstaat*, in which freedom of association and of the press was to be severely curtailed and, on the other, the aspiration that there should be freedom of the churches. This is a useful standpoint from which to turn to the extended theological study by Bonhoeffer headed 'A Theological Position Paper on State and Church'. The date of the document is uncertain (probably sometime after April 1941,) and so is its purpose: an assumption it is a position paper for the Reich Council of Brethren, i.e., the leaders of the Confessing Church in Prussia, is plausible, but so is the possibility the document was written for the conspiracy.[15] To anyone familiar with Bonhoeffer's *Ethics*, the vocabulary and concepts used in the essay are strikingly familiar, in particular foreshadowing his accounts of the divine mandates.

Bonhoeffer begins with parallel accounts of the authority of government and of the pastoral office. Government 'is the power set in place by God to exercise worldly rule with divine authority. Government is the vicarious representative action of God on earth. It can only be understood from above. Government does not emerge from the commonwealth; instead, it orders the commonwealth from above'.[16] Bonhoeffer then describes the pastoral office of the Church in deliberately mirroring terms: 'The pastoral office is the power set in place by God to exercise spiritual rule with divine authority. It emerges not from the congregation but from God'.[17] Immediately, it is clear that Bonhoeffer's understanding of the parallel divine origin of the authority of both worldly government and of pastoral officers of the Church is a restatement of Luther's doctrine of the authority of government and Church. What is also clear is that this formulation is a rejection of a Lockean liberal account of the origin of political authority, that is, of political authority rooted in the social contract. Christians and non-Christians are alike subject to government, and Christians and non-Christians are also alike subject to the claim of Jesus Christ to which the pastoral office bears witness. Bonhoeffer then moves to contrast Luther's account of Church and state with that of an Aristotelian and Thomist position. 'Classical antiquity', Bonhoeffer writes, '... grounded the state in *human nature*. The state is the highest perfection of the rational nature of the human being ... All ethics is political ethics. Virtues are political virtues. This grounding of the state has been taken over in principle by Catholic theology.'[18] This natural theological account had also, Bonhoeffer thought, infected some Anglican and also recent Lutheran theology, an infection which he believed needed curing. The contrast Bonhoeffer draws is recognisable to any student of

---

[14] Ibid., pp. 219–20.
[15] Ibid., pp. 502–503.
[16] Ibid., p. 504.
[17] Ibid., p. 505.
[18] Ibid., pp. 505–506.

political theology as one between an Augustinian account of political authority given by God to restrain the effects of the fall, and a Thomist account, which sees in the basic relation of Adam to Eve a prelapsarian, God-given relation of political authority. Bonhoeffer's theological difficulty with it is that a philosophy of the state grounded in human nature is one not grounded in Jesus Christ. In a particularly lapidary formulation Bonhoeffer remarks that 'there is no immediate connection of government to God; Christ is its mediator'.[19] On what basis, then, might a citizen disobey a government? Bonhoeffer argues that a citizen simply may not disobey a government without becoming guilty. He continues:

> Even where the guilt of government [Obrigkeit] is blatantly obvious, the guilt that gave rise to this guilt may not be disregarded. The refusal to obey within a specific historical political decision of the government, as well as this decision itself, can only be ventured of one's own responsibility. A historical decision cannot be completely incorporated into ethical concepts. There is one thing left: the venture of action.[20]

An act of rebellion against a government is also an act of rebellion against God; but that does not mean there are no circumstances in which a person of strong conscience would not decide upon the venture of action, so long as they do not justify that action, for example on utilitarian or situation ethical grounds. The essay concludes with discussion of Church and state relations in the narrow sense.

The Kreisau Circle

The beating heart of the Kreisau Circle was Helmuth James von Moltke.[21] He was the great great nephew of the Field Marshall Moltke who had won victory in the Franco-Prussian War, for which service the Kaiser gave the money with which he bought the Kreisau estate in Silesia: the name Helmuth carried was, therefore, a useful charm to wear in Nazi Germany, one that opened doors. His mother Dorothy was daughter of the Chief Justice of the South African Union and this gave an international dimension to the family's outlook that was formative for Helmuth. Dorothy and Helmuth's father became committed Christian Scientists and translated Mary Baker Eddy's works into German, though they seem not to have made any attempt to indoctrinate their children. Helmuth was the eldest son

---

[19]   Ibid., p. 511.

[20]   Ibid., p. 518. The idea Bonhoeffer is developing here is plainly that of the structure of responsible life, or of vicarious representative action (*Stellvertretung*). This idea was already present in *Sanctorum Communio* (DBWE 1) and is most fully developed in the second version of the section 'History and Good' in the *Ethics* (DBWE 6, pp. 257–89).

[21]   For biographical details see Günther Brakelmann, *Helmuth James von Moltke 1907–1945* (München, 2007).

and had three brothers and a sister. After study in Breslau, Berlin and Oxford he qualified as a lawyer. To facilitate his intended career in international law he sat examinations for the Bar in London, where he became a member of the Inner Temple. Friendships made during his time in Britain were influential in his later political thinking. He married Freya Deichmann in 1931; they had two sons, Helmuth Casper and Konrad.

Moltke held decidedly socialist views in the run up to war, and was involved, for example, in setting up and running work camps which would later become a model for the US Peace Corps. His known opposition to the Nazis removed some career options, but in 1939 Moltke was drafted into German Military Intelligence by Admiral Canaris to work as an international lawyer. His job, strange as this may seem, was to advise on the legality of military actions during the war. A close reading of his letters during the war reveals a man of conscience repeatedly torn by the very limited impact of his attempts to restrain the worst excesses of German war crimes. In October 1941 Moltke writes to Freya 'The realization that what I do is senseless does not stop my doing it, because I am much more firmly convinced than before that only what is done in the full recognition of the senselessness of all action makes any sense at all.'[22] This insight, so thoroughly anti-Pelagian in tone, seems indeed to have been linked to his growing Christian faith. In the same letter Moltke writes that 'I became aware of a change that has taken place in me during the war, which I can only ascribe to a deeper insight into Christian principles …'[23]

During the war, alongside his legal resistance in military intelligence, Moltke began to engage in conversations that would eventually lead to meetings of a Kreisau Circle. To begin with, conversations were held on a small scale with one or two people. Small groups were formed to discuss, for example, agricultural reform, industrial relations, or Church and state. Names of members of one group were withheld from other groups on security grounds. From the outset it was essential that the Kreisau Circle should be as inclusive as possible. Amongst recruits, therefore, were socialists, trades unionists, as well as more conservative members. Christianity was to be essential to all its deliberations, and this meant – again from the beginning – involving not only Protestant but Catholic members also. After work in small groups, larger groups met, mainly near to Berlin but occasionally at Kreisau, from which the group has taken its name. A series of memoranda were agreed by these 'conferences', on topics such as the structure of the state, the economy, foreign policy and the punishment of criminals and of war criminals. The agreed memoranda were then discretely copied and hidden. Two sets survived, one kept by the Jesuits, another hidden in beehives at Kreisau by Freya. At no point did the group agree who would hold post-war positions of power (as, incidentally, the Canaris group had done). They understood their task as being to think clearly about the future. Crucially, assassination was no part of their conversation. Moltke had several reasons why

---

[22] Moltke, *Letters*, p. 170.

[23] Ibid.

he believed an assassination attempt misguided, two of which he related to the Norwegian Bishop Berggrav in 1943. Firstly, he did not think that a post-war German government could command respect if it proceeded from a murder. Secondly, he felt that for security reasons it was important to keep the Kreisau group isolated from other circles of resistance that were developing.[24] Moltke also shared Karl Barth's view that Germany needed to be completely defeated before she could be rebuilt from the foundations upwards; a military coup would in fact halt the destruction needed for rebuilding to begin.

Moltke and others in the group were arrested in January 1944, six months before the bomb plot, on suspicion of engaging in defeatist conversations. Initially, Moltke was optimistic about the outcome of a trial, but after July 1944 he knew that the outcome of his trial would be his execution. In October 1944, knowing his trial and execution were imminent, Moltke wrote a parting letter to his two sons. In it, he said the Nazis were right to kill him, since he stood against everything they stood for:

> Throughout an entire life, even at school, I have fought against a spirit of narrowness and unfreedom, of arrogance and lack of respect for others, of intolerance and the absolute, the merciless consistency among the Germans, which found its expression in the National Socialist state. I exerted myself to help overcome this spirit with its evil consequences, such as excessive nationalism, racial persecution, lack of faith and materialism.[25]

Though the outcome was clear it was important nonetheless to score some points from the President of the People's Court (*Volksgerichtshof*), Roland Freisler, who was already notorious for his hectoring manner in the trial of members of the White Rose group.[26] In an account of his trial written for Freya, Helmuth reports a number of small victories in his exchanges with his judge. Two points in particular were important, and Moltke relished the moments when Freisler conceded them. The first was that the conspirators were not being condemned for something they had done but rather for something they had thought. Moltke pushed home the lack of a direct connection between the Kreisau group and the July 1944 bomb plotters. Moltke writes to Freya with characteristically forensic coolness that:

> The beauty of the judgment on these lines is the following: it is established that we did not want to use any force; it is established that we did not take a single step towards organization, did not talk to a single man about the question of

---

[24] See Ger van Roon, *German Resistance to Hitler: Count von Moltke and the Kreisau Circle* (London, 1971), p. 276.

[25] Moltke, *Letters*, p.3.

[26] With an irony not wasted on opponents of the Nazi regime Freisler was killed in an air raid in 1945, a freak event that also resulted in the escape of some of those he was interrogating.

whether he was willing to take over any post; it read differently in the indictment. We merely thought, and really only Delp, Gerstenmaier and I ... .[27]

The second important point Moltke was keen to score concerned Christianity. Throughout the trial Freisler insisted that the men owed a duty of loyalty to the Führer, while the accused argued they owed a higher duty to God. It was, for Moltke, significant that they stood condemned simply for doing their duty as Christians. Finally, Freisler yelled "'only in one respect are we and Christians alike: we demand the whole man'".[28] Moltke concluded that 'one thought remains: how can Christianity be a sheet-anchor in the chaos?'[29]

The working documents and memoranda of conferences that survived the dissolution of the Kreisau Circle are all highly condensed. From the documents it is possible to gain a sense of the 'mind' of the group on what were the key challenges facing the reconstruction of Germany. In some areas, however, concrete proposals are included that put flesh on the skeleton frame of post-war Germany. Following Ger van Roon's descriptive account of the documents,[30] four key areas of interest emerge from the Kreisau documents. The group were, firstly, concerned with the cultural formation of a post-war Germany. Christian values were to be basic to German reconstruction, and to the reconstruction of Europe, since Christianity was, the group believed, virtually the only source of values that had survived the chaos of world war. Moreover, the group understood that if violent conflict were to be avoided in the future, it was going to be essential to find a basis for sustained peaceful cooperation between the European nations: Christianity offered the best hope for a cultural basis for a peaceful Europe. Under the rubric of cultural policy the group also considered radical proposals for a reformation of further and higher education in Germany. Technical schools were to play an enhanced role. Beyond them, existing higher educational institutions were to be divided into colleges of further education and Reich universities, the former being essentially teaching institutions and the latter focused essentially on research.

Secondly, the group proposed that, in order to decentralise and redistribute political power Germany should be reconstructed at three political levels. The base unit of political power would be locally elected parishes. Members of parish councils would then elect regional governments, which in turn would elect members to a national Reich government. This proposal took into account existing German political structures, but took them a step further in the direction of radical devolution. In terms of political philosophy the insight that this federal system was designed to embody was that 'The purpose of the state is to provide men with

---

[27]   Moltke, *Letters*, p.404.

[28]   Ibid., p.409.

[29]   Ibid., pp. 404–405.

[30]   Roon, *Resistance*.

the freedom that enables them to perceive the natural order and to contribute to its realization'.[31]

Alongside this federal structure, political power was to be further redistributed by the formation of a national German Trade Union, which would represent workers' interests, but also be a significant player in local, regional and national political economic strategy. The churches too were to play a strong independent role.

Thirdly, the group considered economic policy. They judged that:

> the object of economic activity must be to make the individual person freer by liberating him from subordination to the material world. The object must not be to diminish his freedom by replacing his dependence upon the material world by a dependence upon men – a dependence which is just as great when it relates to an employer as to an official.[32]

Finally, and as one would expect of a group in which Moltke took a lead role, the group took on issues in foreign policy. In order to build peace the group believed that future German economic development should be embedded within a European economic and political union:

> Peace brings with it a united European sovereign state, which extends from Portugal to a point as far east as possible ... they [the member nations] would share at least the following: customs frontiers, currency, foreign policy including defence, constitutional authority and, if possible, economic administration.[33]

The roadmap outlined by the 'Kreisauers' here bears a striking relationship to the post-war development of a European Economic Community and subsequently of the European Union.[34] So striking is the resemblance, indeed, that the extent of the direct influence by the Kreisau Circle on German post-war European policy has

---

[31]   Ibid., p. 313.

[32]   The citation is from Moltke's letter to Einsiedel, 16 June 1940, in Roon, *Resistance*, p. 291.

[33]   Roon, *Resistance*, p. 322. The document continues that Britain and its empire might play an intermediary role as a member of the European 'family' of nations and also as a key partner, in an Anglo-Saxon political and cultural alliance, with the United States.

[34]   For a brilliant if tendentious analysis of the political philosophical streams flowing into the European Union, including that originating in Germany, see Larry Siedentop, *Democracy in Europe* (London, 2000). Siedentop's conclusion is, I fear, all too right, namely that '[t]he attraction of federalism, properly understood, for Europe is that it should make possible the survival of different national political cultures and forms of civic spirit ... Federalism is the right goal for Europe. But Europe is not yet ready for federalism', p. 231.

warranted discussion.[35] Moltke believed that in the end ideas had greater influence than actions. If the measure of influence is the extent to which either ideas or actions demonstrably shape subsequent historical developments then it is certainly tempting to consider the possibility that the Kreisau Circle had greater influence on post-war Germany than did the Canaris conspiracy. But it is the impact of *theological* thinking on the broader philosophy of the group to which I now turn.

Alfred Delp's Contribution

As we have noted, the Kreisau Circle was determined to achieve a broad base for post-war Germany, and that meant including both Protestant and Catholic Christians in their work. The biggest Protestant 'player' in the Kreisau Circle was Peter Graf Yorck von Wartenburg who, like Moltke, was a scion of a famous Prussian military family whose family estates lay in Silesia. Yorck was essentially co-founder, with Moltke, of the Kreisau Circle and shared his profound commitment to Christianity and, for Yorck, the Lutheran 'shape' of that faith was especially well defined. Harald Poelchau, who as Tegel prison chaplain smuggled letters between the Moltkes, had studied theology at Bethel before moving to the University of Tübingen. Poelchau was a religious socialist and was keen to see the Christian Church re-engage with workers and slough off its conservative tendencies. His experiences as a prison chaplain convinced him that capital punishment was immoral. He survived the war.

Though the Kreisau Circle involved several Protestant Christians with ability and integrity, none, it is fair to say, were theologically skilled to the highest level. Consequently, the most expert theological contribution to the group's political philosophy came from one of the Catholic members, the Jesuit sociologist and theologian Alfred Delp.[36] Delp, a convert to Catholicism, had been a novice at Stella Matutina at Feldkirch where he formed a close friendship with his Latin teacher, the theologian Karl Rahner. Delp also came under the influence of the 'new' philosophy of Erich Przywara (to which Bonhoeffer paid attention in *Act and Being*). This led to his first book, a study of tragic existence in dialogue with Martin Heidegger. After ordination, Delp worked from 1939 as a sociologist on the staff of the journal *Stimmen der Zeit*. When the Gestapo closed the journal down in 1941, Delp became a parish priest, but this did not save him when finally

---

[35]   See, for example, Gerhard Ringshausen, 'Europa in den Planungen der Kresauer und des Exils', pp. 3–16, and Franz Graf von Schwerin, 'Moltke und Europa', pp. 17–23, in Ulrich Karpen (hg.), *Europas Zukunft: Vorstellungen des Kresauer Kreises um Helmuth James Graf von Moltke* (Heidelberg, 2005).

[36]   For a study of Delp's social philosophy, see Michael Pope, *Alfred Delp S.J. Im Kreisauer Kreis: Die Rechts- und Sozial – Philosophischen Grundlagen in Seinen konceptionen für eine Neuordnung Deutschland* (Mainz, 1994).

the net closed on the Kreisau Circle. In January, 1945 he was tried with Moltke and executed shortly thereafter.

In his study of Delp's legacy Michael Pope comments that identifying the tracks of individual contributors in the documents of the Kreisau Circle is almost impossible as any information identifying individual authors was deliberately kept off the unsigned memoranda.[37] Nevertheless, Pope succeeds in reconstructing Delp's social philosophy on the basis both of his writings before his involvement with the Kreisau Circle and what *is* known of his work in the last period of his life.

Delp's political thinking had its roots in traditions of Catholic social thought stretching back to Pope Leo XIII's encyclical letter *Rerum Novarum*, which signalled a significant change of direction in Catholic thinking on capital and labour.[38] The distinction drawn by Moltke between 'humanist' values that 'find their clearest expression in Christian moral teaching' and are binding on *all* people of good will, and 'the Christian revelation' recognised by Christians alone, is one that is central to Catholic social thought. With Catholic social thinking in the background Delp developed several viewpoints that would shape his input to the Kreisau Circle. First, Delp – like Bonhoeffer[39] – was keen to underscore that human beings were fundamentally social creatures. Delp believed that the genuine community and order essential for human beings is only possible where there is a sense of encounter with the divine, and even where there is a covenant with God to underwrite it.[40] What this meant in practice, for Delp, was a rejection of any political system, any understanding of the state – whether Communist or National Socialist – in which the state overwhelms the individual. In a powerful rhetorical flourish Delp calls this 'the despotism of the crazy we ... the degeneration into the collective'.[41] It is this insight, on the relation of individual and state that would subsequently underwrite the understanding in the Kreisau documents of the primary duty of the state as being to facilitate human flourishing. Take, for example, the first thesis on the relation between the state and the individual in Moltke's memorandum on 'The Foundations of Political Science', which states unequivocally that:

> I believe that the relationship between the state and the individual can be
> expressed in a single sentence: The purpose of the state is to provide men with

---

[37]   Pope, *Delp*, p. 159.

[38]   For an English edition of *Rerum Novarum* see: http://www.vatican.va/holy_ father/leo_xiii/encyclicals/documents/hf_l-xiii_enc_15051891_rerum-novarum_en.html/ Accessed 17 June 12013.

[39]   For this comparison see Clifford J. Green, *Bonhoeffer: A Theology of Sociality*, revised edn (Grand Rapids, 1999).

[40]   Pope, *Delp*, p. 31.

[41]   Cited in Pope, *Delp*, p. 34.

the freedom that enables them to perceive the natural order [a marginal note explains this as 'just order'] and to contribute to its realization.[42]

Though Christianity may be said to provide the only proper basis for such freedom in (political) community, this did not mean, for Delp, that all citizens are or must be Christian. A 'Christian' state too can degenerate into a form of totalitarianism. This view too is echoed in Moltke's memorandum, in which, in a section on the relation between state and faith, Moltke wrote that:

A) There is no such thing as a theological doctrine of the state, only a doctrine of man in the state; there is, therefore, no Christian state.

B) In formulating these basic principles of the state we proceed from the binding principles of the individual's ethics seen as 'humanist' ethics, and independent of the content of the Christian or any other religious revelation …

The ethical principles from which we proceed are 'humanist'. These are certain binding moral doctrines that are valid for all within Western civilization, and which are independent of the Christian revelation even though for the Christian these principles find their clearest expression in Christian moral teaching.[43]

The distinction made by Moltke between, on the one hand, 'humanist' values that 'find their clearest expression in Christian moral teaching' but which are binding on all people of good will, and on the other of 'the Christian revelation' is a distinction central to Catholic social thought. It is not, however, the only idea present in the Kreisau Circle's memoranda that reflect Catholic social thinking: also important is the principle of subsidiarity. Subsidiarity was defined by John Paul II, in an encyclical letter commemorating the centenary of the publication of *Rerum Novarum*, as the principle that 'a community of a higher order should not interfere in the internal life of a community of a lower order, depriving the latter of its functions, but rather should support it in case of need and help to coordinate its activity with the activities of the rest of society, always with a view to the common good'.[44] This principle, one of several at the heart of Catholic social thought,[45] also underpins the devolved federal structures proposed by the Kreisau Circle for post-war Germany and Europe.

---

[42] Roon, *Resistance*, p. 311.

[43] Ibid., p. 315.

[44] Pope John Paul II, *Centesimus Annus* § ١٩٩١ ,٤٨.

[45] For a succinct summary of six principles of Catholic social teaching see Michael P. Hornsby-Smith, *An Introduction to Catholic Social Thought* (Cambridge, 2006), pp. 104–7.

Theological Commentary and Conclusion

Before commenting on differences between these two resistance groups it is important to take note of connections and overlaps between them. One of the pieces of evidence used against Delp, for example, was that he had visited Stauffenberg in June, 1944 – although the meeting apparently had nothing to do with the bomb plot.[46] We have already seen that Moltke knew both Bonhoeffer and Dohnanyi; he also knew Oster. Admiral Canaris was, of course, ultimately his boss. The proximity of the groups and their differences are most pointedly illustrated in the brothers von Haeften. Hans Bernd von Haeften was a member of the Kreisau group and a committed member of the Confessing Church. Bernd von Haeften did not believe that assassination was either morally or strategically right. However, he had detailed knowledge of the July 1944 plot from his brother Werner von Haeften, who was Stauffenberg's adjutant and friend. When, after the plot failed, Stauffenberg was about to be shot Haeften defiantly jumped in front of him to catch the hail of bullets before the firing squad fired again.[47]

In spite of such overlaps, the two groups had strikingly different approaches to change, and equally striking differences in what changes they aimed at. The Kreisau Circle was engaged in planning a post-war Germany: the Canaris group looked little further than a military coup to remove Hitler. The Kreisau Circle was inclusive and mainly civilian: the Canaris group was mainly military in membership. The Kreisau Circle did not think, as a whole, that assassination was a good basis for political change: the Canaris group was convinced assassination was the only way forward. The Kreisau Circle was federal and European in outlook: the Canaris group was strongly nationalistic. Finally, the Kreisau Circle looked for an inclusive political structure in which socialists, trades unionists, nationalists and others might work together in a civilian government of national unity, giving way very quickly to a multi-party democracy: the Canaris group was deeply suspicious of democracy and believed an authoritarian Rechtsstaat to be the best way forward. If the post-war history of Germany and Europe is our measure, then clearly the Kreisauers got more right than the bomb plotters. Several members of the Kreisau Circle became involved in post-war German politics: Hans Lukaschek, for example, was a minister in the Soviet occupied zone before fleeing to the Allied zone, where he was a minister in the nascent Bundesrepublik. The federal structure of the Bundesrepublik, and the growth of the European Union, while not identical in every respect with the blueprint spelled out in the Kreisau documents, is essentially similar. In spite of serious questions put to it, for example in the 1960s and 1970s by the Red Army Faction, German democracy has proved very successful against the assumptions of Bonhoeffer and others.

---

[46]   Moltke, *Letters*, p. 400, fn.1.

[47]   The incident is reported by Joachim Fest in *Plotting Hitler's Death: The German Resistance to Hitler 1933–1945* (London, 1994) p. 278.

Throughout the chapters in this book it is apparent that untangling the threads of Bonhoeffer's life and thought, his biography and his theology is a task that requires skill and patience. In some ways, it is easy to see why attempting that task may seem undesirable: Bonhoeffer's life may be taken to illuminate his theology and his theology to illuminate his life in return. But might there are also be serious problems in this approach. Let us take politics as a test case. If it really is impossible to untangle his theology from his biography are we obliged to think that since his theology if strong and true so also must be the political decision he took to participate in this particular attempted *coup d'*état? Consider then the possibility that Bonhoeffer's theology of vicarious representative action, of the 'venture of action', is theologically rich and thought-provoking but that Bonhoeffer's political judgement was flawed. Many evaluations of Bonhoeffer take for granted that there were only two possible options for a Christian in his position in war-time Germany: either collude in the evils of Nazism, or resist it to the point where one is prepared to be involved in tyrannicide. Perhaps one of the things that juxtaposing the Canaris conspiracy with the Kreisau Circle achieves is to expose the choice between collusion and tyrannicide as an artificially sharp either/or. At least one other option existed: to *think* the future into existence.

In addition to the straightforwardly strategic political differences between them, then, there were also substantive moral differences. Bonhoeffer was prepared to incur guilt to end evil: Moltke doubted that evil could be ended by an intrinsically evil act. Who was right and who was wrong? Is simply thinking clearly about what needs to change ever really enough, must we not also *do* something to bring that change about? Can a genuinely moral politics ever truly arise from an immoral act of rebellion? Must we choose between the approaches taken by these two groups of brave men and women trying to do right in unrighteous times? To me, the clearest lesson is that earthly politics is imperfectable and therefore that *all* political convictions and actions stand under the judgement of God. The actions of both groups, though different in aim and outcome, both bear witness to God's divine judgement on the pursuit of earthly justice. A final poignant conversation that took place a day after the July 1944 attempt on Hitler's life suggests perhaps a fitting judgement applicable to both groups. Joachim Fest reports that Bonhoeffer's brother Klaus, his sister-in-law Emmi and her brother Justus Delbrück were reflecting on the plot's failure as they cleared rubble from a neighbour's bombed house when Emmi asked the men what they felt about the failure of the plot. After pausing Delbrück replied, 'I think it was good that it happened, and good too, perhaps, that it did not succeed'.[48]

---

[48] Fest, *Plotting*, p. 343.

Chapter 2

An Article Marking the Centenary of Bonhoeffer's Birth: Faith, Political Duty and One Man's Costly Grace

Dietrich Bonhoeffer, born a century ago today,[1] is one of the best-known Christians of the twentieth century. He is one of 10 twentieth-century martyrs commemorated in statues above the west door of Westminster Abbey; his family home is now a museum and several tourist companies offer 'pilgrimages' to sites with which he was associated. He may be the closest thing modern Protestants have to a saint.

If Bonhoeffer was merely the object of a 'cult' or model for piety, marking the centenary of his birth could be kept behind church doors. But Bonhoeffer's legacy raises unsettling questions about the relationship between faith and politics. Bonhoeffer's Christian convictions leach into political action, dissolving easy distinctions between the two.

In 2002, in a speech thanking the *Bundestag* for German support in the War on Terror, President George W. Bush held Bonhoeffer up as a model of fighting tyranny. Paul Hill, an American executed in 2003 for the murder of an abortion doctor and his guard, disturbingly compared Bonhoeffer's opposition to Nazism with his own actions. Such appropriations are not new: since his death, Bonhoeffer's reputation has been conscripted by all kinds of political causes.

Religious leaders in East Germany used his story to prove the Church's anti-Fascist credentials. Opponents and supporters of wars in Vietnam, the Falklands and Iraq used him to shore up their cause. And in the country which executed him for treason, cities have vied to honour him by naming streets and schools after him.

This ought to astonish us much more than it does, for the values that shaped him were not those of modern liberal democracy, but the cultured elitist values of a Germany now long-forgotten, and the thoughtful, deeply held religious convictions to which secularisation makes most Europeans indifferent or suspicious.

When Dietrich Bonhoeffer was born on 4 February 1906, in Breslau (now Wrocław in Poland), he entered a Germany in which Bismarck's land-owning class still had politics in its grip. Beneath the surface seethed the pressures of rapid industrialisation and population growth. Yet even when Berlin collapsed into chaos at the end of the First World War this did not impinge greatly on Bonhoeffer's

---

[1]   This article was published in *The Times* (London) on 4 February 2006, to mark the centenary of Bonhoeffer's birth.

privileged family. He grew up in the educated milieu of Berlin University where his father held, from 1912, the respected chair of psychiatry.

Against the instincts of his empirically inclined family, Dietrich studied theology, gained his doctorate and had qualified as a university lecturer by the time he was 24. After a 'gap year' in New York he was ordained and settled to a career teaching theology.

When Hitler became Reich Chancellor in 1933, Bonhoeffer knew immediately that this was a crisis for Germany, for Europe and for himself. He feared that the popularity of the Nazis threatened decency, law and order.

In the beginning Bonhoeffer put his faith in the Church as a vehicle for opposition. Though junior, he helped to mobilise opposition to state interference in Church life. He attempted – without success – to persuade the nascent World Council of Churches to reject the Nazi state church as heretics, and began to feel frustration for his church's reluctance to stand up for the Jews.

In 1935 he was asked to head a seminary to train pastors for the illegal Confessing Church, established in opposition to the pro-Nazi state church. He thrived in these unusual circumstances, writing two of the books that have made his name. *Life Together* (1938; English 1954) reflects on the life of his seminary, and *The Cost of Discipleship* (1937; English 1959) argues that 'cheap grace is the mortal enemy of our Church. Our struggle today is for costly grace.'

In 1936 the Gestapo began to move against him. It withdrew his teaching licence, forbade him from speaking in public, banned him from visiting Berlin and closed his seminary. Later, they banned him from publishing. In 1939 Bonhoeffer accepted an invitation to lecture in the US but realised he could not live out the war in America. He returned to Germany on the eve of war and agreed, on the urging of his brother-in-law – a senior legal officer in German Military Intelligence – to join the anti-Nazi conspiracy.

In the early years of the war Bonhoeffer worked as a double agent. Ostensibly working for Military Intelligence, he used his church contacts to sound out responses to a possible coup. His texts, published posthumously as *Ethics* (1949; English 1955), debate with breathtaking originality how Christians might conform themselves to Jesus Christ in a post-war, non-religious age.

A message conveyed by Bonhoeffer though Bishop George Bell to the British Foreign Secretary was dismissed by Anthony Eden in a marginal note: 'I see no reason whatsoever to encourage this pestilent priest.' In 1943 Bonhoeffer was arrested on minor charges and imprisoned until evidence linked him to the attempt on Hitler's life in July 1944. He was moved several times, summarily tried and hanged with his co-conspirators, Brigadier Hans Oster and Admiral Wilhelm Canaris, at Flossenbürg concentration camp on 9 April 1945.

Little-known during his life, Bonhoeffer's posthumous publications won huge recognition, placing him in the first rank of twentieth-century theologians.

His decision to join the resistance was not easy. He had been a pacifist since forming a close friendship with a Frenchman in America who, like him, had lost a brother in the First World War. Bonhoeffer had written a book on the Fall:

he understood that killing Hitler was murder and that murder was a sin. But he believed that inaction was also sinful. He never renounced pacifism and refused to justify his actions by arguing that the death of one individual might save the lives of many.

Bonhoeffer's class gave him a sense of duty, and the urbane and humane culture of his family home gave him ground beneath his feet. In this he was no different from the men with whom he was tried, and who died for the same crime without religious convictions.

So what was the difference? What is the role for Christian convictions in politics? In a poem, 'Christians and Heathens', smuggled by Bonhoeffer from prison, he reaches towards an answer. In need, all people seek mercy and bread, whether Christian or not. And God hangs on the Cross for everyone, irrespective of their belief. The difference?

> People go to God when God's in need
> find God poor, reviled, without shelter or bread,
> see God devoured by sin, weakness, and death.
> Christians stand by God in God's own pain.[2]

---

[2]   DBWE 8, p. 461.

PART II
Bonhoeffer and the Bible

Chapter 3
How Theologians Decide: German Theologians on the Eve of Nazi Rule[1]

Kenneth Cracknell[2] believes that a key task of ministerial formation is to give ministers-in-training the tools to 'think theologically'. At least that is the impression he gave of his pedagogical convictions to those of us whom he trained. It is a fine ideal. This chapter explores the role actually played by theology and by other factors in decisions taken by a particular group of theologians at a particular time and place: it is a kind of case study. On this basis I ask, 'Is theology really as important to Christian decision-making as Kenneth believes it is?'

At Pentecost 1932, Leopold Klotz published a volume of essays, which he had himself edited titled: *The Church and the Third Reich: Questions and Demands of German Theologians.*[3] In August 1932 he published a second volume with the same title. The two volumes contain four essays by German theologians, each one expressing a view on the Nazi movement. Volume 2 included the guidelines agreed in June 1932 of the 'German Christian faith movement', the pro-Nazi movement of Protestants that was to play a significant role in German Church life throughout the next decade. The second volume also published correspondence with Hitler's Office and several reviews of the first volume. The contributors were mostly professors of theology; a few were parish pastors. Only three contributors were women. All of the contributors members of the *Landeskirchen*, that is, mostly from Lutheran churches or United Protestant churches such as the Old Prussian Union in which the Lutheran element was predominant.

Collectively the essays are a remarkable source of insight into theological responses to the Nazi movement. It is also a source that has scarcely been tapped. Leonore Siegele-Wenschkewitz offers a useful analysis in her *National Socialism*

---

[1] This chapter is based on the 1999 Annual Hartley Lecture at Hartley Victoria College in Manchester. I am grateful to the College for the invitation to give the lecture and to those who asked questions. I am also grateful to the staff of the Institute of Germanic Studies, London, for assistance in the preparation of this chapter.

[2] This chapter was published in a *Festschrift* in honour of my former tutor, Kenneth Cracknell, at Wesley House, Cambridge.

[3] Leopold Klotz (ed.), *Die Kirche und das dritte Reich: Fragen und Forderungen deutscher Theologen*, 2 vols (Gotha, 1932). Subsequent citations are referenced in the main text by volume number and page number.

and Church,[4] as does Klaus Scholder[5] in his history *The Churches and the Third Reich*, but both analyses are brief and follow historical rather than theological lines. With 43 essays, Klotz's *The Church and the Third Reich* provides the best available 'straw poll' of Protestant theological views of National Socialism in 1932. That the essays were published in 1932 is significant: 1932 and 1933 were decisive years in German history.

A Particular Context for Theological Reflection

By September 1930 the Nazi Party had become the second largest party in the Reichstag. In presidential elections early in 1932 Hitler won a third of the vote against Hindenburg, who had previously been thought unassailable. In the same year in Reichstag elections the Nazis more than doubled their vote. Papen, the conservative Chancellor, busied himself dismantling the Weimar Republic in an effort to establish strong government and, as part of this process, in August 1932 he along with others tried to buy Hitler off by offering him the job of Vice Chancellor. But Hitler was too canny; he turned him down and bided his time. In September Papen's government fell to a no-confidence vote and Germany lurched towards civil war. Surprisingly, in the November 1932 elections the Nazis suffered a dramatic set-back, losing 2 million votes to other parties. Nevertheless, after a short-lived government under General Schleicher, Hitler was appointed German Chancellor on 30 January 1933.[6] By March he had inveigled the Reichstag into passing the Enabling Act, authorising him to rule by decree and was well on the way to a fatal consolidation of Nazi power. It was not only government that the Nazis began changing, however; they embarked swiftly on a dramatic transformation of the whole of German national life. Writing in 1935 an American professor, George Norlin, describes the effects of the transformation that took place in Germany in these two years:

> Between the Germany which I entered in 1932 and the Germany which I left a
> year later there is an astonishing contrast. Then there was division discord lack
> of direction, a feeling of ineffectualness and humiliation, and one could read in
> the faces of the people a sense of the futility of existence. Now all that appears to
> have changed. A people prostrate stands erect, or rather marches with aggressive

---

[4]   Leonora Siegele-Wenschkewitz, *Nationalsosialismus und Kirche: Religionspolitik von Partei und Staat bis 1935* (Dusseldorf, 1978), pp. 27–35.

[5]   Klaus Scholder, *The Churches and the Third Reich: Vol. I, 1918–1934* (London, 1987), p. 143.

[6]   For an overview of the period see Mary Fulbrook, *A Concise History of Germany*, updated edn (Cambridge, 1995), pp. 155–203.

confidence to a common rhythm, shoulders back and eyes shining with faith in the 'New Dawn' of their country.[7]

On the cusp of this transformation Klotz commissioned the 43 essays.

Placing the essays in labelled boxes is not equally straightforward in the case of each essay. While the essays that are explicitly pro-Nazi or anti-Nazi are easy to spot, at either end of the more neutral essays are several contributions that could be placed within the more committed categories. In her analysis Siegele-Wenschkewitz writes[8] that of the 43 essayists 19 are uncompromising opponents of the Nazis (i.e., 44 per cent); 12 (i.e., 28 per cent) are undecided, or see some good in the movement if certain concerns can be addressed; 12 are unreservedly pro-Nazi (i.e., 28 per cent). Though I reckon a couple less to be undecided and a couple more to be anti-Nazi than Siegele-Wenschkewitz, her figures are accurate enough. Siegele-Wenschkewitz notes that in addition to the personal experience of the Nazis essayists refer to three written texts in particular. The first is Hitler's *Mein Kampf*, published in two volumes in 1925 and 1927. It is, as the Duchess of Atholl put it in the mid-1930s in the foreword to a collection of extracts in English, an astonishingly candid book: 'Never can a modern statesman have made so startlingly clear to his readers his ambitions for the aggrandisement of his people.'[9] The second text referred to by Klotz's essayists is the Party Programme in 25 Points of 1920. Hitler co-authored this, and it remained an important text, though by the 1930s Hitler was secure enough progressively to ignore it. Crucially, Paragraph 24 concerned religion and guaranteed the freedom of all religious confessions. Much more than this, however, it states that the Party 'steps out from the standpoint of a positive Christianity, without being bound to its own confession, or to a particular [religious] confession'.[10] It adds that: 'the danger of godlessness and moral decline has never been greater than it is today'.

A third important source is Alfred Rosenberg's *The Myth of the Twentieth Century* which became the best-known of several attempts to state a version of Christianity which was mixed with Nordic, or '*Völkisch*', elements. G.K. Chesterton, the English Catholic novelist, sensed in it 'the strange staleness which makes the racial religion stink in our nostrils with the odours of decay'.[11] He also demolished its arguments, suggesting that Rosenberg read Homer if he seriously believed that honour was a peculiarly Nordic virtue. But the book was hugely influential. Rosenberg, who wrote one of the reviews of Klotz's first volume

---

[7]   George Norlin, *Hitlerism Why and Whither: Some Aspects of a Religious Revolution* (London: A Friends of Europe Publication #22, 1935).

[8]   Siegel-Wenschkewitz, *Nationalsosialismus*, p. 27.

[9]   *Germany's Foreign Policy as stated in 'Mein Kampf' by Adolf Hitler* (London: Friends of Europe publications, #38).

[10]   The paragraph is quoted in full by Ina Gschlössl in Klotz, *Kirche*, vol. 2, p. 56.

[11]   In *Germany's National Religion*, foreword by G.K. Chesterton (London: Friends of Europe publications, #13, undated, but probably 1933).

that is published in the second, became a Nazi politician and was executed in 1946 by the Nuremberg Tribunal. Myth was widely referred to by Klotz's essayists, though even the most pro-Nazi voices found his book cranky. And so to the essays themselves: first, to anti-Nazi voices, then to those who were undecided, and finally to pro-Nazi essayists.

Anti-Nazi Voices

Amongst anti-Nazi essayists were a small number who belong to political or other groups that were explicitly attacked by the Nazis. Two contributors, Gotthilf Schenkel (vol. 1, 99–114), a Stuttgart pastor, and Paul Tillich (vol. 1, 126–8), a Professor in Frankfurt-am-Main (to English-speaking readers the best known of all the contributors) were both committed socialists. Schenkel's essay begins with an account of his meeting with Mahatma Gandhi who told him, 'Christianity is very good, but Christians are very bad.' Schenkel agreed. In his experience the Church had failed signally to engage with socialism. In both its Communist and Social Democratic forms, socialists had been severely criticised by individual Christians and by the Church. The Proletariat had been largely excluded from a Church that was predominantly middle-class. There was a desperate need, Schenkel continued, for the Church to engage in social action and for religious socialism to be accepted into the mainstream. He found the greeting 'Heil Hitler!' to be offensively blasphemous, since only Christ deserved the honour this greeting implies. The heroism of Hitler, based on self-assertion, compared poorly for Schenkel with that of Christ, which is based on service, mercy, and sharing the loads of others. Tillich submitted ten theses. Like Schenkel, he pleaded for a more consistent attitude in the Church towards party politics: a critical approach to socialism was not matched in his experience with a similarly critical approach to Nazism. Tillich is one of several contributors who contrasted the cross of Christ with the Swastika, in German '*Hakenkreuzes*', the 'hooked cross'.

Two authors found themselves excluded on the basis of race. N. Rudnitzky (vol. 2, 85–91), a preacher in Berlin, was a Christian of Jewish ethnic origin and wrote consciously with this as his starting point. Beginning with the unity between Man and Woman in the creation narrative he makes a powerful case for the unity of the nations in the eyes of God: what God joins, human beings cannot separate. As St Paul put it in his speech to the Athenian philosophers in Acts 17:26, 'From one ancestor he made all nations to inhabit the whole earth.' Rudnitzky also argued that the Jewish people are God's chosen people and noted that the Nazi programme promise to protect religious freedom in the name of a 'positive Christianity' does not include those of Jewish origin.

Theodor Devaranne (vol. 2, 32–7) found himself doubly excluded by Nazism. On the one hand, as a Christian of Huguenot descent, he perceived a fundamental flaw in Nazi conceptions of Germanness. Rosenberg had argued that 'There can only be nationhood where there is German blood': Devaranne retorts that there can be. Nationhood is not, he argued, a matter of blood, but of shared language, culture, Spirit and faith. Only when *faith* is valued more highly than *race* as the basis of nationhood, Devaranne concluded, will he feel welcome as a German. Devaranne was also excluded on the basis of his job as a director of foreign missions. Hitler, in *Mein Kampf*, had sneered at foreign missions, writing that 'while the mortal struggle for the Nation rages in Europe, off go the pious Men to save Africans'. Any Christianity outside Germany, Hitler had written, was merely a bastard offspring. Devaranne replies with justice, courtesy and love that that it is the missionary task to proclaim the Gospel around the world. Out of this must grow national Churches each with their own national forms: a German Church in Germany, but a Japanese Church in Japan and African Churches in Africa.

One did not need non-German ethnic origins to see that the racial hatred of the Nazis was wrong from the Christian viewpoint. Lilly Farnke (vol. 2, 133–6) from Heidelberg observed a hiatus between the Nazi's would be piety and the brutality of their anti-Semitism. She noted that while other churches hesitated following violence directed against those attending synagogues in 1931, the Quakers had taken public action in defence of the Jews. Their magazine had lamented the desecration of Jewish graveyards and an open letter had called on churches to defend the Jews. It is one of only a few examples of an essayist looking outside their own religious tradition for resources to sustain an argument.

Ina Gschlössl (vol. 2, 55–61), an assistant pastor in Cologne, contrasted the aggressive nationalism of the Nazis with the teaching of Christ. She could not stomach an ideology that valued 'my country right or wrong' above the command to love. She was also one of many, on both sides of the argument, who considered theologically relations between Church and state. For Lutherans this is a famously difficult issue. Put rather crudely, Luther taught that Church and state had divinely appointed spheres of influence and only where the other 'kingdom' exceeded their boundary should the civil magistrate or prince interfere in the life of the Church or the Church interfere in the life of the state. Even where this doctrine is not explicit in Gschlössl's essay and others, the issue is there between the lines. Yet, as Gschlössl showed, such a doctrine has biblical origins. She quoted Jesus' saying 'render unto Caesar what is Caesar's and unto God what is God's'. This doesn't mean that one should pay an oppressor tribute; rather, that before every other debt God must be given what belongs to Him. Gschlössl also dismissed Alfred Rosenberg's programme from the perspective of objective science and history, as mere Pseudo-science and 'immanent Pantheism'.

Gschlössl's astonishment at the lack of academic objectivity in Nazi ideology is a repeating theme. Paul Fiebig (vol. 1, 25–30), a pastor and professor in Leipzig, proceeded, as he puts it, from the perspective of New Testament science and a German spirit of scientific thoroughness and objectivity. On this basis Fiebig's critique of Nazi anti-Semitism is devastating. For Protestant theology the New Testament is fundamental and makes clear that Jesus, the twelve Apostles and Paul, were Hebrew-speaking Jews. To understand the origins of Christianity properly, therefore, theology must attend to the study of Judaism. Fiebig's essay asked whether the 'third Reich' would permit such study to continue. Secondly, Fiebig argued that careful biblical study makes clear that Jesus' struggle was not with Judaism as such, as the German Christians asserted but with all forms of religious hypocrisy. Jesus had nothing, for example, against legal regulations, only their abuse and certainly nothing against Jews as such. Fiebig concluded that the lessons of New Testament study did not sustain theological anti-Judaism, but a call for the Church to challenge all abuses of legal power.

Also basing his argument self-consciously on objective historical method, Friedrich Heiler of Marburg University accused the 'German Christians', in their rejection of the Old Testament as Scripture, of succumbing to the Marcionite heresy. Using Dogmatic rather than biblical theological argument, perhaps echoing Kierkegaard, Richard Mumm (vol. 1, 77) wrote: 'This is the decisive question: if the contemporary will bow to the eternal, or if the contemporary will surpass the eternal.'

Undecided Contributors

The rigour of academic objectivity is less obvious amongst those essayists who were neutral or undecided. In one of the intellectually weakest essays in the collection Heinrich Weinel, a professor in Jena, seems overwhelmed by the concrete reality of National Socialism's existence: it is here, he argued, and it can't just be ignored. The self-assurance and egoism of the Nazis worried Weinel. Yet, he argued, he loved his country and so did the Nazis. Weinel distinguished, as did several contributors between the National Socialist political party and the Nazi movement, a much broader phenomenon.[12] This, at least, is a useful insight: its supporters regarded Nazism not merely as a potential government, but as a national revival. Weinel concluded that Christians must work within Nazism and turn to Nazi's the spiritual weapons of love.

Professor Johannes Hempel of Gottingen University (vol. 1, 44–52) was similarly conciliatory in tone. Like many Germans he believed Hitler was more disciplined than the more thuggish elements of his movement. Hempel advised a pastoral attitude to Nazis, rather than blunt condemnation. He believed that the Church had, in any case, contributed to its own conflict with 'Nazi theology'. The critique of the Old Testament and Jewish roots of Christianity promoted by pro-Nazi Christians follows on from liberal biblical criticism: if some parts of the biblical canon may be challenged as science or history, why not the whole of the Old Testament? Still, Hempel concluded that Adolf Hitler's features must not be laid over the unique image of Jesus Christ the Saviour. Thus Hempel instances a characteristic feature of most of the 'undecided' essays: even where some features of the Nazi movement are viewed positively, there is a desire to resist

---

[12]   In 1932 the term 'Nazi movement' was generally used; the term Nazi Party became the dominant term later.

excesses that are blasphemous. Also ambivalent was Ernst Bizer (vol. 1, 9–16), a pastor in Goppingen. Bizer expressed fascination with what he perceived as parallels between National Socialism and Christianity. Both, for example, have an eschatology: Christians have the Kingdom of God (the 'Reich Gottes'); Nazis have the 'third Reich'. For both the Christian and the Nazi, Bizer added, the path towards the realisation of that eschatology is said to involve suffering and sacrifice in the name of the goal. On the other hand he also noted parallels between Marxism and Christianity. Bizer was critical of key aspects of the Nazi programme and wrote that 'The idea that a Jew cannot be a Christian is as un-Christian as one can get'. He called on Christians actively to engage in politics and to change the Nazi party from within.

Several undecided essayists use practical political, rather than theological, arguments to justify their ambivalence. Alfred Depuhl (vol. 1, 16–20), a Hannover pastor, touched on the political dilemma facing Protestants. In Protestant Church circles, he wrote, it is common to say that Church and politics don't mix. Yet German Roman Catholics have their own political party, the Centre Party, giving them a clear lead in influencing the life of the nation. Walter Künneth (vol. 1, 65–72), a teacher of apologetics in Berlin, registered his concern that if the Catholic Church managed to negotiate a political and religious settlement with a Nazi Government it would be a tragedy for Protestantism. It is the Protestant Church, Künneth asserted, that is the most truly 'German' Church. Künneth then added a valuable point: the reason the Protestant Church must get right its relation to the state is that Luther's doctrine of the two kingdoms, far from requiring a rigid separation of Church and state, requires the Church to establish limits to state power and influence.

Pro-Nazi Essays

With the final group of essays voicing pro-Nazi views there is a noticeable shift of style, vocabulary and method. Blood and race, nation and national character, duty and responsibility, sacrifice and honour are terms that appear frequently. The revolutionary character of the Nazi movement is adduced to deny the ultimate authority of Scripture and tradition. Sloganising becomes common. Siegfried Nobling (vol. 2, 79–85), a Berlin pastor, was not unrepresentative when at the end of his essay he exclaimed:

> Our politics is Germany
> Our culture is race
> Our religion is Christ.

Some ideas and themes held by anti-Nazi or neutral essayists re-appeared in the third group: the injustice of the Versailles settlement rankled with all the essayists. Wilhelm Schubring (vol. 1, 115–19), a Berlin pastor, raised what had been touched upon by Johannes Hempel, that to balk at pro-Nazi biblical exegesis simply exhibited the same kind of inbred conservatism with which the Church had reacted to post-Enlightenment biblical critics. Nazism, Schubring emphasised, was a spiritual revolution, not merely a political programme.

Almost all pro-Nazi contributors were explicit about their enthusiasm for the revival in German national confidence they were sure the Nazis promised. Amongst these was Pastor Johannes Bruns (vol. 2, 19–24), who asserted that Christians were not obliged merely to discuss the Nazi movement, but had a 'Sacred duty' to pray for its success. Bruns believed that nationhood was amongst the greatest gifts bestowed by God, for 'Blood' is the decisive factor in all aspects of life. 'A Jew', Bruns wrote, 'is rejected as a Jew. A German by virtue of being German is virtually free of sin.' Because of this, Bruns continued, the Old Testament must be rejected by Germans and concluded: 'God bless National Socialism!'

Two contributors deployed practical political arguments to make their case. Pastor Ernst Bublitz from Nackel (vol. 2, 24–7) believed that the Germans are a naturally pious people, and that National Socialism arose out of that piety and expressed it. The concepts that expressed German natural piety, he continued, were nation, state, culture and blood community. Bublitz recalled the impact on him of hearing Hitler speak: 'over the gathering his [Hitler's] voice was spread out like a holy consecration': far from being paganism, he argued, this German 'religious revival' was pure Lutheranism. Bublitz applauded Hitler for keeping open dialogue with Rome by not responding to the ban the German bishops had made on Catholics joining the Nazi Party.[13] Gerhard Heinzelmann, a Cologne pastor, also addressed political questions. A great confusion faced Protestants who asked, he wrote, who they should vote for:

> The Communists address themselves to the Proletariat, Marxist Socialists to the working-class; the Liberal party (increasingly individualistic) looks to the cultured middle-class for support; the ultramontanists [i.e., the Centre Party] are the arms of Rome within the German people; the Conservatives lack a living empathy for the people. (vol. 2, 61–7)

But Heinzelmann concluded dramatically, the National Socialists are a party for every German. If one does not vote for the Nazis, then whom, he asked should one vote for? Even amongst Christians, then, who were prepared to vote Nazi, there may have been some sense that the choice was not ideal.

Several of the pro-Nazi essayists also pointed out that one of National Socialism's great strengths was its ability to attract the young. Like the working-class, the young had, for one reason or another, felt excluded by the Church. Now, here was a movement that included them. More than this, though, was the feeling that there was something unstoppable, something vigorous about Nazism that

---

[13]   The ban was lifted in July 1933 as part of the Concordat between the Roman Catholic Church and the Third Reich.

was sweeping Germans up. The characterisation of both Fascism and National Socialism as vigorous and new, movements for today's generation seems to have been one of their most seductive ploys. Other parties in Germany had existed before the war; the Nazis were new. There was a decisive break between those who had fought in the war and those who had been too old to do so. In Britain Oswald Mosley MP described his British Union of Fascists in very similar terms:

> This age is dynamic, and the pre-war age was static … The men of the pre-war generation are much 'nicer' people than we are, just as their age was much more pleasant than the present time. The practical question is whether their ideas for the solutions of the problems of the age are better than the ideas of those whom that age has produced.[14]

Corroborating Evidence

How representative are the essays I have examined? Klaus Scholder believed that the proportions of pro-Nazi, neutral and anti-Nazi views contained in the essays 'may have accurately reflected the actual position'[15] of Protestant theological opinion and Scholder is the most reliable German Church historian of this period. Two other essays published just a little later by better known theologians provide interesting points for comparison. In May 1933 Rudolf Bultmann commented on the task of theology in, as he euphemistically put it, 'the present situation'. It was not, he began, his intention to express a political view, nor to exclaim joyfully about political events. His task as a theologian, Bultmann argued, was to ask what his responsibility was towards the possibilities presented by events. Like so many of Klotz's contributors, Bultmann asserted that 'faith in God and nationality stand in a positive relation, insofar as God has placed us in our nation and state'.[16] Nevertheless, he added, 'nothing that encounters us as a phenomenon within the world is directly divine'[17] which means, he spells out, that no state and no nation is sin-free. The criterion for evaluating the functions of nationhood in concrete terms is love. He concludes by deploring the defamation of German Jews.

A month later Dietrich Bonhoeffer published an article on 'The Church and the Jewish Question' which has since been fine tooth-combed by both hagiographers and character assassins searching out evidence of his theological virtues or vices.[18]

---

[14] Cited in Mark Mazower, *Dark Continent: Europe's Twentieth Century* (London, 1998), p. 137.

[15] Scholder, *Churches*, vol. 1, p. 143.

[16] Rudolf Bultmann, *Existence and Faith* (London, 1964), pp. 187–78.

[17] Bultmann, *Existence*, pp. 187–78.

[18] Two recent examples of each are Ruth Zerner, 'Church state and Jewish Question', in John W. de Gruchy (ed.), *The Cambridge Companion to Bonhoeffer* (Cambridge, 1999), 190–205; and Kenneth Barnes, 'Dietrich Bonhoeffer and Hitler's

To be sure there are some of each in the essay which I don't want to analyse here. But one quotation reinforces the impression of the dilemma posed to Church–state relations by the Lutheran doctrine of the two kingdoms. In the essay Bonhoeffer wrote that:

> There is no doubt that the Church of the Reformation is not encouraged to get involved directly in specific political actions of the state. The church has neither to praise nor to censure the laws of the state. Instead it has to affirm the state to be God's order of preservation [Erhaltungsordnung] in this godless world. It should recognize and understand the state's creation of order – whether good or bad from a humanitarian perspective – as grounded in God's desire for preservation in the midst of the world's chaotic godlessness.[19]

That Bonhoeffer's thinking on Church–state relations continued to evolve to the point where he was willing to participate in a 'tyrannicide' indicates sufficiently the limits of the view expressed here. What is interesting about it for our purposes is that these remarks would not seem at all out of place in Klotz's volumes. Bonhoeffer's biographers are right to highlight original aspects of his theology, but in the context of the Klotz essays, it can also be demonstrated that Bonhoeffer occupied the same world as other German theologians in the 1930s. He is properly understood against that backdrop and not as a thinker *sui generis* as it is sometimes implied he was.

Many have suggested on the basis of the theology of Bonhoeffer, Bultmann and the Klotz contributors that at the heart of the Lutheran tradition there are two deep flaws that made it almost impossible for Lutherans to think clearly in relation to Hitler. These were, they argue, Luther's teaching on the Jews and his doctrine of the two kingdoms. In the early years of the Reformation some Jews warmly welcomed Luther's work. In the late fifteenth and early sixteenth century there had been several brutal anti-Jewish pogroms. Luther, who repeatedly emphasised the Jewish origin of Jesus, who read Hebrew and taught from the Old Testament, seemed to promise better. However, at the end of his life Luther's anti-Jewish polemic, most noticeable in the 1543 polemic 'On the Jews and their Lies', had become distressingly wrongheaded; even other Reformers distanced themselves from it. Ekkehard Stegemann,[20] on whom these last remarks are based, acknowledges that Christianity, particularly its Lutheran form, has been stamped with anti-Judaism. Stegemann explains the shift away from Luther's more open attitude to the Jews early in the Reformation, as the result of his progressive

---

Persecutions of the Jews', in R.P. Ericksen and S. Heschel (eds), *Betrayal: German Churches and the Holocaust* (Minneapolis, 1999), pp.110–28.

[19]   DBWE 12, pp. 362–3.

[20]   E. Stegemann, 'Die Stellung Martin Luthers und der Evangelischen Christen zum Judentum', in Wolfgang Stegemann (ed.), *Kirche und Nationalsozialismus*, 2nd edn (Stuttgart, 1990), pp. 121–38.

disappointment that the Jews had failed to convert to Protestant Christianity as he seems genuinely to have thought they would.

As we have seen, the doctrine of the two kingdoms certainly played a role in shaping Lutheran attitudes to the Nazis. Yet, like Luther's anti-Judaism, this has complex origins that include New Testament texts such as Romans 13. Neither did the doctrine cease to develop once Luther had articulated it: the Western Protestant tradition's separation of theology and politics also, for example, owes something to Immanuel Kant.[21] Confronted by the possibility that Lutheran theology proved particularly ill-equipped to cope with National Socialism, a glance sideways at the record of other churches proves salutary. For example, Herbert Strahm's dissertation *The Episcopal Methodist Church in the Third Reich (1933–45)*[22] shows that the Nazis brought out the worst in the Methodist Church too. Among factors that led to Methodist quiescence towards the Nazis some would be farcical if the consequences were not so shameful. The Nazi's discouraged drinking and smoking amongst the young and encouraged health and sport. Methodists therefore saw in the new state a potential partner in their own moral crusade against alcohol and tobacco. But it was what Strahm calls the 'minority complex' of the Episcopal Methodist Church that proved decisive. The Church, which originated in the United States and was still structurally linked with American Episcopal Methodism, was sensitive about its Germanness in a culture where that was becoming an increasingly important commodity. Moreover, the Church had always felt itself to be overshadowed by 'state Churches'. In the first months of Nazi rule there was a genuine possibility that Methodism would be forced to become part of a new United Reich Church. Thus in 1935 when Church leaders successfully negotiated a status as a legally registered body there was widespread satisfaction. Strongly oriented towards evangelism, Strahm argues that Episcopal Methodists thought the Nazi state provided better opportunities for mission than the Church had ever had. In return the Church was only too pleased to agree to political neutrality which had in any case been its previous practice. Strahm concludes that this 'was too high a price'. The Church spoke not one word during the whole period to challenge the state. In his examination of the evidence, Strahm uncovered plenty of examples of Methodists in the SS but not one example of a Methodist resister. A firm stance against alcohol and an overriding drive to

---

21   Oliver O'Donovan recalls that Kant wrote: 'I can actually think of a moral politician, i.e., one who so interprets the principles of political prudence that they can be coherent with morality, but I cannot think of a political moralist, i.e., one who forges a morality to suit a statesman's advantage' (*Perpetual Peace, AA* VIII., 372), cited in Oliver O'Donovan, *The Desire of the Nations: Rediscovering the Roots of Political Theology* (Cambridge, 1996). O'Donovan's thesis that theology is intrinsically political and that political theology really needs to be *theological* is especially apposite in the context of this study.

22   For a summary see Herbert Strahm, 'Die Bischöfliche Methodistenkirche im Dritte Reich (1933–1945)', in Michel Weyer (ed.), *Der kontinentaleuropäische Methodismus zwischen den beiden Weltkriegen* (Stuttgart, 1990), pp. 93–132.

preserve a Methodist identity proved on their own to be as inadequate a basis for Methodist Church witness in Nazi Germany as they would be today. This brief comparison with the Episcopal Methodist Church does nothing to excuse Klotz's Lutheran theologians, but it suggests that the shadow the Nazis cast showed up the peculiar blemishes in all Germany's theological traditions. It certainly showed up deeper-seated ambiguities in the Christian tradition as a whole.

Conclusions

It is time to begin drawing some conclusions and the first requires a little patience to do so properly. What attitude should be assumed towards Christian theologians who either supported Hitler or preferred to wait and see before committing themselves? As I have presented the contents of Klotz's collection of essays I have found myself being impaled as on the horns of a dilemma. The dilemma is this: on the one hand, the more one reads the arguments of those who saw good in the Nazi movement the more appalling becomes the extent of the failure of theology. On the other hand, the more the reasons for that failure are exposed, some, at least, of the reasoning for it becomes intelligible. There were various reasons why people became Nazis. Some became wholehearted Nazis, others retained reservations. Can one understand how theological mistakes came to be made and still condemn those who made the mistakes? Bernhard Schlink's novel *The Reader* is a sensitive and intelligent exploration of just this dilemma. Faced with the discovery that his former lover is implicated in crimes against Jews, the novel's protagonist reflects:

> I wanted simultaneously to understand Hanna's crime and to condemn it. But it was too terrible for that. When I tried to understand it, I had the feeling I was failing to condemn it as it must be condemned. When I condemned it as it must be condemned, there was no room for understanding ... I could not resolve this. I wanted to pose myself both tasks – understanding and condemnation. But it was impossible to do both.[23]

One way for theologians and Church historians to deal with this dilemma to deny it and simply condemn the failure of the Churches without entering into the context in which that failure occurred. Two books, published this year more or less do just this. John Cornwell, a Catholic journalist and historian has written a compelling account of the life of Eugenio Pacelli, the Vatican diplomat who served as Papal Nuncio in Germany from 1917 to 1929. He then served as Cardinal Secretary of State and was responsible for the Concordat between Hitler and the Vatican signed in 1933. Pacelli became Pope in 1939 and died in 1958. With the title of the biography the author already declares his hand: *Hitler's Pope: The Secret*

---

[23]   Bernhard Schlink, *The Reader* (Phoenix, 1997), p.156.

History of Pius XII.[24] Cornwell set out to write a conventional defence of Pope Pius XII. But, he writes, in the middle of his research he found himself 'in a state I can only describe as moral shock. The material I had gathered, taking the more extensive view of Pacelli's life amounted not to an exoneration but to a wider indictment.'[25]

Cornwell makes two particularly damning charges. Firstly, he alleges that Pacelli tended towards anti-Semitism. The evidence for this is an account of a meeting between a Bolshevik revolutionary, who was Jewish and a member of staff in Pacelli's Munich Nunciature during the Munich Communist uprising in 1919. While Pacelli did not himself write the report, it traded in historic anti-Semitic caricatures, which Pacelli retailed without comment to his Vatican superior. Later, Cornwell describes the deportation of Roman Jews under Pacelli's Vatican windows. Pacelli's flat refusal to speak out in defence of the Jews is certainly a gross failure but the evidence that this failure was due to anti-Semitism is not strong: the second charge, that Pacelli allowed his deep distrust of Communism to influence his relations to Fascist and Nazi regimes is better substantiated. Yet, in my view, Cornwell has blemished an otherwise readable and necessary book by exaggerating Pacelli's failures, and overestimating the role he might have played in opposing the Nazis. Describing the cover photograph a note tells us that it shows Pacelli leaving the presidential palace in Berlin in 1939, thereby underlining Cornwell's tendentious title. But, as the reviewer in *The Economist* points out (10 September 1999) the photograph is in fact taken in 1927, and the jack-booted soldiers flanking Pacelli serve the Weimar Republic not the Nazis. The mistake is probably not Cornwell's but his publisher's, but it serves to emphasise the book's exaggerated claims.

The second book also has a telling title: *Betrayal: German Churches and the Holocaust.*[26] A collection of nine essays, *Betrayal* presents an indictment of the Churches from which Klotz's essayists came. The essays contain undeniable truths. Christian anti-Judaism prepared the ground, as several essays demonstrate, for Nazi anti-Semitism. But, as with the Cornwell biography, the evidence is not presented with the detachment the subject demands. The introduction suggests that Luther introduced a sharp distinction between 'law' and 'gospel', which led to what proved to be a dangerous contrast between Judaism and Christianity.[27] He did, but that theological insight is only now being made: in the 1930s and 1940s such a distinction was not unreasonably thought to be genuinely Pauline. Heschel's essay points out that Protestant theologians presented first-century Judaism as a degenerate faith, which Jesus opposed, and so they opposed it as well. It is not a view of Judaism I subscribe to, but was it as 'irrational' in 1933 as she insists? Doris Bergen asserts that 'the vast majority of Protestant clergy

---

[24]   John Cornwell, *Hitler's Pope: The Secret History of Pius XII* (London, 1999).

[25]   Cornwell, *Hitler's Pope*, p. x.

[26]   Ericksen and Heschel, *Betrayal*.

[27]   Ibid., p. 15.

and lay-people remained neutral in the conflict' in the Church,[28] but surely that is a matter of interpretation not of fact, as the Klotz essays show. In January 1934 Martin Niemöller's Pastor's Emergency League, which had sprung up to defend the Church against the depredations of the pro-Nazi German Christians, had over 7,000 members, 37 per cent of all serving Protestant clergy.[29] Kenneth Barnes describes Dietrich Bonhoeffer's decision to go to London in 1933 as a 'cowardly flight'.[30] But Bonhoeffer was only 27 years old; he longed to experience parish life, he loved travel, and he had felt crushed by his heavy responsibilities in the Church struggle.

My point is that it is all too easy to make condemnatory remarks about Christian responses to Nazism, or the lack of them, with the benefits of hindsight. Members of the Confessing Church had not seen Spielberg's film *Schindler's List*. What Klotz's essays show us, if nothing else, is that the theological decisions his essayists had to take in 1932 were far from clear. Theological errors were certainly made, but judging those decisions from a pluralistic, post-Holocaust perspective of the late twentieth century simply leads to a moral smugness with no useful lessons teach. Morality, like history, is lived forwards and without hindsight. Ethical decisions, when no outcome is certain, are often inherently risky. The tricks demanded of us in this process are, first, to learn from the mistakes of those who came before us; and second, as far as is bearable, to remain hoisted on the horns of the dilemma between condemning the errors of the past and understanding how they could have been made. To understand how the churches could have failed so signally does not mean 'forgiving and forgetting'. Rather, it requires us to understand how they came to make their errors. This surely is a better way of ensuring that their mistakes are not repeated than simply condemning them, as though we ourselves could never behave the same way in similar circumstances. This may seem a meagre conclusion to reach after so much effort, but some historians and theologians still manage to overlook it.

The Place of Theology in Coming to Decide

So much for a proper sense of history, what about the proper sense of theology in which Kenneth Cracknell places so much hope? In my view the evidence I have presented sends out conflicting messages about the use of theology in the decision-making of theologians on the eve of Nazi rule. Those who were most immune to the charms of the Nazi movement were protected not by their theology, but by a prior identification with a group excluded by Nazi ideology. For those, like Paul Tillich, with a prior ideological commitment (to socialism), the Nazis were enemies. Others, such as the Huguenot Theodor Devaranne, were excluded on the

---

[28]	Ibid., p. 46.

[29]	Klaus Scholder, *The Churches and the Third Reich*, vol. 2 (London, 1988), p. 22.

[30]	Scholder, *Churches*, vol. 2, p. 120.

basis of race. Socialists and non-Germans were generally 'immune' to the Nazis, Christian or not, although they might then link together theological reasons (e.g., God is the God of all nations) with the ground of their exclusion (not belonging to the 'German race'). Did theological factors not play a leading role in the decision-making of theologians who rejected German Christian exegesis and the crack-pot ideas of Alfred Rosenberg as 'unscientific'? Again, I suggest it is not clear that theology was the decisive factor. It is true, and it is a credit to German biblical scholarship, that several of the clearest essays in Klotz's collection opposing Nazi ideology argue on the basis of evidence that Jesus and the Apostles were Jewish, etc. But is this not simply sound historical method? The canonicity of the Old Testament is a theological matter to be sure, but historical research is also able to establish the parameters of orthodox Christian theology.

Where did the theological fault lines run in the essays? One is certainly the presence of anti-Judaism in the Christian tradition. Another fault line, whether it was Luther or Kant or the writers of the New Testament who cracked it open, concerns the proper relationship between Church and the state. It is clear that when the Church identifies with one political party disaster follows. No political party has all the answers. There is anyway, often not one Christian point of view on political issues, but several. On the other side, however, it is essential that Christians are involved in politics. Many Christians voted for the Nazi Party because of a lack of viable alternatives. If many Christians had been actively engaged in politics during the Weimar Republic perhaps there would have been political alternatives to the Nazis and democracy might have taken root. Christians have duties to civil society. Oliver O'Donovan takes the point one stage further when he writes that: 'Theology must be political if it is to be truly evangelical. Rule out the political questions and you cut short the proclamation of God's saving power; you leave people enslaved where they ought to be set free from sin – their own sin and others.'[31] And that is a statement that Kenneth Cracknell would endorse.

---

[31] O'Donovan, *Desire*, p. 3. O'Donovan's book would be amongst the first places I would look to develop the conclusions hinted at in these closing sentences.

Chapter 4

'In the Bible it is God who speaks':
Peake and Bonhoeffer on Reading Scripture*

The A.S.Peake Memorial Lecture 2006

There is a touching moment in Leslie S. Peake's memoir of his father. Narrating his earliest memory of the biblical scholar the son recalls that his father 'had a horror of cruelty in any of its forms, and especially the cruelty that kept birds in cages'. As the venerable scholar convalesced after an operation his young son entertained him by singing a verse that ran:

> It's only a bird in a gilded cage,
>   A beautiful sight to see,
> You'd think she was happy and free from care,
>   She's not, though she seems to be.[1]

It is whimsical, I realise, but I sense in this childish rhyme an intimation of Peake's attitude to the Bible. For Peake, the Bible resembled a bird locked in a gilded cage waiting for the compassionate biblical scholar to open the door to its message. With wanton cruelty the passage of time and generations of theologians had locked away the meaning of the Bible; his vocation was to release it so that the history of God's revelation could be heard again. Peake believed that biblical criticism, with its scientific tools of textual reconstruction and historical enquiry, could reconstruct a generally accepted account of the meaning of biblical texts and convey it to a lay readership. Only by this means, Peake thought, could the Bible be saved for a generation squeezed between sceptical modern critics who would discard Scripture and traditionalists intent on the irrational assertion of the Bible's verbal inspiration and historical, scientific and theological inerrancy.

Dietrich Bonhoeffer belonged to a different generation. In 1929, the year in which Peake died, Bonhoeffer was 23 and already embarked on a promising academic career. Two years earlier he had defended his doctoral thesis. In August 1929 as Peake went under the knife in the operation from which he never

---

* I am grateful to the Trustees of the Peake lectureship for the invitation to give this lecture, and to all those who contributed to the evening. I am also grateful to Andrew Mein for conversations during the preparation of the paper; the chapter's deficiencies, however, are all my own.

[1] L.S. Peake, *Arthur Samuel Peake: A Memoir* (London, 1930), p. 291.

recovered, Bonhoeffer was writing the *Habilitation* thesis on the doctrine of revelation that would qualify him as a university lecturer.[2] For Bonhoeffer, biblical criticism was *not* the key that released the meaning of Scripture. The knowledge that Christian faith is about is like other kinds of knowledge in many respects, his thesis argued, but in other respects is best regarded as a distinct kind of knowing. Historians and theologians, he thought, traded in different kinds of knowledge. If biblical critics were not for Bonhoeffer, as traditionalists claimed, the Bible's jailors, they were certainly not its liberators. As a student in the University of Berlin, Bonhoeffer had been trained (amongst others by Adolf von Harnack, who Peake admired greatly) skilfully to wield the tools of scientific biblical criticism. In 1928 his examiners judged his Old Testament exegesis 'good' and his New Testament exegesis 'sufficient'.[3] But Bonhoeffer had come to believe that the tools of biblical criticism were incapable of penetrating the surface of Scripture. What he aimed at in Bible reading was a post-critical approach that achieved – in a phrase coined later by Paul Ricoeur – a 'secondary *naïveté*', a reading that moves beyond critical methods in order to attend humbly to the Word of God speaking in the Bible. In 1936 Bonhoeffer wrote explaining his approach and his dissatisfaction with biblical criticism to his agnostic brother-in-law Rüdiger Schleicher:

> First, I want to confess quite simply that I believe the Bible alone is the answer to all our questions, and that we only need to ask persistently and with some humility in order to receive the answer from it. One cannot simply read the Bible the way one reads other books. One must be prepared to really question it. Only then will it open itself up. Only when we await the final answer from the Bible will it be given to us. That is because in the Bible God speaks to us. And we cannot simply reach our own conclusions about God; rather we must ask him. He will only answer us if we are seeking after him. Naturally, one may also read the Bible like any other book – from the perspective of textual criticism, for instance. There is nothing to be said against that. But that will only reveal the surface of the Bible, not what is within it. [tr. amended][4]

Bonhoeffer knew how this would sound to his sceptical brother-in-law, and concedes in his letter that he is prepared to live with the possibility of sacrificing his intellect with respect – and only with respect – to God. Reading the Bible, Bonhoeffer appears to say, is not a question of technical skill: if that were true the meanest contemporary scholar would be a better reader of the Bible than the greatest saints and scholars of the pre-modern Church. Bible reading for Bonhoeffer is a matter of attentiveness and faith. The Word of God in the Bible does not lie buried

---

[2]   Bonhoeffer's habilitation thesis, *Akt und Sein*, was accepted by Berlin University in 1930.

[3]   DBWE 9, pp. 183–4.

[4]   Dietrich Bonhoeffer, *Meditating on the Word*, ed. David M. Gracie (Cambridge, MA, 1986), pp. 43–4; German original in DBW 14, pp. 144–5.

under the alien cultures and foreign languages of the Biblical writers, awaiting the biblical scholar to sweep away the centuries of dust: it is a gift God is free daily to give – or withhold – to each faithful reader in her unique situation.

Contrasting Peake and Bonhoeffer in this way involves a certain violence towards the evidence: as an exegete Peake was more guided than he knew by what Henry Rack terms his 'liberal evangelical faith';[5] and as a theologian Bonhoeffer retained more of his biblical critical training than he was prepared to acknowledge.[6] But there is enough truth in this contrast to make it worth reflecting upon. For Bonhoeffer, Peake's generation represented an approach to Bible reading that had signally failed to articulate God's Word to the world: a generation of biblical scholars and dogmatic theologians had failed the men in the trenches and were now repeating their theological and political error in their response to Nazism. In the Church struggle Bonhoeffer learned to distrust any ground outside the Bible, suspecting that even in the supposed objectivity of scientific biblical criticism he would find an echo of his own opinions rather than the sovereign Word of God. In men like Peake, Bonhoeffer thought he saw a generation that had called the Bible before the bench of human reason, thereby taming God's Word by making it subject to scholarly interpretation. As Bonhoeffer argued in his Christology lectures of 1933, it is not the job of the human *logos* to make sense of the *Logos* of God; it is the job of God's *Logos* to make sense of us.

The contrast I have sketched above appears to impale us on the horns of a dilemma: is biblical criticism the key to the Bible or a tool kit capable of merely scratching its surface? Must we chose either historical criticism or what Bonhoeffer calls 'theological interpretation'? I want to suggest that this choice is artificial and unhelpful. That is, though there are indeed substantive differences between Peake and Bonhoeffer it may not be necessary to choose between them. Though they differ fundamentally in their respective *construals*[7] of the way God is revealed through Scripture, I want to suggest that contemporary debates within and between the guilds of biblical scholarship and systematic theology are, uneasily and untidily, feeling towards ways of reading the Bible that have taken both Peake and Bonhoeffer's perspectives into account. I want to add that in one key respect – the relation of Christianity to Judaism – contemporary scholarship has moved beyond both men making them seem oddly antique in their biblical exegesis.

---

[5]   Henry Rack, 'A.S. Peake memorial lecture: A.S. Peake – Liberal evangelical', *Epworth Review*, 31/3 (July 2004): 48–53.

[6]   See, e.g., Georg Huntemann, who argues that 'Dietrich Bonhoeffer participates, first of all, in the schizophrenia of modern theology which on the one hand analyses the Bible critically, but then nevertheless allows the critically analysed text to stand as God's word', *Der Andere Bonhoeffer: Die Herausforderung des Modernismus* (Wuppertal, 1989), p. 112, my translation.

[7]   I refer here to David Kelsey's *Uses of Scripture in Recent Theology* (London, 1975).

It is reasonable to ask what the point of such a comparison is: it is unlikely that Bonhoeffer had ever read Peake; certainly there is no record of his having done so. If the Trustees for the Peake Lectureship had not hit upon the idea of marking the centenary of Bonhoeffer's birth by graciously inviting me to give this year's lecture, Peake and Bonhoeffer might never have been mentioned in the same breath. One possible reason a comparison may be worth attempting is implied in what I have already said: Bonhoeffer's hermeneutic – his theory of how the Bible should be interpreted – was hammered out against that generation of biblical scholars in which Peake is numbered. Comparing them may help us fathom what Bonhoeffer is doing when he reads the Bible. Interesting as this project might be, I'm not sure it would justify the effort. Yet the dialogue between theology and biblical scholarship is no less pressing a task now than it was for Peake or Bonhoeffer. My hope is that in rehearsing some issues raised by the two men's uses of the Bible I may contribute modestly to that ongoing conversation.

A.S.Peake and the Nature of Scripture

John T. Wilkinson commented that Peake wrote 'some twenty books of solid scholarship, a large number of important monographs [and] a colossal quantity of articles and book reviews';[8] this is, perhaps, a somewhat generous assessment. Many of the volumes of 'solid scholarship' to which Wilkinson refers are, by today's scholarly standards, not classifiable as instances of constructive scholarship but attempts, as Peake puts it in the commentary that bears his name, 'designed to put before the reader in a simple form, without technicalities, the generally accepted results of Biblical Criticism, Interpretation, History and Theology'.[9] With some exceptions, Peake's main contribution lay in mediating critical scholarship to lay readers. This is no bad thing and it helps give some sense of what made him tick: Peake was foremost a polemicist. If Bonhoeffer's biblical hermeneutic is a reaction against Peake's generation, Peake's own biblical hermeneutics are no less a reaction against the past. He was driven by his conviction that traditionalists, not least those in evangelical traditions such as his own Primitive Methodist Church, had wrongly dismissed the contribution of critical scholarship to Bible reading. In his 1897 book *A Guide to Biblical Study*,[10] his 1913 book *The Bible: Its Origin, its Significance and its Abiding Worth*,[11] and again in his 1922 book on *The Nature*

---

[8] John T. Wilkinson, *Arthur Samuel Peake* (London, 1971), p. 85; this volume also includes a useful select bibliography of Peake's writings, pp. 161–67.

[9] A.S. Peake, *Peake's Comentary on the Bible* (London, 1920), p. xi.

[10] A.S. Peake, *A Guide to Biblical Study* (London, 1897).

[11] A.S. Peake, *The Bible: Its Origin, its Significance and its Abiding Worth* (London, 1913).

of Scripture,[12] Peake states and restates a strikingly coherent[13] case concerning the nature of critical biblical scholarship and the nature, value and message of the Bible that such scholarship makes available.

One immediate impression one gains from these books is Peake's view of Scriptural authority, or rather his lack of one. Until the second Vatican Council and the publication in 1965 of *Dei Verbum* on 'The Dogmatic Constitution of Divine Revelation',[14] which declared that Scripture and tradition are twin forms of the one Revelation to which the Church is subject, one could have been forgiven for thinking that in Western Christianity there were essentially two ways to understand the authority of the Bible. Either (as the Church of Rome was supposed to believe) Scripture is authoritative because the Church declares it so; or (as the Reformers taught) Scripture alone is authoritative for the Church, and is so because it is intrinsically inspired – literally 'in-breathed' by God. Peake subscribed to neither position. For a man so interested in Church unity he was signally uninterested in the Church. Like von Harnack, for Peake the Christian religion was primarily a question of personal salvation in which the Church plays little role except as a fellowship of believers in which the individual might hear God's Word preached. Certainly Peake displays little sense of the Church's potential role as a community in which an individual's interpretation of biblical texts may be tried and tested. More surprisingly for a Protestant he rejects expressly any notion that the Bible is authoritative because it is inspired. For Peake, critical biblical scholarship has emancipated us from 'a mechanical view of inspiration' that held that 'from the first page to the last the Bible was written under the direct inspiration of the Holy Spirit'.[15] Quoting 2 Timothy 3:16 (though interestingly omitting the biblical reference) Peake rejects the view that all Scripture, because inspired by God, is 'profitable for doctrine, for reproof, for correction, for instruction in righteousness'. This view has, he argues, become progressively less credible and 'the facts are so clearly against it that only a preconceived theory could have made men blind for so long'.[16] His reason for this conclusion is simple: to any unprejudiced reader, contended Peake, it is clear that the Bible 'is not throughout on the same level, whether of historical accuracy, or moral insight, or theological correctness'.[17] In Peake's opinion, the Bible is a record of God's progressive revelation; it is not that revelation itself. Revelation, in other words, is an historical process. What the Bible gives us is a record of human experience of revelation in which it is

---

[12]   A.S. Peake, *The Nature of Scripture* (London, 1922).

[13]   Wilkinson detects some development in Peake's understanding and use of the Bible in the period spanned by these books (cf. Wilkinson, *Peake*, chapter 5 'The Interpreter of the Bible', pp. 84–123) and is surely right to do so; but the very great *consistency* of Peake's fundamental views on the Bible throughout his career is nonetheless striking.

[14]   *The Documents of Vatican II*, ed. W.M. Abbott SJ (London, 1966), pp. 107–32.

[15]   Peake, *Nature*, p. 200.

[16]   Ibid., p. 201.

[17]   Ibid., pp. 201–202.

not the biblical writers who are inspired, but the people of Israel to which they belonged. Intelligent readers will take the Bible as a whole rather than fixating on particular texts.

Traditional accounts of the authority of Scripture were not the only ancient doctrines and practices of the Church that Peake distanced himself from: he also rejected two ways of reading the Bible with ecclesial pedigrees reaching back to the New Testament. Firstly, Peake regarded the allegorical interpretation of biblical texts as little more than a form of primitive superstition that is simply disallowed for modern readers: in this he was and is not unusual. But more significantly, he also rejected as entirely without value or propriety Christological interpretations of the Old Testament, that is readings of Old Testament texts in which the person of Christ is 'read back' into the text.[18]

The issue that best displays Peake's view of Scripture is his understanding of the relation between the Old and the New Testament. In Peake's earliest commentary, on *The Epistle to the Hebrews*,[19] Peake associates himself with what he takes to be the message of that letter: 'Christianity [he writes] is that heavenly original of which Judaism is the flickering and insubstantial shadow'.[20] The Old Testament represented for Peake, unwittingly echoing Hegel, a 'lower stage of religion'[21] that has been superseded by Christianity.[22] For Peake, the primitive religion of the Old Testament is a problem to be overcome by Christian apologetics; he is unembarrassed by the resemblance between his view of the Old Testament and that of the Gnostic heretic Marcion. The Old Testament cannot serve as a basis for personal or social ethics. The vital aspect of Old Testament texts is not the message its authors convey, but, taken as a whole, its record of a deepening experience of God. Only by recognising its limitations may a modern reader love it.

For Peake, the Bible must be read with the same critical faculties as any other book. Biblical texts, he thought, have a single meaning that can accurately be recovered by biblical scholars, a meaning on which scholars could achieve a high degree of consensus. Biblical scholars, thought Peake, had achieved permanent agreement on certain textual and historical conclusions, for example about the sources that make up the Pentateuch. He was certain of the achievements of biblical scholarship and sure that they must be accepted by any rational individual who objectively surveyed the evidence.

---

[18]   For a good example of a Christological interpretation of an Old Testament text, see Charles Wesley's identification, in the hymn 'Come, O thou Traveller unknown', of Christ with the stranger encountered by Jacob at Peniel in Genesis 32.

[19]   Published in *The Century Bible* (Edinburgh, 1904).

[20]   Cited in Wilkinson, *Peake*, p. 110.

[21]   Peake, *Nature*, p. 140.

[22]   Ibid., p. 178.

Bonhoeffer and the Theological Interpretation of Scripture

Dietrich Bonhoeffer disagreed with very nearly every single point detailed in my summary of Peake's view of the nature and value of the Bible. For Bonhoeffer, the Bible can be read as one reads any other book, but that will only scratch its surface. He viewed the Old Testament as a book of Christ and routinely engaged in Christological readings of Old Testament texts. He believed the Bible – even the Old Testament – could serve as a guide for Christian social and personal ethics. He suspected that dismissals of the authority of Scripture were simply pretexts for disobedience to the divine command. For Bonhoeffer, for example, a reader of the Sermon on the Mount simply has to face up to the possibility that Jesus means exactly what he says and calls the Christian to simple obedience to his command. Thus, when Jesus tells the rich young ruler to sell his possessions and give to the poor, Bonhoeffer suspects that interpretations which suggest Jesus does not *really* intend that a reader of this story should also sell his possessions for the poor may be evasions of the true cost of discipleship. For him, the archetype of the typical modern reader of the Bible is the cunning serpent, who, with his 'pious question'[23] 'did God really say … ?' asks the ultimately godless question of the critic.

Perhaps the only item on which Bonhoeffer would have agreed with Peake is that the Bible matters. Dietrich Bonhoeffer was a profoundly biblical theologian. Of the five books he published during his lifetime three 'are meditative interpretations of the Bible from an ethical-pastoral perspective'.[24] Bonhoeffer wrote numerous works of biblical exegesis including texts on the Ten Commandments, the Psalms, on the books of Ezra and Nehemiah, on the temptation narratives and on the Lord's Prayer. A hundred or so of his biblically oriented sermons are extant and from prison he wrote to Eberhard Bethge that he was reading 'a lot … especially the Bible'.[25] Almost his last earthly act was to reflect on two biblical texts for fellow prisoners on Low Sunday, 1945.

Yet even as an undergraduate student, Bonhoeffer's approach to the Bible was beginning to create tension between him and his theological teachers and peers. In 1925, when he was still in his teens, Bonhoeffer received the lowest mark he achieved for any paper in dogmatic theology for his essay on the question 'Can one distinguish between a historical and a pneumatological interpretation of Scripture, and how does dogmatics relate to this question?'[26] Already the precocious student had begun to raise questions about the historical critical method that were as troubling to his own professor as they would have been to Peake had he received the essay to mark. 'Regarding the form of the Bible', Bonhoeffer writes:

---

[23]   DBWE 3, pp. 103–10.

[24]   See Gerhard Krause's entry on Bonhoeffer in the *Theologische Realenzyklopädie*, vol. 7 (Berlin/New York, 1981), p. 57ff.

[25]   DBWE 8, p. 62.

[26]   DBWE 9, pp. 285–300.

with this approach [i.e., historical criticism] the concept of the canon disintegrates and becomes meaningless. Textual and literary criticism are applied to the Bible. The sources are distinguished, and the methods of the history of religions and form criticism fragment the larger and even the remaining short textual units into little pieces. After this total disintegration of the texts, historical criticism leaves the field of battle. Debris and fragments are left behind. Its work is apparently finished.[27]

'None of us', Bonhoeffer concedes late in the essay, 'can return to a pre-critical time' and he accepts that even the 'spiritual' interpreter has to use historical critical methods since, first and foremost, a reader of the Bible is faced with written texts that are the words of real human beings. But, he concludes in an early echo of Karl Barth, while for the historical critic Scripture is merely an historical source, for the spiritual interpreter 'scripture is a witness'.[28]

Bonhoeffer worried Berlin's theological professors. He was, as one senior Berlin theologian, Professor Arthur Titius told a friend in 1933 when Bonhoeffer quit his teaching post to become a pastor in London, the 'best hope' in the faculty; but in spite of protestations from, among others Adolf von Harnack, Bonhoeffer had fallen under the spell of dialectical theology and in particular of Karl Barth, whose commentary on Paul's letter to the Romans had shaken the foundations of the early twentieth-century consensus on how the Bible should be read. We get some sense of the flavour of such controversy from the Old Testament scholar Gerhard von Rad's post-war recollection of a conversation with Bonhoeffer as the two peers meandered home following the von Rad's lecture on Psalm 51 at the University of Jena:

> When we walked home together, we discussed the need for historico-critical research which I passionately defended against a counter-current which was arising during the Church struggle. I did not in the least understand my companion, and we quarrelled. Nowadays I would more easily comprehend his concern without giving up mine.[29]

Where was all this coming from? From Barth certainly, but not only from Barth. Bonhoeffer's view of the Bible was being shaped not only by new approaches to exegesis that rejected the liberal theological presuppositions of historical critics such as A.S.Peake, but by his theological discovery of the *sanctorum communio*, the holy community of the Church, as the primary context in which the Christian reads the Bible. The Bible for Bonhoeffer is above all the *Church's* book, and when Christians read it they read it with the eyes of faith. From the early thirties

---

27   Ibid., p. 286.

28   Ibid., p. 296.

29   Gerhard von Rad, 'Meetings in Early and Late Years', in W-D Zimmermann and R.G. Smith (eds), *I knew Dietrich Bonhoeffer* (London, 1973), p. 177.

there were also increasingly *political* reasons why Bonhoeffer was reading the Bible. The impact on biblical studies of anti-Semitism was beginning to be felt and there was a serious possibility, under pressure from the pro-Nazi German Christians who were gaining influence in both Church and academy, that study of the Old Testament might be excluded from the curricula of both seminary and university. In this heady atmosphere Bonhoeffer made the decision in the winter semester of 1932/3 to lecture on the first three chapters of the book of Genesis. The decision was doubly bold. Dogmatic theology, then as now, did not by and large undertake theology by engaging with biblical texts; Bonhoeffer risked rejection by theologians for reading the Bible, and by biblical scholars for intruding into areas where he could claim no expertise. His choice was bold too because by January 1933, before his lectures had reached their conclusion, the arch-anti-Semite Adolf Hitler had been appointed Reich Chancellor, changing for good the political geography of Germany and Europe.

Bonhoeffer's approach to the interpretation of the Bible had altered very little since his formational essay on spiritual interpretation. In a brief introduction to the published version of the lectures Bonhoeffer attempts to express the tension that, in his view, characterises the relationship between the Church and the world: 'The church of Christ witnesses to the end of all things. It lives from the end, it thinks from the end, it proclaims its message from the end.'[30] How is it possible for the Church, which exists in time like every other institution, or the Christian, who lives like every other individual in the middle of time and history, to speak authoritatively of the beginning of the universe and of the end point of time to which the world is travelling? This human impossibility is made possible on the basis of the witness of Scripture, which knows Christ as the beginning and the end. The Church can do this because it is founded on the witness of Scripture. There is no other church than the Church of Holy Scripture. In this Church, 'the story of creation must be read in a way that begins with Christ and only then moves toward him as its goal'. The term Bonhoeffer now uses to describe this thoroughly Christological hermeneutic method is 'theological exposition', and Bonhoeffer insists, against Peake, that it takes 'the Bible as the book of the church and interprets it as such'.[31] His subsequent remarks are worth quoting in full:

> Its method is a continual returning from text (as determined [here again is Bonhoeffer's concession] by all the methods of philological and historical research) to this presupposition. This is the objectivity in the method of theological exposition. And on this objectivity alone does it base its claim to have the nature of a science.[32]

---

[30] DBWE 3, p. 21.

[31] Ibid., p. 22.

[32] Ibid., p. 23. Bonhoeffer amplifies precisely this view of biblical interpretation in the letter he wrote to his brother-in-law, cited at the beginning of this chapter: 'This is how I read the Bible now. I ask of each passage: What is God saying to us here? And I ask God

Bonhoeffer's view of the Bible, his approach to reading it, and his critique of the limitations of the historical critical method raise questions no less difficult than Peake's approach. The most significant of these difficulties concerns a tension between Bonhoeffer's comment to Rüdiger Schleicher that the reason he found himself turning more and more to the Bible in the context of the Church struggle was because in all other texts he feared meeting merely an echo of his own interpretation. What was distinctive about Bonhoeffer's experience of reading the Bible relative to other texts was its *otherness*, the alien qualities of its culture, languages and theology. Yet, properly undertaken, it is precisely the otherness of the biblical text that historical criticism helps to establish. This results in some very pressing questions about the quality of some of Bonhoeffer's exegesis. For example, in his study of Ezra and Nehemiah Bonhoeffer utilises the story of the rebuilding of the walls of Jerusalem and the restoration of Jewish religion following the rediscovery of the scroll of the law, in relation to the German Church struggle. Ezra and Nehemiah, he interprets, teach the importance of theological purity as a basis for the life of God's people: just so, the Confessing Church has to defend its theological purity against the German Christians. To my mind, deploying the books of Ezra and Nehemiah in this way, that is in a way in which Bonhoeffer's own context is the decisive factor in reading the biblical texts, entails precisely the risk that its otherness, that otherness established by historical criticism, is kept out of the picture.

There is much more to be said about Bonhoeffer's view of the Bible, not least on his understanding of the relation of the Old and the New Testaments.[33] But in order to achieve a more tangible grasp of the practical exegetical consequences of Peake and Bonhoeffer's biblical hermeneutic it is helpful briefly to compare and contrast their respective readings of the same text. One obvious comparison is between the editor's own commentary on the book of Genesis in *Peake's Commentary on the Bible* and Bonhoeffer's interpretation of the first three chapters of that book in *Creation and Fall*; only 13 years elapsed between the publication of Peake's commentary and that of Bonhoeffer.

---

that he would help us hear what he wants to say. So, we no longer look for general, eternal truths, which correspond with our own "eternal" nature and are, therefore, somehow self-evident to us. Instead we seek the will of God, who is altogether strange to us, whose ways are not our ways and whose thoughts are not our thoughts, who hides himself from us under the sign of the cross, in which all our ways and thoughts have an end. God is completely other than the so-called eternal verities.' Bonhoeffer, *Meditating*, p. 45; German original, DBW 14, p. 146.

[33]   See, e.g., Martin Kuske's splendid monograph, *The Old Testament as a Book of Christ* (Philadelphia, 1976).

Peake on Genesis

Peake begins his commentary, predictably enough, with the question of sources. Rejecting what he terms 'persistent assertions to the contrary'.[34] Peake asserts that the 'there is no room for reasonable doubt' that the book of Genesis is comprised for the most part of three documentary sources and goes on to emphasise that the text is characterised by 'internal inconsistencies' and 'intrinsic incredibilities'.[35] Singling out the creation narrative he takes pains to iterate that 'the narrative of creation cannot be reconciled with our present knowledge except by special pleading which verges on dishonesty'.[36] Peake is clear that the proper approach to the text is one of 'dispassionate enquiry' that distinguishes history and myth, though he adds that myth, like poetry, may often be an effective means to convey religious truth. This insight is the basis for his reading of the first 11 chapters of the book, in which what was once naked myth has been, as he puts it, 'purified' by the religious genius of the Israelites. On this basis Peake is able to write that 'it is not the explicit formulation of principles and beliefs, nor even these distilled from the narrative' that is precious, 'it is the narratives themselves as they stand which yield us most for edification, guidance and inspiration'.[37] The texts are neither science or history, Peake is saying, but their capacity to instruct remains intact. One way in which to understand how the texts arrived at their present form, Peake continues, is to see that 'many of the stories are aetiological, that is, that they supply an answer to the question: What gave rise to such customs, instincts, conditions, names, such as those with which we are familiar?'[38]

This is one way that Peake, to select an example, treats the story of the woman's conversation with the serpent in Genesis 3 and its consequences: the story, Peake explains, accounted for the Hebrews for the pangs of childbirth: God's everlasting punishment for the woman's disobedience. In the body of his commentary, however, Peake by and large contents himself with re-narrating the biblical story. Like Bonhoeffer, as it happens, Peake asserts that it is mistaken to associate the serpent with the devil; the text is quite explicit in making the serpent simply one amongst the creatures made by God. But Peake distinguishes himself from the approach Bonhoeffer would later take in stating that 'there is no Messianic reference' in the text, thereby ruling out the link that Bonhoeffer will make between the text of Genesis 3 and the apostle Paul's understanding of Christ as the new Adam who in his person reconciles fallen Adam with God.

---

[34]   Peake, *Commentary*, p. 133.

[35]   Ibid., p. 133.

[36]   Ibid., p. 133.

[37]   Ibid., p. 134.

[38]   Ibid., p. 134.

Bonhoeffer on Genesis

In contrast with Peake, Bonhoeffer sets out not from the question of the sources of the book of Genesis, but from a theological discussion of how Christians may speak of the beginning of time. No one 'can speak of the beginning but the one who was in the beginning'. Because of this, 'God alone tells us that God is in the beginning; God testifies of God by no other means than through his word, which, as the word of a book, the words of a pious human being, is wholly a word that comes from the middle and not from the beginning.'[39] The beginning described in Genesis 1 is not to be thought of in temporal terms; but as something unique, a limit beyond which human beings cannot go. The character of this beginning, Bonhoeffer asserts, can only be known in the resurrection, which is, like God's creation, a creating out of nothing.

It is clear to Bonhoeffer that the first chapters of the book of Genesis contain more than one narrative of creation. But while this fact cannot be ignored, Bonhoeffer is not anxious about it. If the first creation narrative is for Bonhoeffer, about humankind for God thought out from above; then the second is about God for humankind, thought out from below. The two narratives therefore complement rather than contradict one another. The anthropomorphisms of the Yahwist account of the creation of Adam (in Genesis 1–2:4a) are, Bonhoeffer acknowledges, insupportably childlike. However, he asserts that 'in being distinguished as the word of God it [the story] is quite simply the *source* of knowledge about the origin of humankind'.[40] It expresses the physical nearness of the Creator to the creature, but also God's omnipotence. 'Who can speak of these things', he asks, 'except in pictures? Pictures after all are not lies; rather they indicate things and enable the underlying meaning to shine through.'[41]

In the space available it is possible to give but one example of the theological interpretation Bonhoeffer engages in the lectures. In the centre of Eden stand two trees: the tree of knowledge of good and evil, and the tree of life. Bonhoeffer mentions historical critical treatments of the trees, but only to dismiss them by reiterating that 'our concern is the text as it presents itself to the church today'. On this basis Bonhoeffer titles his treatment of the serpent's discussion of the trees with Eve 'the pious question'. The serpent is not, for Bonhoeffer, an incarnation of the devil, but one of God's creatures who becomes an instrument of evil. By spelling this out Bonhoeffer sidesteps the question of how evil came into the world, justifying the evasion on the basis that the biblical narrative of the Fall does not address the question either. The serpent is subtle: to begin with he does not dispute God's Word. His question, 'Did God really say?' is apparently innocent. Bonhoeffer describes his exchange with Eve as the first religious conversation and the first theological debate. But the question opens up a brave new world

---

[39] DBWE 3, p. 30.

[40] Ibid., pp. 75–6.

[41] Ibid., p. 81.

of possibilities unsuspected by Eve in her innocence. 'The decisive point', Bonhoeffer explains:

> is that through this question the idea is suggested to the human being of going behind the word of God and now providing it with a human basis – a human understanding of the essential nature of God. Should the word contradict this understanding, then the human being has clearly misheard.[42]

So what, Bonhoeffer continues, 'is the real evil in this question?':

> It is not that a question as such is asked. It is that this question already contains the wrong answer. It is that with this question the basic attitude of the creature toward the Creator comes under attack. It requires humankind to sit in judgement of God's word instead of simply listening to it and doing it. And this is achieved by proposing that, on the basis of an idea, a principle, or some prior knowledge about God, humankind should now pass judgement on the concrete word of God.[43]

When Eve still resists temptation, the serpent takes a more aggressive line, suggesting to Eve that God's prohibition of the tree's fruit is intended to prevent Eve and Adam becoming '*sicut deus*', like God: eat of the fruit, lies the serpent, and you too can be like God. Eating the fruit removes a limit, as the serpent suggested it would, and makes Eve and Adam *sicut deus*, at the centre, but alone. Is it going too far to speculate that this '*sicut deus*', this placing of oneself at the centre instead of God, is the position in which Bonhoeffer suspected the historical critic had placed himself and his discipline?

Evaluation and Conclusions

It is of course clear that reading Peake and Bonhoeffer on Genesis is not to compare like with like: a critical commentary facilitating biblical study and a lecture in dogmatics by a private lecturer free to choose his topic and the way he handles it would result in different treatments even if the authors were in substantial agreement. Yet, even when we have taken this into account the distance between them is great. So who is right? Which side of the fence do I want to choose? At the beginning of this chapter I suggested that putting the question in this way is artificial. Both Peake and Bonhoeffer, for different reasons, address questions of the nature of the Bible and the function of historical criticism in a polemical mood: both men, that is, are keen to present the questions as though every reader of the Bible must choose between historical critical and theological modes of reading. But is this really the case? I want in this concluding section to identify several

---

[42]   Ibid., p. 106.
[43]   Ibid., pp. 107–108.

avenues of enquiry along which, with more time, I would want to journey further with the issues raised by comparing Peake and Bonhoeffer.

Let us make the most obvious point first: historical criticism is not what it was. The historical criticism that Peake is writing about, the historical criticism Bonhoeffer is writing about, and historical criticism as it is practised today by Old and New Testament scholars, though they are clearly variant forms of the same practice, are not identical. Bonhoeffer's view of historical criticism is skewed by the fact that the variant form with which he was in contact was German historical criticism. German forms of biblical scholarship were particularly fixated on textual and redaction criticism. Confronted with biblical scholarship that occupied itself almost entirely with textual and redaction criticism, it is easy to see why Bonhoeffer might feel frustrated at the lack of theological interest in biblical criticism.

Contemporary biblical scholarship resembles no more the view Peake had of it. Peake was impressively confident in the achievements of biblical scholarship. Surveying his discipline Peake displays pride in the rational consensus on key issues, such as the construction of the Pentateuch, on which he and his peers were agreed. Today, it seems to me as an outsider, Old and New Testament scholarship are more controverted and less coherent. Some biblical scholars do share many of Peake's assumptions; but increasingly many do not. Peake, for example, believed both that biblical scholars generally agreed about the sources that make up the book of Genesis, agreed about when it was constructed, and that these kinds of conclusions represented considerable scholarly achievements that help modern readers to make better sense of the texts. Today, few if any of these assumptions are universally shared within biblical scholarship. Some biblical scholars assert that redaction criticism has proved a bit of a blind alley, a way of heated disagreements that ultimately boil down to simple matters of opinion. Some biblical scholars are now suggesting that scholarship should set questions of source criticism aside and deal only with the text in its final received form. Peake was confident that the text had a meaning, that the meaning of the text was what the original writer meant it to mean, and that the biblical critic was in a position to recover that meaning. Once again, while some biblical scholars continue to hold this view, others, drawing for example on post-war developments in philosophical hermeneutics, believe the idea that texts have a single definitive meaning is a chimera that will always elude the critic's grasp. Neither Peake nor Bonhoeffer could have foreseen the impact on biblical scholarship that liberationist and feminist theory have had, for example in raising political questions about whose interests are served in the construction and interpretation of biblical texts. The more recent growth in social scientific interpretations of biblical texts[44] is raising no less interesting and promising questions about the role and nature of biblical criticism. While some biblical critics still conceptualise their discipline as a science separate from theology, and defend as Peake did, the ideal of the biblical critic as a dispassionately objective

---

[44]   For an introduction to this approach, see D.G. Horrell (ed.), *Social Scientific Approaches to New Testament Interpretation* (Edinburgh, 1999).

scientist in the classic rationalist Enlightenment mould, a growing number are accepting that this ideal can no longer be maintained. A smaller number of biblical scholars have begun to argue not only that theological presuppositions may creep up on biblical scholarship unawares, but have embraced the aim of an openly theological approach to biblical scholarship in ways that acknowledge complex interactions between the written text, the Church and the world.[45]

But perhaps more than liberation, feminist or social scientific influences on biblical scholarship, the Holocaust is proving to have an impact on biblical scholarship that neither Peake nor Bonhoeffer could have predicted. Peake subscribed to the view that the Old Testament must be regarded as a partial and imperfect introduction to the fullness of revelation in Christ. Like Hegel he regarded Judaism as a primitive religion that achieves its perfect form in Protestant Christianity. Bonhoeffer's relation to Judaism has been much discussed, and he has variously been hailed as part of the problem of Jewish–Christian relations and as a model for good conduct in Christian relations to the Jews. The truth probably lies somewhere in between. This is not the place to go into this topic in depth; here it is enough to say that recent developments in biblical scholarship that arise directly and indirectly from the challenges raised by the Holocaust for Jewish–Christian relations make Bonhoeffer's biblical exegesis look their age. One consequence of the Holocaust for biblical scholarship has been the recent development of Jewish biblical scholarship alongside Christian biblical scholarship. Dialogue between Christian and Jewish readers of biblical texts is taking place more and more and, while this need not disallow Christological readings of the Old Testament such as those Bonhoeffer routinely deployed, it is putting them in a different light. Similarly, the so-called new readings of Paul, which have called into question assumptions about the apostle's supercessionist theology shaped by centuries of Christian anti-Semitism, not least disturbingly displayed in Martin Luther's writings, have radically altered New Testament scholarship in ways that make the later sections of Bonhoeffer's book *Discipleship* seem oddly antique.

It is certainly true that Bonhoeffer raises for us several still unresolved questions about biblical criticism. Some forms of scholarly enquiry into the Bible, for example patterns of Bronze and Iron Age settlement, may not raise very many theological questions; but it seems entirely reasonable to me for theologians to feel frustration with biblical scholarship if, for example, it undertakes *textual* enquiry into the relationship between the books of Judges and Kings without interest in questions of their *theological* relationship. Peake approached the Bible as a historian and made historical critical questions primary in his reading of biblical texts. Bonhoeffer approached the Bible as a theologian and made theological questions dominant in his reading of biblical texts. To my mind, historical approaches and theological approaches to reading the Bible may legitimately be distinguished.

---

[45]   e.g., Francis Watson, *Text, Church and World: Biblical Interpretation in Theological Perspective* (Edinburgh, 1994).

Peake came dangerously close to making historical critical readings of the Bible the only legitimate way of reading biblical texts. Bonhoeffer came dangerously close to making theological interpretation the only legitimately *Christian* way of reading the Bible. Somewhere between these reactionary extremes lies a much less tidy, and potentially much richer – richer that is for the Church – *modus vivendi* for biblical scholars and theologians, in which their respective methods of reading engage in a dialogue that permits far greater interpenetration of insight between the disciplines than either Peake or Bonhoeffer envisaged. Bonhoeffer thought a fence stood tall between historical critical and theological interpretation of the Bible and insisted that readers chose which side to sit on. I agree that the fence is there: but I also think that it is in the mutual interest of biblical criticism and theology that it should never be so tall as to prevent these neighbouring communities of Bible readers from talking.

Chapter 5
Guilt and Promise in Bonhoeffer's 'Jonah'[1]

b. Megillah 31a – On the Day of Atonement we read 'After the death' [Lev 16] and for *haftarah*, 'For thus said the high and lofty one' [Isa 57.15]. At *minchah* we read the section of forbidden marriages [Lev 18] and for *haftarah* the book of Jonah.

(Directions in the Talmud for texts to be read at Yom Kippur)

Jonah[2]

They screamed in the face of death, their frightened bodies clawing
at sodden rigging, tattered by the storm,
and horror-stricken gazes saw with dread
the sea now raging with abruptly unleashed powers.

'Ye gods, immortal, gracious, now severley angered,
help us, or give a sign, to mark for us
the one whose secret sin has roused your wrath,
the murderer, the perjurer, or vile blasphemer,

who's bringing doom on us by hiding his misdeed
to save some paltry morsel of his pride!'
This was their plea. And Jonah spoke ''Tis I!'
In God's eyes I have sinned. Forfeited is my life.

'Away with me! The guilt is mine. God's wrath's for me.
The pious shall not perish with the sinner!'
They trembled much. But then, with their strong hands,
they cast the guilty one away. The sea stood still.

Introduction

Guilt and promise are at odds: guilt pulls life into the past, promise pushes life into the future. Guilt draws a life back to things that have been and that cannot be changed; promise directs a life forward to things that are not, but which can

---

[1]   This chapter is a significantly revised version of a paper given in Oxford on 6 January, 2006, at the conference *Bonhoeffer's theology through the lens of his poetry*. I am grateful to all who commented on the paper, and in particular to Bernd Wannenwetsch for editorial guidance.

[2]   DBWE 8, pages 547–8.

yet be. Yet though guilt and promise appear opposing forces, in God they are eventually reconciled. In the atonement effected by Jesus Christ, God leads human beings from sin to the promise of new life; in Him, guilt is transformed into promise.

Bonhoeffer's 'Jonah' is a poem in which the transformation of guilt into promise is transfixed in a moment of its happening; a moment in which a life configured by Jonah's past sin is reconfigured towards its future by God's promise. Bonhoeffer's 'Jonah' imagines a crisis in which a past act which cannot be changed is placed humbly into the hands of God, who alone stills storms and calms seas. In confessing his guilt, Jonah confesses God.[3] In this poetic re-narration of an episode in the biblical book of Jonah – at a point in time when Bonhoeffer himself was about to be cast into the malevolent sea of *fin de règne* Germany under National Socialist tyranny – we sense Bonhoeffer entrusting his life to the judgement and promise of God.

It is tempting, in reading Bonhoeffer's 'Jonah', to be drawn into a quest for meaning; but whose quest, and which meaning? The quest and the meaning of the author/s of the biblical book of Jonah? Bonhoeffer's quest for meaning in the biblical book of Jonah? Or *our* quest for meaning in Bonhoeffer's poem? These are seductive questions: but if Bonhoeffer is to be believed, all quests for meaning – existential and hermeneutical – need to be understood in the light of what in the scriptures is called promise. Writing not long before he wrote 'Jonah', Bonhoeffer warned Bethge:

> Again and again in these turbulent times, we lose sight of why life is really worth living. We think that our own life has meaning [*Sinn*] because this or that other person exists. In truth, however, it is like this: If the earth was deemed worthy to bear the human being Jesus Christ, if a human being like Jesus lived, then and only then does our life as human beings have meaning [*Sinn*] … The unbiblical concept of 'meaning' [*Sinnes*], after all, is only one translation of what the Bible calls 'promise' [*Verheißung*].[4]

The search for meaning and the hearing of promise are related but not identical events. The point is amplified by Heinz Eduard Tödt, who explains that for Bonhoeffer, the term *promise* 'points out that something, brought from God by the gospel, comes to meet the human being, whereas meaning is something that the human being looks for in human life and in its surroundings, in the past, the present, and the future – often enough in vain'.[5] A promise, then, is something given and

---

[3]   For a rich display of the profound interconnectedness of these two senses of 'confession', see Augustine, *Confessions*, trans. Henry Chadwick (Oxford, 1991).

[4]   DBWE 8, p. 515; DBW 8, p. 573.

[5]   Heinz Eduard Tödt, *Authentic Faith: Bonhoeffer's Theological Ethics in Context*, ed. Glen Harold Stassen, trans. David Stassen and Ilse Tödt (Grand Rapids, 2007), pp. 16–17.

received, while meaning is something one searches for oneself. Accepting this, we may decide that in reading Bonhoeffer's 'Jonah', a distinction needs to be drawn between seeking meaning and being receptive to promise. Good textual exegetes come in many forms and may hold many convictions; but promise is something one only prepares for in a mind-frame of what Simone Weil called *attente de Dieu*. It is this sense of waiting on God that Bonhoeffer's poem conveys, and which commentary on the poem should pray, if dimly, to reflect.

The essay that follows proceeds in three stages. In the first stage, I want to turn attention away from Bonhoeffer's poem towards the biblical book of Jonah. My intention here is to situate Bonhoeffer in a community of interpretation and to probe the question of why this particular book was the one that proved fit for purpose at this decisive moment in his life. Turning back to Bonhoeffer, I next want to situate the poem in time and place before, thirdly, reading the poem in light of the themes of guilt and promise adumbrated above – themes brought into focus through Bonhoeffer's understanding of vicarious representative action (*Stellvertretung*). These are not the only interesting or possibly fruitful directions one might take in reading the poem, but they are I hope, ones that arise naturally from the text of the poem itself.

The Book of Jonah: A Whistle-Stop Tour[6]

Why Jonah? Of all the passages in all the books in all the Bible, Bonhoeffer walks in to this one: why? We can readily understand why a 'profoundly biblical theologian',[7] at a key moment in his life, might use a biblical passage or a biblical book as a still to condense thoughts and feelings to their essence; but what was it about *this* book that drew Bonhoeffer to it? In early December 1943, Bonhoeffer wrote that for some months 'I notice more and more how much I am thinking and perceiving things in line with the Old Testament; thus in recent months I have been reading much more the Old than the New Testament.'[8] And yet there is no

---

[6]   This section is indebted to several commentaries on the book of Jonah, including James Limburg, *Jonah* (London, 1993); R.B. Salters, *Jonah & Lamentations* (Sheffield, 1994); Jack M. Sasson, *Jonah* (New York, 1990); Jonathan Magonet, *Form and Meaning: Studies in the Literary Techniques of the Book of Jonah* (Sheffield, 1983).

[7]   Gerhard Krause's telling phrase in his entry on Bonhoeffer in the *Theologische Realenzyklopädie*, vol. 7 (Berlin/New York, 1981), p. 57.

[8]   DBWE 8, p. 213. For Bonhoeffer's use of the Bible see also Walter Harrelson, 'Bonhoeffer and the Bible', in Martin E. Marty (ed), *The Place of Bonhoeffer* (London, 1963), pp. 115–42; Stephen J. Plant, 'Uses of the Bible in the Ethics of Dietrich Bonhoeffer', unpublished doctoral dissertation, Cambridge University, 1993; E.G. Wendel, *Studien zur Homiletik Dietrich Bonhoeffers* (Tübingen, 1985). For Bonhoeffer's use of the Old Testament see Martin Kuske, *The Old Testament as the Book of Christ* (Philadelphia, 1976); and Martin Hohmann, *Die Korrelation von Altem und Neuem Bund* (Berlin, 1979).

indication that Bonhoeffer had the book of Jonah in mind. Prior to writing the poem, Jonah's story left scarcely any trace on Bonhoeffer's theology. Bonhoeffer neither underlined nor made marginal notes on the text of Jonah in his *Lutherbibel*; he mentions Jonah in an undergraduate essay in connection with repentance;[9] in 1937 he again mentions Jonah, this time as God's witness, in a circular letter to the Finkenwalde brethren;[10] and a year later we once again find a passing mention in a lecture on theology in the Confessing Church.[11] But compared to his engagement with the book of Genesis, or with the Psalms, or with the books of Ezra and Nehemiah, or in his sermons with other major and minor prophets, Bonhoeffer's engagement with the book of Jonah prior to writing the poem appears, on the basis of what he wrote, to have been slight. At least once Bonhoeffer had unflatteringly been likened to Jonah – when Karl Barth instructed Bonhoeffer in London to stop 'playing Elijah under the juniper tree or Jonah under the gourd' and to return to Germany 'with all guns blazing'[12] – but this was more than a decade before the poem was written and refers to quite a different episode in the story of Jonah to that taken up by Bonhoeffer in 1944. Which still leaves the question 'why Jonah?'

The biblical book of Jonah has several unusual features. The eponymous prophetic books of the Bible generally contain three elements, though typically *not* in equal proportions: they contain direct and indirect words given by God through the prophet to the people; words addressed by the prophet to God (for example in prayer or in lament); and material relating to the biographical experiences of the prophet. The book of Jonah has all three, but material detailing the biography of Jonah is proportionately its main focus. This makes it – by comparison with the other prophetic books – the only prophetic book to be *primarily* about the prophet. In his *Ethics* Bonhoeffer had argued that, for Christians, what matters is not to pattern one's life on some biblical character – such as Abraham or Peter – but to be conformed to the '*Gestalt*' – the form or character – of Jesus Christ.[13] Does Bonhoeffer now identify himself with a moment in Jonah's story, an aspect of his experience or a feature of his character?

A second unusual feature of Jonah is that it is the only prophetic book in which the prophet is sent to proclaim his message in a foreign land. When Bonhoeffer arrived in America in 1939 it immediately became clear to him that he had made a mistake. One of the reasons he gave to Reinhold Niebuhr for his decision to return to Germany was that he felt the necessity of living through 'this difficult period

---

[9] DBWE 9, p. 250.

[10] DBW 14, p. 286.

[11] DBWE 15, p. 431.

[12] DBWE 13, p. 39; the instruction stung Bonhoeffer, who sent Barth's letter to his father for his professional psychiatric opinion! Franz Hildebrandt sometimes addressed Bonhoeffer as 'my Dove' (Jonah in Hebrew means 'dove'), but this relates to their mutual pacifism.

[13] See Plant, *Uses*, pp. 79–154.

of our national history with the Christian people of Germany'.[14] Is it possible that Bonhoeffer should see himself in the story of a prophet whose calling was to a nation other than his own? The identification seems odder still if we recall that one of the explanations offered by some for why the book of Jonah was written is that its apparently universalist message was intended to counter the exclusivist outlook reflected in the books of Ezra and Nehemiah. In a sermon of January 1936, and again at greater length in a Bible study given to students on 21 April 1936, Bonhoeffer drew from the story of Ezra and Nehemiah the theological conclusion that just as 'the Jewish people must be pure because they are God's own chosen people ... God's church-community may not be tainted through heathen elements.'[15]

A third unusual aspect concerns what genre Jonah belongs to. The book can be broken down into several episodes: Jonah's call and decision to run from it; the sea voyage and its stormy outcome; the fish that swallows Jonah and his prayer in the fish's belly; Jonah's prophecy to the Ninevites and their repentance; Jonah's anger with God's mercy; God's dialogue with Jonah seated beneath a miraculous bush. But what sort of book is it? If it contains too much biographical material and too little oracular text to fit neatly with the other minor prophets, is it best classified as history or legend, didactic story, parable or allegory? Or is it a 'chowder' of several genres?[16] One intriguing possibility is that it takes the form – very loosely speaking – of a 'midrash' either on the miraculous exchanges between God and Elijah in the book of Kings or more likely, on Exodus 34:6–7a, cited in Jonah 4.2b as a summation of the book's message: 'The Lord, the Lord, a God merciful and gracious, slow to anger and abounding in steadfast love and faithfulness, keeping steadfast love for the thousandth generation, forgiving iniquity and transgression and sin.' The body of biblical commentary termed 'midrash' arose, properly speaking, in the Rabbinic schools in the early centuries of the Christian era. They varied in form and content, but tended to be characterised by use of story to convey meaning and by the use of questions that, by interrogating characters in the story, serve as a literary device to put the hearer in the place of the character questioned. Is this method foreshadowed in Jonah? There are 14 questions in the book of Jonah: seven addressed to Jonah, and seven addressed by Jonah to God – a symmetry that can hardly be unintended. This suggests that the book was developed as an interactive story to be spoken and heard with a view to instructing listeners willing to participate in its narrative twists and turns.

Finally, the book of Jonah is unusual because of the extent of uncertainty about its setting. Other prophetic books, to be sure, lack an explicit social and political context, but their contents usually lead commentators to agree about their likely *Sitz im Leben*. The text of Jonah, however, leads to no such consensus about when, where or why it was written. Though it is clear from Jonah 1:1, and from the

---

[14] DB-EB, p. 655.

[15] DBW 14, pp. 930–45.

[16] Yvonne Sherwood, *A Biblical Text and its Afterlives: The Survival of Jonah in Western Culture* (Cambridge, 2000).

reference to Jonah the prophet in 2 Kings 14:23–27 that it is intended to be *set* in the eighth century BCE, the book itself is adrift from a historical context. It is likely to have been written towards the end or soon after the end of the exile. But – even for the shrewdest commentator – fixing its date can only be a matter of guesswork. Which leaves us still with the question why did *this* book draw Bonhoeffer in?

Jonah: A Biblical Text and its Afterlives

If Bonhoeffer himself won't give us a direct answer to that question perhaps an answer is suggested by the history of the book's interpretation. Fortuitously, just such a history exists: in colourful imagery invited by the fabulous qualities of the book of Jonah itself, Sherwood's, *A Biblical Text and its Afterlives: The survival of Jonah in Western Culture*, gives us a glimpse 'into the tailor's shop and gourmet restaurant that is the interpretive history of the book of Jonah'.[17] Sherwood's analysis helps us to see Bonhoeffer within the community of readers stretching from the Patriarchs, through rabbis and Reformers, and on into the nineteenth century, when the plausibility or implausibility of a sea creature that could swallow a man became a battleground for those slugging out the factual truth of the biblical record. What is often true in the history of biblical interpretation is particularly true in the case of Jonah: 'knowledge and meaning are *agglutinative* ... new products can be made by bringing together existing traditions and recombining them'.[18] Readers of Jonah, even new readers interpreting the story in new situations, stand on the shoulders of readers before them.

For the Patriarchs, Jonah and Jesus were typological twins.[19] This was not only because, as Augustine observed, '[t]o the healthy and pure internal eye [Christ] is everywhere',[20] but also because the gospels themselves warranted typological comparisons between Jonah and Jesus. For Luke the correlation has to do with judgement and repentance: 'just as Jonah became a sign to the people of Nineveh, so the Son of Man will be to this generation' (Luke 11:30). Matthew shares with Luke an emphasis on judgement but adds, 'just as Jonah was for three days and three nights in the belly of the sea monster, so for three days and three nights the Son of Man will be in the heart of the earth' (Matthew 12:40), drawing an analogy between Jonah in the whale and Jesus in the tomb. From the loam of these typologies, elaborate analogies bloomed for both Patriarchs and rabbis in which ship, sailors, waves and fish were symbolically employed: the ship became the Church, humanity or the synagogue; the sailors became the apostles, Romans or Jews opposed to Christ; the storm became humankind's affliction, the storms that

---

[17]   Sherwood, *Biblical Text*, p. 1.

[18]   Ibid., p. 5.

[19]   Ibid., pp. 11–21.

[20]   Augustine, *On Christian Doctrine*, trans. D.W. Robertson (New York, 1958), p. 13; cited in Sherwood, *Biblical Text*, p. 11.

shipwrecked Peter or Paul, or the work of the devil; the fish came to symbolise the devil, its jaws representing the jaws of hell, or even the concept of time, consuming all things; the Ninevites then represented either the gentiles or (for Bede) the splendid Church. However, above all, Jonah proved a wonderfully malleable symbol. For most of the Patriarchs, Jonah represented Christ (the exception was Augustine, who saw in him *both* Christ and fleshly Israel); for some rabbis, and for later Christian interpreters, Jonah was the Torah-bound Jew, a personification of cruel law, clinging to the letter while God goads him with mercy. For Jerome he was a nationalist, defending Israel against the widening of God's mercy to mere gentiles; while for Luther, struck by the animistic reference of his Hebrew name, Jonah was the dove who pointed towards the Holy Spirit.

It does not matter how much or, as seems more likely, how little of this history of interpretation Bonhoeffer was conscious of or influenced by in his own appropriation of Jonah. What matters are the possible interpretations that this history invites. Sherwood's conclusion is that:

> [m]eme-like, the book seems to cue in a whole range of survivals/mutations: with its chowder-like mixtures of death wishes and aqua-psalms and shivering ships, the book spawns comic riffs on prophets 'snoring slobberingly' *and* serious meditations on the alienation and powerlessness of the human protagonist; and by anticipating the alliterative, cartoonish, paranomastic, and associative linguistic effects through which the Rabbis, Auster and the *Gawain*-poet will go on prolonging and stretching the life of the 'Word', it seems to inaugurate and legitimate an expansive approach to interpretation.[21]

Jonah is a questioning and nonconformist book that delights in questioning and nonconformist readings, a story begging to be remade and retold, a book richly empathetic to human beings and 'lacking in reassurance of the comfort of the divine'.[22] Why did Bonhoeffer fix his eye on the book of Jonah? Might the answer simply be that it presents an especially suitable surface for a palimpsest on which Bonhoeffer could inscribe his own meaning? That is part of the answer, but I do not think it is the whole answer. For that, we need to return to where we began, to the themes of guilt and promise in this episode in the book of Jonah and their resonance with Bonhoeffer's own situation.

Bonhoeffer's 'Jonah' in its *Sitz im Leben*

The catastrophic failure of the 20 July bomb plot set the scene for the events leading up to the composition of 'Jonah'. Many whose involvement was immediately clear were unhesitatingly executed; others lasted only as long as their interrogation. The

---

[21] Sherwood, *Biblical Text*, p. 291.

[22] Ibid., p. 291.

plotters were intelligent calculators of risk, and it was clear that it was only a matter of time before nooses tightened around all their necks. The Allied landings in Normandy and the inexorable advance of the Soviet army, however, meant that there was always a chance that the war would end before their execution. Bonhoeffer, aware of all the ramifications, worked on determinedly with his prison theology and waited to see how events would unfold.

The answer came on 22 September 1944, when the Gestapo discovered records of the Abwehr conspiracy, which General Beck – against the advice of Hans von Dohnanyi that they should be destroyed – had ordered to be held in a branch of the Military Intelligence in Zossen. Probably acting on information yielded in the files, on 1 October the Gestapo arrested Bonhoeffer's brother Klaus. A day later Corporal Knobloch, the guard with whom Bonhoeffer had planned to escape Tegel prison, called at the Schleicher home to say that Dietrich had called off escape plans to avoid making matters worse for Klaus and of placing his fiancée and family in further danger.[23] The arrest of Dietrich's brother-in-law, Rüdiger Schleicher, followed on 4 October and of his Confessing Church colleague Friedrich Justus Perels on 5 October. This was the date on which he wrote 'Jonah'. Eberhard Bethge was arrested a few days later. Unaware that the snare was closing on Bethge himself, Bonhoeffer passed the poem to Maria von Wedemeyer with the instruction: 'please type out the poem and send it to Eberhard. He'll know who it's from without being told', adding 'You may find it a trifle incomprehensible. Or will you?'[24] On 8 October, as he had been expecting, Bonhoeffer was transferred to the Gestapo prison in the cellar of the Reich Central Security Headquarters at Prinz Albrecht Strasse. He was able to send only one more poem beyond this before communication with his family ceased. The poem 'Jonah' can be placed, then, very precisely at the moment at which Bonhoeffer gave up his plans for escape and accepted the likelihood of death. It was written in the days in which he finally accepted what must for some weeks have been increasingly obvious, that his survival could only come about at the cost of unacceptable risk to others. But the urgency of this immediate context should not replace, but complement wider contextual cues. Bonhoeffer's sense of responsibility extended beyond his immediate family and friends to the conspiracy, to the Church and to Germany. The essay for co-conspirators, 'After Ten Years' – which contained insights Bonhoeffer found important enough to incorporate into his *Ethics* – wrestled with the moral impact on the conspirators of a decade of secret opposition and dissimulation. And the Church too had failed, leading Bonhoeffer to draft a post-war confession of guilt. The likelihood of death acted as a lens focusing reflections on guilt and promise that had kept Bonhoeffer company since the early thirties.

---

[23]   EB-DB, pp. 826–8. The friendly guard, Knobloch is given the rank of 'corporal' by Bethge; in other accounts he is given the rank of 'sergeant'.

[24]   *Love Letters from Cell 92: Dietrich Bonhoeffer, Maria von Wedemeyer, 1943–1945*, ed. Ruth-Alice von Bismarck and Ulrich Kabitz, trans. John Brownjohn (London, 1994), p. 225.

Bonhoeffer's 'Jonah'

The poem is short – after 'Christians and Heathens', it is the next shortest of the prison poems. Its four stanzas, each of four lines, follow a disciplined ABBA rhyming pattern.[25] Both the brevity of the poem and the tightness of its form help convey the tense mood of the poem's subject matter, a tension emphasised by the staccato effect of some of the poem's short phrases and sentences, e.g. in the last line of the third stanza, 'Ich sündigte vor Gott. Mein Leben ist verwirkt' ('I sinned against God. My life is forfeit'). This is especially effective in the last line of the poem, in which Bonhoeffer uses a phrase taken directly from his 1911 Stuttgart edition of the *Lutherbibel*: 'Da stand das Meer' – 'the sea was still'. At key moments, such as the final line and in the preceding stanza when Jonah owns up to his responsibility for God's anger saying 'Ich bin es' – 'I am the one' – Bonhoeffer pares his language down to words of one syllable. If indeed Bonhoeffer is identifying with Jonah at this point, what is he guilty of? What is the sin to which Bonhoeffer owns up? In popular reception of the book (in medieval as well as modern times) Jonah and the whale have been as inseparable as Laurel and Hardy: the medieval scribes and modern children's book illustrators had a whale of a time picturing one in particular of the book's episodes. It is therefore striking that Bonhoeffer's poem re-narrates what is effectively scene two of the drama of Jonah (Jonah 1:4–16), and concludes at the instant *before* the great fish rears its head. Possibly, in its title and leading character, Bonhoeffer's poem evokes the whole drama of the book, but its focus is very narrowly on one aspect of Jonah's story and its cut-off point – the storm stilled as Jonah sinks beneath the waves (v. 15) – seems quite deliberate in ignoring the book's voracious co-star. Yet though Bonhoeffer decided to focus the action of the poem on vv. 4–15, it then follows the biblical account very faithfully. The biblical story is beautifully crafted in a symmetrical pattern:

A The Lord hurls a storm
B The sailors pray
C The sailors act
D The sailors question Jonah
E Jonah speaks
D The sailors question Jonah
E Jonah speaks
C The sailors act
A The storm ceases

---

[25] The 1953 SCM translation of *Letters and Papers from Prison* makes no attempt to use rhymes. Bronwnjohn, in *Love Letters from Cell 92* (London, 1992), does use rhymes at the end of a number of lines but is relaxed about the poem as a whole. Edwin Robertson's translation in *The Prison Poems of Dietrich Bonhoeffer* (Guildford, 1998) manages an English version with an ABBA rhyming pattern.

Bonhoeffer reduces the elements of the story somewhat, but retains the essential symmetry of the pericope:

A The storm breaks
B The sailors pray
C Jonah speaks
B the sailors act
A The storm ceases

The first stanza describes, in compelling physical detail, a fearful storm that beats the ship in which Jonah is travelling. The second stanza and the first two lines of the third stanza are in direct speech reporting the prayer of the sailors asking that the guilty one be identified.[26] In the following six lines, Jonah answers, first acknowledging his guilt, and then instructing the sailors to cast him overboard, since the pious shall not share the sinner's fate. In the closing lines, trembling, the sailors cast Jonah overboard, and the sea is stilled. Bonhoeffer's decision to end the poem *before* the prophet is saved from drowning, focuses attention on Jonah's willingness to sacrifice himself for his fellow travellers. The theme, in other words, is not so much Jonah's salvation, but his willingness to die for the salvation of others, even though they are not fellow countrymen (since they have no knowledge of Yahweh until Jonah names Him). A natural supposition is that Bonhoeffer senses here an intimation of the conspirators' willingness to sacrifice themselves for the German people. The fact that he cuts off the poem at v. 15 heightens the sense that this is what he intends to convey, since it means he does not attend to the sailors' assertion of the sovereignty of Yahweh above all other gods in v. 16. Neither is this the only key theme excluded by the poem's narrow focus: the narrator seems to draw everything towards the 'punch-line' in Jonah 4:2, which sums up the story with the mercy of Yahweh who may change his mind about punishing the sinful where there is true repentance.[27] For Bonhoeffer, the penultimate note of guilt in the last line is followed not by the ultimate affirmation of God's mercy, but with the more open end 'the sea was still'. This is Jonah in

---

[26]   Jack M. Sasson points out that the book of Jonah here echoes the role played by storms in extra-biblical literature in the ancient world. The assumption that storms are called up by gods to punish evildoers was also widespread: *Jonah* (New York, 1990), pp. 90ff.

[27]   Johann Christoph Hampe, *Prayers from Prison* (London, 1977) interprets the story in terms of the Church – recalling early Christian interpretation linking the story of Jonah to the sacrament of Baptism. Hampe even suggests equivalence between Jonah asleep in the ship's hold while storms rage with the failure of the German Church to wake up to the storms of ideology and war. Edwin Robertson favours a more personal interpretation that connects Bonhoeffer's intentions in the poem with his own role and that of his co-conspirators: 'Bonhoeffer moves from punishment for his guilt, the sacrifice of his righteousness ... to see that his death, like that of many others after the failure of the July bomb plot, is for the salvation of Germany': *The Prison Poems of Dietrich Bonhoeffer* (Guildford, 1998) p. 99.

close-up, with all attention focused on God's judgement, a judgement expressed in the powerful imagery of the stilled sea. But the judgement Bonhoeffer is concerned with is not simply an event in which God and Jonah alone are involved: it is a judgement that impacts upon the sailors' lives too. Jonah's acknowledgement of guilt and his instruction to cast him overboard suggests *both* acknowledgement of guilt *and* a taking of responsibility for the lives of others. Described in this way, does Jonah appear to be an archetypal *Stellvertreter* – one who stands in place of others? Is Jonah's action in telling the sailors to cast him overboard, an instance of *Stellvertretung*, of vicarious representative action?

Guilt, Promise and 'the structure of responsible life'

'Vicarious representative action' was one of Bonhoeffer's longest standing and most cherished theological and ethical ideas – one that he had been thinking through since writing *Sanctorum Communio*.[28] The fullest expression of the theme, however, unfolds in the fragment 'History and Good' in Bonhoeffer's *Ethics*. There, vicarious representative action is described as a form of responsible life, that is, of a life 'lived in answer to the life of Jesus Christ'.[29] Less complete forms of responsibility do exist in other moral systems, to be sure, but in the strict sense Bonhoeffer's unfolding of 'responsibility' 'denotes the complete wholeness and unity of the answer to the reality that is given to us in Jesus Christ'.[30] Such responsibility is accountable not to criteria such as usefulness, or adherence to a principle (such as honour), or to an abstract ideal such as patriotism. It is accountable only to Jesus Christ in his 'Yes and No to our life'. There are two aspects to this *representivity*. The first is that the vicarious representative represents Jesus Christ.[31] This is because the *Stellvertreter* gives up any attempt to justify himself; '[r]ather' continues Bonhoeffer, 'I take responsibility and answer for Jesus Christ, and with that I naturally also take responsibility for the commission I have been charged with by him.'[32] Yet, secondly, the vicarious representative also represents other people. Taking up responsibility is always something embedded in social structures – such as the family, government, or work place; responsibility is always responsibility for another *person*.

Towards the end of the fragment[33] Bonhoeffer sums up his attempt to grasp the 'structure of responsible life' under the rubrics of 'vicarious representative action, accordance with reality, [and] taking on guilt'.[34] Taking on guilt (*Schuldübernahme*)

---

28   For this point, see DBWE 6, p. 257, fn. 38.
29   Ibid., p. 254.
30   Ibid., p. 254.
31   Ibid., p. 255.
32   Ibid., pp. 255–6.
33   Ibid., p. 289.
34   Ibid., p. 289.

rolls together a free acceptance of one's own guilt and a taking on of the guilt of others (e.g., of church, or of nation).[35] Bonhoeffer writes:

> Those who in acting responsibly take on guilt – which is inescapable for any responsible person – place this guilt on themselves, not on someone else; they stand up for it and take responsibility for it. They do so not out of a sacrilegious and reckless belief in their own power, but in the knowledge of being forced into this freedom and of their dependence on grace in its exercise.[36]

The poem 'Jonah' distils Bonhoeffer's sense of what is involved in vicarious representative action. In doing so, something of the flavour of Bonhoeffer's action in taking responsibility transfers to his representation of Jonah, as an Islay malt whisky takes on the flavour of the sea beside which it is distilled and aged.

If this is indeed what is going on in Bonhoeffer's poem, then we have here a reading of the Jonah story in perfect harmony with the centuries-old Jewish tradition, prescribed by the Talmud, of reading Jonah on the festival of atonement.

---

[35] Ibid., p. 289 (see the footnote by the editor of the English translator, p. 288, fn. 159).
[36] Ibid., p. 282.

Chapter 6

The Evangelisation of Rulers:
Bonhoeffer's Political Theology

Bonhoeffer's chaplaincy to students at the Charlottenberg Technical College in Berlin was always an uphill struggle. He had been assigned the role following his ordination and his first semester in post, in his own words, had the appearance of being 'almost completely unsuccessful'.[1] In November 1932 Bonhoeffer pinned to his notice board a plaintive note addressed to the joker who had three times removed the chaplaincy programme for the term.[2] In the winter semester Bonhoeffer tried Bible studies on current topics, but with no greater success. Yet the four services he conducted for students at Trinity Church were, as he put it in his end of year report, 'conspicuously well attended by students'.[3]

On 26 February 1933, therefore, as Bonhoeffer began the service marking the end of the winter semester, he may have had a sense of occasion. It had been an eventful term, one that had begun in the dying days of the Weimar Republic and was ending as the third Reich was being born. Bonhoeffer's sermon was based on several verses from Chapters 6, 7 and 8 of the book of Judges that condense the story of Gideon. It would have been plain to his student congregation that these Bible verses were concerned with the politics of Israel in the period of the Judges. Less plain was that his sermon was also an exercise in political theology, understood, using Oliver O'Donovan's definition, as a reflective practice whose task 'is to shed light from the Christian faith upon the intricate challenge of thinking about living in late-modern Western society'.[4] In the first part of this chapter I ask what light this sermon sheds from the Christian faith on the political challenges Bonhoeffer and his students faced. In the second part I explore the sources on which Bonhoeffer's political theology draws and identify two of his key insights.

To grasp what Bonhoeffer is doing in his sermon we must first take note of the significance of the date on which he preached it. From the late 1920s the Nazi Party had become increasingly successful in elections to the German Reichstag

---

[1]   See Bonhoeffer's annual report to the Berlin Consistory, DBWE 12, pp. 118–20.

[2]   Ibid., p. 69.

[3]   Ibid., p. 119.

[4]   Oliver O'Donovan, *The Ways of Judgment* (Grand Rapids, 2005), p. x. I am also indebted to O'Donovan's *The Desire of the Nations* (Cambridge, 1996), for the phrase 'the evangelization of rulers'.

(parliament).[5] The rule of law hung in the balance and politically motivated violence became commonplace. In one incident, several Nazis beat a Communist sympathiser to death in Potempa, a Silesian village, and were condemned to death. Hitler sent the men a telegram expressing his solidarity with them and a Nazi newspaper reported that one of the condemned men had said: 'This telegram and his [Hitler's] picture will be the small altar before which I shall pray daily'.[6] In presidential elections Hindenburg proved hard to beat, but in April 1932 Hitler polled 37 per cent of votes to Hindenburg's 53 per cent. After declining Chancellor Papen's offer of the Vice Chancellorship, Hitler endured a frustrating winter until Hindenburg finally appointed him Chancellor on 30 January 1933. Most Germans were delighted. That evening the Brownshirts and the SS, groups with a history of internecine conflict, marched together through Berlin. Within weeks of taking office Hitler freed the killers from Potempa. Still many, including the theologian Karl Barth, initially judged Hitler's appointment to be an inconsequential shuffling of the deck of right of centre leaders.[7] But the Bonhoeffer family saw immediately that the consequences of Hitler's appointment were serious. On the evening of 30 January Dietrich's brother-in-law Rüdiger Schleicher, on arriving home, announced: 'This means war!'[8] The following day Bonhoeffer made his own views public in a radio broadcast on the 'Younger Generation's altered view of the concept of the Führer'. Unfortunately, Bonhoeffer overran his allotted time and the broadcast was cut off with the result that the theological conclusion was lost. His full script concluded: '… the leader points to the office; leader and office, however [point] to the ultimate authority itself before which Reich and state are penultimate authorities. Leader and office that turn themselves into gods mock God …'.[9] It is the same insight Bonhoeffer would glean from the story of Gideon.

In the weeks that followed Hitler's appointment the Nazis moved with astonishing speed and organisational skill to fix themselves in a position of complete power. A key moment was the burning of the Reichstag, the national parliament building in Berlin, on the evening of 27 February. The fire was started by a Dutchman Marinus van der Lubbe, whose lapsed Communist Party membership enabled Hitler to portray his arson as an attack on the state and on

---

[5]   For details of the historical events discussed in this section see Ian Kershaw, *Hitler 1889–1936: Hubris* (London, 1998), pp. 314–495.

[6]   See DBWE 12, p. 462, fn.6, and Klaus Scholder, *The Churches and the Third Reich, Vol. 1: 1918–1934* (London, 1977), p. 180.

[7]   Karl Barth to Anna-Katharina Barth, 1 February, 1933, cited in Scholder, *Churches*, Vol. 1, pp. 221 and 624.

[8]   DB-EB, p. 237.

[9]   DBWE 12, pp. 281–2. See also Bonhoeffer's circular note to friends explaining that he had overrun and that this distorted what he aimed to say (DBWE 12, p. 91); the incident has sometimes been misrepresented as if Bonhoeffer was cut off by a producer put out by the anti-Nazi tenor of the address.

28 February he enacted his 'Order for the protection of People and State'. It was the first of several legal moves giving Hitler total power.

Such detailing helps situate Bonhoeffer's sermon in its context, a month after Hitler took office as Reich Chancellor and 48 hours before the first of the legal acts that would replace the Weimar Republic with the Nazi Third Reich. In spite of what we know to be Bonhoeffer's political views, his sermon makes no explicit mention of Hitler. We may assume that many of the students in his congregation were Nazis; but it was not reluctance to offend that accounts for why Bonhoeffer does not name Hitler in his sermon. When preaching Bonhoeffer preferred to let the Bible do its own work theologically and politically.[10] In times of crisis or confusion Bonhoeffer instead urged theologians and preachers to 'go back to the very beginning, to our wellsprings, to the true Bible, to the true Luther', as he put it in November 1933, adding that: '[o]ne should keep on, ever more undaunted and joyfully becoming a theologian 'aletheuntes en agape' [speaking the truth in love]'.[11]

Bonhoeffer carefully prepared for his sermon. In his copy of the *Lutherbibel* he has underlined the key verses and at one point (Judges 7:2) he substituted Luther's phrasing with his own translation in such a way as to emphasise God's reluctance to let Israel take credit for its victory.[12] He begins with a summary of his main point:

> This is a passionate story about God's derision for all those who are fearful and have little faith … it is a story of God's mocking human might, a story of doubt and faith in this God who mocks human beings, who wins them over with this mockery and with love.[13]

If Gideon is a 'hero', he is not, for Bonhoeffer, a Teutonic hero like Wagner's Siegfried, who succeeds by cunning and the power of his own arm. Gideon is merely a creature, called to do God's will, coaxed round by teasing and love to obedience to God. In a side swipe at the Nazi killer from Potempa worshipping Hitler at his small altar, Bonhoeffer insists that the Church has only one altar: the altar of the Most High, the Almighty, the Creator, the Lord. If we grasp only one thing of Bonhoeffer's theopolitics, let it be this: '[a]nyone who wants to build an altar to himself or to any other human is mocking God'.[14] Faith, Bonhoeffer

---

[10]   See Bethge's comment on Bonhoeffer's preaching in DB-EB, p. 235: 'Though he took liberties with his text, he avoided modernist tricks that twisted the meaning, and did not comment directly on current political or church events.'

[11]   DBWE 1, p. 435.

[12]   See note 2, DBWE 12, p. 461, which reports Bonhoeffer's handwritten marginal note in his copy of the *Lutherbibel*.

[13]   Ibid., pp. 461–2.

[14]   Ibid., p. 463.

tells his student congregation, has the quality of pointing away from oneself to the one we obey.

In a neat rhetorical move, Bonhoeffer turns next from Gideon as a historical figure, to one whose situation is recognisable in his own context. Bonhoeffer offers his congregation Gideon as a type or figure for the Protestant Church, called to proclaim God to the nation, but in every way without influence, powerless and undistinguished. What can such a Church do? His answer is that the Church is able to follow its calling simply because 'God is with us'. To make the point, God orders Gideon to dismiss the army he has assembled and, in doing so, Gideon gives God the glory. In a conclusion that points a way towards the coming Church struggle with the Nazi state, Bonhoeffer says 'it does seem crazy, doesn't it, that the church should not defend itself by every means possible in the face of terrible threats coming at it from every side'.[15] The basic insight here is Pauline: God's grace is sufficient for us, for God's power is made perfect in weakness (see 2 Corinthians 12:9). The insight is a refraction backwards through time of the one Bonhoeffer would articulate from prison in the phrase 'only a suffering God can help': God's lordship, God's rule, God's politics, God's power, is seen most clearly in Jesus' nailed and outstretched hands: 'The cross of Jesus Christ – that means God's bitter mockery of all human grandeur and God's bitter suffering in all human misery, God's lordship over all the world.'[16]

What are we to infer from the Gideon sermon about Bonhoeffer's political theology? I want to turn first to the sources of Bonhoeffer's thinking, before exploring two of its key elements. I present these points in sequence, but they may also be conceived as a rudimentary systematically interrelated political theology, with each point informing the others.

'Wellsprings'

On 5 March, a few days after his end of semester service, Bonhoeffer went with his friend Franz Hildebrandt to the polls for the Reichstag elections. Hildebrandt, ever the convinced Protestant, voted for the Protestant Christian People's Party; but Bonhoeffer voted for the Catholic Centre Party on the pragmatic basis that it was the only party with half a chance of standing up to Hitler.[17] If Lutheran perspectives shaped Bonhoeffer's politics they did not do so in a *tribal* fashion, as if his ecclesial community was simply one more political party whose interests he was duty bound to defend. Yet, as we have already noted, Bonhoeffer wrote at the end of 1933 that periods of crisis should drive theologians 'back to the very beginning, to our wellsprings, to the true Bible, to the true Luther'.[18] The

---

[15]   Ibid., p. 466.
[16]   Ibid., p. 467.
[17]   DB-EB, p. 266.
[18]   DBWE 12, p. 435.

Gideon sermon tells us several things about how the Bible sheds light on unfolding political events. A first point to note is that the Bible, for Bonhoeffer, meant both the Old and the New Testaments, which together constitute the Bible as the Church's book.[19] This may seem obvious to most Christians, but it was by no means so obvious in Bonhoeffer's context, in which a strong Marcionite tendency existed in liberal Protestantism that judged the New Testament superior to the Old, which consequently was virtually excluded from theological discourse. By 1933 this liberal prejudice was already being used to warrant a denial of the Old Testament as Christian Scripture on far uglier anti-Semitic grounds. It is, therefore, all the more striking that so many of Bonhoeffer's biblical studies with a political flavour from 1933 to 1945 were based on Old Testament texts: Genesis 1–3 is used to reveal the basis on which human life is preserved; a study of the Psalms treats political themes such as law, kingship and the punishment of enemies, another on Ezra and Nehemiah sees in the rebuilding of a wall around Jerusalem an analogy of the theological truth that *extra ecclesiam nulla salus* – outside the Church there is no salvation. One consequence of Bonhoeffer's attentiveness to Old Testament as well as New Testament texts may be to balance a tendency observable in some Christian political theology that proceed more narrowly on New Testament texts alone.[20] New Testament texts reflect contexts in which the early Church was a minority outwith political power; they either perceive authorities as beastly persecutors or as established by God but without being godly. While some Old Testament texts likewise reflect an experience of political exile, others, like the book of Judges, wrestle with the messier experience of the exercise of power by God's servants: Gideon, Samuel, Saul, David and Nehemiah, who, with their compromises and frailties, lived out their political lives within the penultimate in ways that directed the eyes of their people to the ultimate.

A second point to take note of concerning Bonhoeffer's political use of biblical texts is his expectation that in the Bible God really does speak to the Church about concrete contemporary situations. Bonhoeffer does not discern in the Bible – as for example did the Anabaptist revolutionaries at Münster between 1532 and 1535 – a blueprint drawn by God for a theocracy that can and should be built by Christians now on earth; but he does believe that an authentically Christian politics is one that seeks to discern God's will for today in Scripture.

The second wellspring Bonhoeffer identified as central for theologians facing a crisis is the theology of Martin Luther. Making sense of Luther's political theology is challenging, not least because the treatises from which his political thought is in the main derived were responsive to particular and very different challenges. This has two consequences: firstly, it makes knowledge of context important for an intelligent understanding of any particular treatise written by Luther; secondly, it makes it hard to derive a consistent theopolitical position based on Luther's

---

[19]   See Martin Kuske, *The Old Testament as the Book of Christ* (Philadelphia, 1976).

[20]   I am thinking here, e.g., of John Howard Yoder's influential *The Politics of Jesus* (Grand Rapids, 1972).

writings.[21] To add to these challenges, from 1933 pro-Nazi Lutheran theologians began to debase the currency of Lutheran theopolitical vocabulary by claiming Luther as father of German nationhood, a promoter of Christian anti-Semitism,[22] and crucially as author of an understanding of an human society described in terms of inviolable orders of creation. Nonetheless, Bonhoeffer's political theology is shaped by Luther in four ways:

- Firstly, Bonhoeffer shares with Luther a fundamentally Augustinian conceptualisation[23] of politics structured by two realms: a temporal realm and a spiritual realm. For Luther, the spiritual realm comprises Christians only but the temporal realm comprises both Christians and non-Christians. Crucially, the authority of both realms is derived from God.
- Secondly, the two realms place limits on each other's authority. Temporal authority only extends to bodily life; the life of faith should be free of interference by temporal rulers. But the converse is also true: spiritual authority, while it may offer counsel to a godly temporal ruler, has no authority to impede the state in the exercise of its authority over bodily life.
- Thirdly, Luther – like Augustine developing his political theology under the shadow of political chaos and violence – affirmed the value of political order. Like Augustine, but unlike Thomas Aquinas, Luther understood political authority as a remedy for sin: if all the world were genuinely Christian, there would be no need for temporal authorities, such as soldiers, police or magistrates at all, since Christians do not make war, murder, rape or steal.
- Fourthly, Luther bulked out his understanding of the two realms with a political theology he, indeed, thought rather more important: a theology of orders of creation and preservation, to which he sometimes gave the alternate term the three estates. The first estate is the Church, since one is claimed by God before one has any other relationship. The second estate

---

[21]   As examples see the contrast between the 1520 treatise *To the Christian Nobility of the German Nation*, which defends temporal rulers against Papal interference in the exercise of their responsibilities and the 1523 treatise *Temporal Authority: To What Extent it Should be Obeyed*, which sets limits to the rights of temporal rulers to interfere with freedom of religious conscience.

[22]   Alas not, in this case, without justification.

[23]   Opinion divides over what Augustine's two cities theology intends, between those who think Augustine means that citizens of the earthly and the heavenly cities *cooperate* in a limited sense; or whether all Augustine's talk of intermingling is merely a qualification of the fundamental point, which is that the two cities are in *competition* with each other. For a representative of the first approach see R.A. Markus, *Saeculum: History and Society in the Theology of Augustine* (Cambridge, 1970). For an advocate of the second, more 'combative' approach see Gregory W. Lee, 'Republics and their loves: Rereading *City of God* 19', *Modern Theology*, 27/4 (2011): 553–81.

is the household, which includes not simply marriage and the relationship of parents and children, but in the broadest sense economic life, all, that is, needed for the sustenance of life, farming, commerce, work. The third estate is government, understood broadly as princes and rulers and the magistrates and soldiers and tax collectors who do their bidding.

We can grasp little of Bonhoeffer's originality until we see it essentially as biblical exegesis undertaken from within a confessionally Augustinian and Lutheran tradition.

Bonhoeffer is explicit about these two wellsprings; but there is a third that we must take note of: Bonhoeffer's political roots in a very particular culture and family within a broader German context. That culture is nowhere better displayed than in Bonhoeffer's attempts, while in prison, to turn his hand to writing fiction. While imprisoned in Tegel, Bonhoeffer began to write a drama a novel and a short story. In his letter to Eberhard Bethge of 18 November 1943, Bonhoeffer describes his intention in these fragments as being 'to rehabilitate middle-class life as we know it in our families, specifically from the Christian perspective'.[24] For our purposes, what we must take note of is that it was this same middle-class, family-based culture, undergirded by roots in a Christian culture, both Protestant and Catholic, that characterised those with whom Bonhoeffer cooperated in the anti-Nazi resistance. The central figure in the hub of resistance in which Bonhoeffer played a relatively minor role was Admiral Wilhelm Canaris the head of the Abwehr, German Military Intelligence, with whom Bonhoeffer would later be hanged. The conspirators who belonged to the so-called Canaris conspiracy[25] held common values and political views rooted, like Bonhoeffer, in the German middle class. By the time Germany invaded Poland in September 1939, the Nazis had successfully expunged most opponents on the political left; socialists, Communists and trades unionists. Josef Goebbels's process of conforming all German social life to Nazi forms, a policy termed *Gleichschaltung* 'coordination' or 'bringing into line', had destroyed all possible centres of anti-Nazi opposition. Only the German military retained any degree of autonomy. There, among the officer class, there remained a few individuals with serious doubts about the course on which Hitler had steered the German nation. Though Bonhoeffer's immediate family did not include military officers, contact was established through his brother-in-law Hans von Dohnanyi, who became a lawyer in Canaris' office. Unsurprisingly, the conspirators were cagey about writing down their political views; but from what Bonhoeffer's sister and other survivors have written, certain core values and political commitments emerge. They include a commitment to the rule of law, a sense of the importance to government of a lively civil society, and roots in Catholic and Protestant moral

---

[24]   For this link see p. 200, fn.18, in the editor's afterword to DBWE 7.

[25]   For this term and an historical study of the resistance group to which Bonhoeffer belonged see Roger Maxwell and Heinrich Fraenkel, *The Canaris Conspiracy: The Secret Resistance to Hitler in the German Army* (London, 1969).

traditions. They were suspicious of liberal democracy because it placed too much trust in the will of the people. On the evidence of the popularity of the Nazis they judged that popular political opinion was not always in the best interests of the nation or of the people. They understood political authority to derive not from the people but from God. Some considered a restoration of a monarchy desirable. They distrusted revolutionary change, and, following the manifest failings of the Weimar Republic, judged that political democracy was not likely to be viable in Germany for years, possible decades, after the end of war. Their preference was for an interim government by the military, giving way steadily to government by a civilian elite. This preferred political system reflected their conviction that of those to whom much had been given much was expected; political service, like resistance to tyrants, was a question of serving the common good.

Like many first attempts at creative writing individual characters in the writing fragments are recognisably based on Bonhoeffer's immediate circle, his family and friends, or are composites of several of them. In the drama the character of Christoph is based on Bonhoeffer himself. To Christoph, another character, Heinrich explains the basis of Christoph's moral and political values, so at odds with the rootlessness of Nazi revolutionaries:

> People like you have a foundation, you have ground under your feet, you have a place in the world. There are things you take for granted, that you stand up for, and for which you are willing to put your head on the line, because you know your roots go so deep that they'll sprout new growth again. The only thing that counts for you is to keep your feet on the ground.[26]

Bonhoeffer's political theology, then, draws from these sources – Bible, Luther and cultural tradition. We turn now to two key elements in Bonhoeffer's theopolitical thinking, both discernible in his Gideon sermon, but developed more fully in the unfinished fragments written by Bonhoeffer towards an *Ethics*[27] between 1940 and 1943.

The Structure of Responsible Life

The first is Bonhoeffer's understanding of what, from the beginning of 1942, he had come to term the 'structure of responsible life'. In his end of term sermon almost a decade earlier Bonhoeffer was already clear about where Gideon's authority to exercise political office came from: it came from God. Any pretence that the source of Gideon's authority came from his own greatness or from his tribe is mocked by God and, at the end of the story, Gideon's rejection of attempts by the Israelites to redirect Gideon's source of authority into a hereditary monarchy

---

[26]   DBWE 7, p. 68.
[27]   DBWE 6.

is rejected. Though Samuel would eventually find Israelite pressure to anoint a hereditary monarch irresistible, Bonhoeffer's exegetical conclusion here is that the exercise of political authority comes from God and is therefore ultimately accountable to God.

In the *Ethics* Bonhoeffer continued to maintain that conviction, but now in a more sophisticated way, holding accountability to God in tension with taking full responsibility for one's own actions. In the second draft of his section on 'History and Good' Bonhoeffer writes that in acting responsibly '[p]rimarily ... I do not take responsibility for myself, for my actions; I do not justify myself (2 Corinthians 12:19). Rather, I take responsibility and answer for Jesus Christ, and with that I naturally also take responsibility for the commission I have been charged with by him (1 Corinthians 9:3).[28] He continues that responsibility means responsibility exercised in concrete social and political relationships:

> Responsibility is based on vicarious representative action [*Stellvertretung*]. This is most evident in those relationships in which a person is literally required to act on behalf of others, for example, as a father, as a statesman, or as the instructor of an apprentice.[29]

The examples are not randomly chosen; one is from a domestic context, the next political, and the third socio-economic. A year later, when retracing his steps in reflecting upon vicarious representative action, Bonhoeffer gives three slightly different examples of social structures in which it is undertaken: 'a church, a family, or a government'.[30] The examples employed have in common that the one who stands in the place of, or who acts for another, is in a social relationship in which God is encountered 'within an earthly relationship of authority, within an order that is clearly determined by above and below'.[31] Understanding that such apparently hierarchical forms of relating may be misunderstood and abused, Bonhoeffer sharpened his definition by insisting that the divine authority for such social structures may not be invoked by those above to enforce obedience upon those below, or that such structures exist in the interests of those above. Crucially, such relations were always between people. The nature of this final clarification is visible in the warmth of relationship in the examples Bonhoeffer uses to unpack his thinking about relations between an office holder and those he (and Bonhoeffer typically means *he*) is responsible for: 'A father acts on behalf of his children by working, providing, intervening, struggling, and suffering for them. In doing so he

---

[28]   Ibid., pp. 255–5.

[29]   Ibid., p. 257.

[30]   Ibid., p. 391.

[31]   Ibid., p. 391. When Karl Barth, who never lost his social democratic instincts for all that he purified his theology of the social gospel, commented on Bonhoeffer's posthumously published *Ethics* it was this he had in mind when he found a 'suggestion of North-German patriarchalism': K. Barth, *Church Dogmatics*, III:4 (Edinburgh, 1961), p. 22.

stands in their place.'[32] Within such relationships too, the one who is 'below' also has obligations; thus, for example, as Bonhoeffer wrote in a study of truth telling while a prisoner in Tegel, a son rightly denies his father is regularly drunk when asked about it by a teacher, because his relationship to his father requires loyalty.

A year later, in the section of his *Ethics* on which he was working when he was arrested in April 1943, Bonhoeffer reflects on the divinely commanded or mandated nature of the social structures in which vicarious representatives act. As we have seen, Bonhoeffer inherited from Luther a theological vocabulary concerning orders of creation. Bonhoeffer was still using that vocabulary in 1933 when he lectured on Genesis 1–3 at the Humboldt University in Berlin,[33] but was already beginning to refashion Luther's theological thinking in response to a misuse of this same vocabulary by pro-Nazi theologians who saw in the rise of Nazism a new revelation from God for the German people. By the time he worked on *Ethics* during the war Bonhoeffer prefers to write in terms of 'divine mandates'[34] that are implanted in the world from above and hold divine commissions. The mandates – Church, marriage and family, culture and government (elsewhere Bonhoeffer includes work and friendship) – exist for and not in competition with one another. The authority and sphere of operation for each mandate is limited because God is the source of its authority; it is limited by each other mandate (such, for example, that government has no mandate to alter to alter the institution of marriage); and it is also limited by those below within each mandate (children placing proper limits on their parents, a wife placing proper limits on her husband, a citizen placing proper limits on her government, etc).

Bonhoeffer's understanding of social relationships was, even as he was writing about them, beginning to sound oddly archaic. But being out of date is not, of course, the same as being wrong. As one learns in any basic ethics course, an argument that argues that because things *are* this way they *ought* to be this way is logically fallacious. But at a simple level of interpretation, for many – perhaps most – contemporary people in Europe and in North America, steeped in the egalitarian language of human rights, Bonhoeffer's account of the responsibility of those above to act vicariously for those below within mandated social structures can seem like listening to a voice from a different era.

The Penultimate and the Ultimate

A second element in Bonhoeffer's theopolitics already discernible in the Gideon sermon, but developed most fully in the *Ethics*, concerns the relationship between penultimate and ultimate things. As we have seen, though Bonhoeffer does not use the terms 'penultimate' and 'ultimate' in his Gideon sermon, he had already linked

---

[32] DBWE 6, pp. 257–8.

[33] See DBWE 3.

[34] Though he is explicit in saying that he is writing of 'orders', see DBWE 6, p. 390.

them to politics in his radio talk on 'The Younger Generation's altered view of the concept of the Führer' a matter of hours after Hitler's appointment as Chancellor. In the Gideon sermon, the penultimate and ultimate are clearly discernible beneath the surface.

It is tempting to think that the terms 'penultimate' and 'ultimate' can be mapped straightforwardly onto politics by locating all politics in the penultimate and the life of faith in the ultimate. But the simplicity of this formula is deceptive. For a moment, consider a phrase lifted from the middle of the Magnificat, Mary's joyous song in Luke's birth narrative (Luke 1:52–53):

> He has brought down the powerful from their thrones,
> and lifted up the lowly;
> he has filled the hungry with good things,
> and sent the rich away empty.

The terms used by Mary/Luke are certainly political; but do they speak of penultimate or ultimate things? In my view, they are both at once. On the one hand, such political vocabulary may be articulated in purely penultimate ways, speaking of a penultimate, a this-worldly, political revolution. On the other, the same words used by Christians may speak of a more than this-worldly; an ultimate turning of things on their head. Like all theological language, that is, theopolitical words and concepts work because, on the one hand, they are recognisably and intelligibly similar to the ways we use the same words and concepts in day to day political discourse while, on the other, these same words and concepts are transformed when we use them theologically. Political and theopolitical words and concepts are not identical, but are analogously related.

In his *Ethics* Bonhoeffer does not couch his discussion in terms of the grammar of political theology; yet his discussion of the ways in which penultimate and ultimate things are related to each other provides a good example of such a grammatical rule in operation. For Bonhoeffer, grace alone, faith alone, are ultimate: '[i]t is faith alone that sets life in a new foundation, and only on this foundation can I live justified before God'.[35] God's Grace and faith in God are ultimate things because they alone consummate human life. They are ultimate qualitatively, in that there is nothing beyond them and in that they mark a complete break with penultimate things. But they are also ultimate temporally[36] in the sense that they are always preceded by penultimate things. Penultimate things are not, Bonhoeffer continues, interesting therefore for their own sake, 'as if they had some value of their own'; rather, theology speaks of penultimate things because they precede and in some way prepare for the coming of the ultimate[37] in a Christian's life.

---

[35] DBWE 6, p. 147.

[36] Ibid., pp. 149–50.

[37] Ibid., p. 151.

For Bonhoeffer, Christians have often tended to relate the penultimate to the ultimate in one of two mistaken ways. Either they have solved the relation between the penultimate and the ultimate radically by seeing the ultimate as a complete break with penultimate things, or they have solved the relationship through a compromise in which the 'ultimate stays completely beyond daily life' serving in the end as a kind of divine preservation or even validation of penultimate things rather than as a judgement on them. Bonhoeffer sees merit in both, but also error. His own solution is to understand penultimate things as a preparing of the way for ultimate ones. Radicalism would renounce the world, while compromise would embrace it. But the incarnation of Jesus Christ, Bonhoeffer continues, makes nonsense of both approaches. Time and eternity, the life of this world and the life of God, are brought together in Jesus Christ in whom God enters into the world, the ultimate entering into the penultimate. For this reason, the 'Christian life neither destroys nor sanctions the penultimate',[38] just as Christ's resurrection does not abolish the penultimate as long as life on earth continues, even though 'eternal life, the new life, breaks ever more powerfully into earthly life and creates space for itself within it'.[39] The perspective of this ultimate enables us to see what being authentically human looks like; the ultimate thus *empowers* life within the penultimate.

What light does this shed on how Christians engage with the world? Bonhoeffer spells out what he means in an extended example worth citing at some length:

> The hungry person needs bread, the homeless person needs shelter, the one deprived of rights needs justice, the lonely person needs community, the undisciplined one needs order, and the slave needs freedom. It would be blasphemy against God and our neighbor to leave the hungry unfed while saying that God is closest to those in deepest need. We break bread with the hungry and share our home with them for the sake of Christ's love, which belongs to the hungry as much as it does to us … To bring bread to the hungry person is preparing the way for the coming of grace.
>
> What happens here is something penultimate. To give the hungry bread is not yet to proclaim to them the grace of God and justification, and to have received bread does not yet mean to stand in faith.[40]

Bonhoeffer concludes that this does not mean that for Christians to prepare the way for Christ it is enough to give bread to the hungry or shelter to the homeless, since: 'everything depends on this action being a spiritual reality, since what is at stake is nor the reform of worldly conditions but the coming of Christ'.[41]

---

38   Ibid., p. 159.
39   Ibid., p. 158.
40   Ibid., p. 163.
41   Ibid., p. 164.

Bonhoeffer's Politics and Ours

Gideon was not, in Bonhoeffer's sermon, the saviour of his people: God alone saves. Any delusions of grandeur Gideon had, religious, political or military were lovingly and laughingly mocked by God. Yet that is not to say Gideon was unimportant to God, or played no role in the unfolding of God's purposes for Israel. Gideon took vicarious representative action – on behalf of God God's people in defending them against the Midianites. Further, in his obedience to God, Gideon prepared the way for God's self-proclamation by such an astonishing victory over his people's enemies.

The resistance hub in which Bonhoeffer played a part acted also for the common good. Those who hazarded their lives on the successful working of bomb fuses in Oberstleutnant Claus Graf von Stauffenberg's briefcase on 20 July 1944, acted in what they took to be the national interest; they were vicarious representatives acting, as they saw it, on behalf of the German people. Was their vicarious representative action also a preparation for Christ, or did it remain in the penultimate, merely as paving the way for the end of Nazism in Germany? Their actions did not have the element of the proclamation of God's purposes that might permit us to view it as a preparation for the ultimate.

And what of Bonhoeffer – in whose place did he stand? Did his act of political resistance pave the way for God's ultimate word of grace? In the Church struggle, Bonhoeffer was in earnest in resisting, on Lutheran grounds, state interference in the Church's proclamation. But, like Gideon, he was aware of the loving teasing mockery of God for the poor Church in its struggles; he recognised the importance of not taking oneself too seriously. When he became involved in the Canaris conspiracy, much was changed. Though he was a pastor who took his office very seriously, Bonhoeffer seems reluctant to see his actions as representing the Church; he may have intended to resign after the war from his ecclesial office, precisely so as not to associate the Protestant Church with his actions as a conspirator against the state. With his fellow conspirators he too viewed himself as standing in for other Germans. But the element of self-mockery, of *hilaritas*, is gone; indeed Bonhoeffer seems concerned that that involvement in conspiracy may have damaged the conspirators morally and politically, asking them in a privately circulated essay written in January 1943, 'Are we still of any use?' Bonhoeffer lived this disturbing double life conscious of doing so under God's judgement and trusting in the power of God's ultimate word of forgiveness. In resisting Hitler he stood on the line limiting the state's authority over Germans and over the German Church: 'here I stand, I can do no other'. To do so was to proclaim the Gospel of Christ. The Nazis were not listening; the Church today still has both the need, and the time, to do so.

PART III
Bonhoeffer and Ethics

Chapter 7
Ethics and Materialist Hermeneutics

In the English translation of Bonhoeffer's *Letters and Papers from Prison* the following paragraphs are appended to the 1942 essay 'After Ten Years':

> It remains an experience of incomparable value that we have for once learned to see the great events of world history from below, from the perspective of the outcasts, the suspects, the maltreated, the powerless, the oppressed and reviled, in short from the perspective of the suffering … But this perspective from below must not lead us to become advocates for those who are perpetually dissatisfied. Rather, out of a higher satisfaction, which in its essence is grounded beyond what is below and above, we do justice to life in all its dimensions and in this way affirm it.[1]

Bonhoeffer's remarks on perspectives on history provide a useful commentary on the viewpoint from which his *Ethics* were written. With fellow conspirators, Bonhoeffer claims to have learned to see things from below, and from this new standpoint urges that a 'higher satisfaction' be sought with foundations beyond all talk of above and below.

This chapter addresses the question: can a foundation of life, of ethics and of theology truly constitute a gospel of liberation for the poor, or is a gospel of liberation a message which neither desires, nor believes it possible, to stand anywhere other than unreservedly alongside the poor, seeking to view history from below. In particular, I wish to examine the relationship between Bonhoeffer's uses of the Bible in the *Ethics* and the bourgeois liberal class and its ideological commitments out of which his biblical hermeneutics flow.

Any critique of Bonhoeffer's theology treads on holy ground. Bonhoeffer's courage and integrity as an opponent of Nazism mark every page of the *Ethics*. Constrained by his participation in the resistance movement to mystery and camouflage, Bonhoeffer's *Ethics* boldly condemn Nazism's iniquitous policies towards the mentally disabled, and demand Christian action on behalf of the Jews: '[d]riving out the Jew(s) from the West must result in driving our Christ with them, for Jesus Christ was a Jew'.[2] Bonhoeffer's existential solidarity with victims of Nazism furnishes his voice with a radical authenticity amongst those who struggle for liberation. For example, James H. Cone, writing on Bonhoeffer's reputation for radical theology, states:

---

[1] DBWE 8, p. 52.
[2] DBWE 6, p. 105.

[W]hat most white Protestant professors of theology overlook is that these are the words of a prisoner, a man who encountered the evils of Nazism and was killed in the encounter. Do whites really have the right to affirm God's death when they have actually enslaved men in God's name? It would seem that unless whites are willing to endure the pain of oppression, they cannot authentically speak of God.[3]

However, Bonhoeffer's existential commitment to liberation is not sufficient to establish the ideological foundations of his *Ethics*. In his *Biblical Hermeneutics and Black Theology in South Africa* Itumeleng J. Mosala contends that:

Existential commitments to the liberation struggles of the oppressed are inadequate because those who are committed in this way are still ideologically and theoretically enslaved to the dominant discourses in the society.[4]

Because Bonhoeffer's unique skills as a theologian are combined with his integrity as a member of the resistance, he is a formidable conversation partner for Mosala's attempt to liberate the Bible from its hermeneutical captivity to the ideological assumptions of white, patriarchal Western society. Mosala makes 'the historical-materialist method of analysis usually associated with the name of Karl Marx rather than the idealist framework that makes up the history of ideas – abstracted from concrete historical and social relationships – the focus of its analysis.'[5] Mosala's materialist approach to biblical hermeneutics, based on methods associated with the names of Norman Gottwald, Marvin Chaney, Robert Coote and others, develops a search for weapons of liberation. A key category in this search is that of *struggle*, for this is the motivating force of all human society. For Mosala, the category of struggle becomes a factor at two crucial points in the hermeneutical process:

[T]he search for biblical-hermeneutical weapons of struggle must take the form, first of all, of a critical interrogation of the history, culture, and ideologies of the readers/appropriators of the biblical texts.[6]

Thus, Mosala argues that the perspective from which one begins to read the biblical texts is a crucial determining factor in the hermeneutical process. The second point where the category of struggle gains purchase is 'in one's understanding of the history, nature, ideology, and agenda of the biblical texts'[7] themselves. Using the same tools with which the perspective of the reader is interrogated, a biblical

---

[3]   James H. Cone, *Black Theology and Black Power* (New York, 1969), p. 99.

[4]   Itumeleng J. Mosala, *Biblical Hermeneutics and Black Theology in South Africa* (Grand Rapids, 1989), p. 4.

[5]   Ibid., p. 4.

[6]   Ibid., p. 8.

[7]   Ibid., p. 9.

hermeneutics of liberation addresses 'the question of the material conditions that constitute the sites of the struggles that produced the biblical texts.'[8] In practice, such an approach involves Mosala in exploring the ways in which the lives of the biblical peoples were affected by their relationship to the means of material production. Mosala penetrates the biblical texts by asking such questions as: In whose interest is this passage written? What material conditions are reflected in the texts as we receive them? And how may this text now be related to our struggle for liberation, the struggle to liberate our productive forces? For liberation is not only moral and spiritual, but material as well.

Mosala's materialist approach makes a number of valuable hermeneutical gains. Firstly, Mosala 'is deliberately oblivious to the notion of "scriptural authority", which is at the heart of traditional biblical scholarship'.[9] For Mosala the Bible is both a site and a weapon of struggle; to accord to it an authority which may not be questioned is to allow its ideological presuppositions to go unchecked. Mosala argues that:

> The insistence on the Bible as the Word of God must be seen for what it is: an ideological maneuver [*sic*] whereby ruling class interests evident in the Bible are converted into a faith that transcends social, political, racial, sexual, and economic divisions. In this way the Bible becomes an ahistorical, interclassist document.[10]

A second hermeneutical gain made by Mosala arises out of this genuinely critical approach to biblical texts. By treating each text as a site of struggle, materialist hermeneutics denies the possibility of escapist textual selectivity. Mosala allocates a full chapter to a critique of black and liberation hermeneutics which treat the Bible as though it has been written from a single liberating perspective, ignoring texts which do not fit easily into the liberation mould. Mosala contends that:

> the only adequate and honest explanation is that not all of the Bible is on the side of human rights or of oppressed and exploited people … oppressive texts cannot be totally tamed or subverted into liberating texts.[11]

A biblical hermeneutic is not liberating merely because it is read in the context of a struggle for liberation. Black and liberation theologies must also effect a theoretical break with dominant bourgeois/liberal hermeneutical assumptions.

Mosala's description of materialist black hermeneutics provides a basis for conversation with the ideological perspective and biblical hermeneutics of Bonhoeffer's *Ethics*. What may be said of the ideological standpoint from which Bonhoeffer approached the documents he wrote between the summer of 1940,

---

8   Ibid., p. 9.
9   Ibid., p. 11.
10   Ibid., p. 18.
11   Ibid., p. 30.

and his arrest on 5 April 1943? Bonhoeffer's *Ethics* is a political text. As a text of the resistance, Bonhoeffer's *Ethics* struggle to provide a theoretical and theological basis for a reconstruction of a post-Nazi German state. Christoph Strohm and James P. Kelley's paper on *Church and Public Policy*[12] details the political influences on Bonhoeffer's formation. Drawing on research into the political perspectives of Gerhard Leibholz and Hans von Dohnanyi, Strohm and Kelley suggest that the resistance group of which Bonhoeffer was a part was based upon a rejection of Nazism, and a search for a non-collectivist democratic alternative. Strohm and Kelley suggest that this circle:

> saw the decisive alternative between a collectivistic, pseudo-religious, 'totalitarian state' and an 'authoritarian state' which continued to respect the liberal heritage of the last centuries.[13]

Bonhoeffer saw the political task as essentially a restorative one, re-establishing liberal, yet still authoritarian structures of society. Larry Rasmussen perceptively sums up Bonhoeffer's position:

> Rule by elites is not of itself misrule for Bonhoeffer. He was totally opposed to totalitarian rule, insisted upon the rule of law, believed in a distribution of powers, and promoted the guarantee of certain rights. But he was not in principle opposed to all forms of strong government and he was not an unqualified democrat. He probably was closest to a studied, morally responsible Prussian conservatism.[14]

The most significant consequences of Bonhoeffer's political viewpoint are embodied in his theology of the mandates, which Bonhoeffer drafted in the summer of 1940 in 'Christ, Reality and Good' and re-worked again in early 1943 in the section on 'The Concrete Commandment and the Divine Mandates' Bonhoeffer understands by the term mandate:

> the concrete divine commission grounded in the revelation of Christ and the testimony of scripture; it is the authorization and legitimization to declare a particular divine commandment, the conferring of divine authority on an earthly institution ... The bearer of the mandate acts as a vicarious representative, as a stand-in for the one who issued the commission.[15]

---

[12] James P. Kelley and Christoph Strohm, 'Church and Public Policy: Bonhoeffer's Early Critique of Nazi Policy', unpublished paper presented at the American Academy of Religion, 1987.

[13] Ibid., p. 8.

[14] Larry Rasmussen, *Dietrich Bonhoeffer: His Significance for North Americans* (Minneapolis, 1990), p. 47.

[15] DBWE 6, p. 389.

The mandates establish the human person 'always … within an earthly relationship of authority, within an order that is clearly determined by above and below'.[16] For Bonhoeffer, there are qualitative differences between the relations established between the superior and the inferior within the divine mandates, and within merely earthly orders. The relations are regulated to prevent abuse by God who confers the commission, by the other mandates, and by the rights of the inferior party within the relationship. Simple examples of the relationship are offered, between father and son, master craftsman and apprentice. In his final draft Bonhoeffer lists as mandates Church, marriage and family, culture and government.

For Bonhoeffer the mandates are to be viewed from the standpoint of their foundation in Christ. Doubtless, Bonhoeffer's attempt to rework Luther's *zwei-Reich-lehre* is an improvement on the theology of orders proposed by Paul Althaus and by Emil Brunner's *The Divine Imperative*,[17] but it is surely not an ethic which allows for liberation from below. Bonhoeffer's mandates theology seeks to re-establish a tolerant authoritarianism which, while providing safeguards for the inferior, legitimates the retention by the superior of control and power. Karl Barth's comments on Bonhoeffer's *Mandatsbegriff* are telling:

> Is it enough to say that these particular relationships of rank and degree occur with a certain regularity in the Bible, and that they can be more or less clearly related to Christ as the Lord of the world? Again, does the relationship always have to be one of superiority and inferiority? In Bonhoeffer's doctrine of the mandates, is there not just a suggestion of North German Patriarchalism? Is the notion of authority of some over others really more characteristic of the ethical event than that of the freedom of even the very lowest before the very highest?[18]

Bonhoeffer's claim to rest the mandates on a Scriptural foundation leads well into a materialist interrogation of the hermeneutical perspectives undergirding the *Ethics*. At a precociously early stage in his theological career, Bonhoeffer began to develop an original approach to biblical hermeneutics which departed significantly from the Ritschlian, liberal school of theology in Berlin. In a 1925 essay for Reinhold Seeberg, Bonhoeffer argues for a radical distinction between historical and spiritual biblical hermeneutics: 'Scripture is only a *source* for history. For spiritual interpretation, scripture is a *witness*.'[19] This distinction was further developed in *Creation and Fall*. Here, encouraged by Barth's method in his commentary on Romans, Bonhoeffer developed an interpretation of the Bible as the book of the Church. Thus writes Bonhoeffer:

---

[16] Ibid., p. 391.

[17] Emil Brunner, *The Divine Imperative* (London, 1937).

[18] Karl Barth, *Church Dogmatics*, III/4 (Edinburgh, 1990), p. 22.

[19] DBWE 9, p. 296.

When Genesis says 'Yahweh,' it 'means' from a historical or psychological point of view, nothing but Yahweh; theologically, i.e., from the viewpoint of the Church, however, it is speaking of God. For in the whole of Holy Scripture God is the one and only God [der Eine Gott]; with this belief the church and theological science [Wissenschaft] stand or fall.[20]

Bonhoeffer's allegiance to the Bible as the Word of God allows no critical questioning of the perspectives from which individual texts are written. At Finkenwalde in a paper on 'The presentation of New Testament Texts', Bonhoeffer clarified the relation between the Word of God, and the Word of God in Scripture:

The norm for the Word of God in Scripture is the Word of God itself, and what we possess, reason, conscience, experience, are the materials to which this norm seeks to be applied. We too may say that the Word of God and the word of man are joined in Holy Scripture; but they are joined in such a way that God himself says where his Word is, and he says it through the word of man.[21]

Bonhoeffer's finely nuanced position is not antagonistic to criticism per se. In a fascinating letter to Rüdiger Schleicher, Bonhoeffer distinguishes the Bible from other books, for in the Bible it is God who speaks:

Naturally, one can also read the Bible like any other book-from the perspective of textual criticism, for instance. There is nothing to be said against that. But that will only reveal the surface of the Bible, not what is within ... This is how I read the Bible now. I ask of each passage: What is God saying to us here? And I ask God that he would help us hear what he wants to say ... Does this somehow help you understand why I am prepared for a *sacrificium intellectus* – just in these matters, and only in these matters, with respect to the one, true God![22]

Bonhoeffer's approach to biblical interpretation is not without points of contact with Mosala's materialist hermeneutics. Both approaches avoid the escapism of textual selectivity. In the theological climate of his day, Bonhoeffer was unusual in according to the Old Testament equal canonicity with the New. Bonhoeffer's deep dissatisfaction with the ability of liberal biblical hermeneutics to furnish an adequate theological response to Nazi ideology also resonates with materialist hermeneutics' attempt to allow the Bible to speak to the present age. In this limited sense, the Bible is for Bonhoeffer a weapon of liberation. Yet the biblical

---

[20]   DBWE 3, p. 23.

[21]   DBW 14, 399–421; English translation from *No Rusty Swords*, ed. Edwin H. Robertson, trans. John Bowden (London, 1977), p. 309.

[22]   Dietrich Bonhoeffer, *Meditating on the Word*, ed. and trans. David M. Gracie (Cambridge, MA, 1986), pp. 44–6; German original DBW 14, pp. 145–7.

texts themselves cannot, with Bonhoeffer's hermeneutical presuppositions about the Bible as the Word of God, be treated as themselves sites of struggle. Outside the *Ethics* the classic example is Bonhoeffer's study on the books of Ezra and Nehemiah[23] through which he authorises the anathematisation of the theologically impure German Christians. Because the Bible is perceived as witness to the Word of God, Bonhoeffer does not have the critical framework with which to critique these two books, and to discern in them precisely the same racist ideology as he is struggling to oppose in Nazism.

Bonhoeffer's *Ethics* is a richly diverse collection of essays comprised of incomplete and various entry points to his subject matter. Begging the question of how Bonhoeffer intended each new entry point to relate to that which preceded it, what we are left with is a plurality of approaches to ethics, a plurality of motifs characterising the ethical life, and a plurality of approaches to biblical hermeneutics resting on the common hermeneutical assumptions I have outlined.

The editors of the new edition of Bonhoeffer's *Ethics* divide the manuscripts into five working periods. Using this chronological sequence as the basis of my reading of the *Ethics*, and taking the third working period on 'History and Good' as belonging thematically with the motif of the first working period, I discern four motifs, or approaches to ethics within the manuscripts. In the first approach, characterised by the phras 'Ethics as Formation', Bonhoeffer proposes that the reader be conformed to the 'Gestalt Jesu Christi'. The term 'Gestalt', which has usually been translated as 'form' may also carry the sense of 'character. ' Guided by this insight, I suggest that Bonhoeffer's approach in this method has much in common with the notions of character formation advocated by the proponents of narrative theology. In the second approach to ethics, characterised by the term 'Ultimate and penultimate things', Bonhoeffer offers the only sustained engagement in the *Ethics* with micro-ethics, or with issues of concrete morality: abortion, suicide and euthanasia. This motif, deeply influenced by the conversations with Roman Catholic theologians at the Ettal monastery where Bonhoeffer worked during this period, places the biblical, final word of justification alongside his penultimate struggle with concrete moral issues. However one enters the moral maze, the final word is the word of forgiveness spoken by God. The third approach in the *Ethics* begins with Nietzsche's direction to ethics to step 'beyond good and evil', and relates the Bible to the ethical life by means of the motif of 'Proving the will of God'. The final motif concerns 'ethics as command' and develops an approach to ethics in the light of Bonhoeffer's reading of Karl Barth's *Church Dogmatics* II/2, returning at many significant points to the perspective of *Discipleship*.

One of the most striking features of Bonhoeffer's *Ethics* is the manner in which these various motifs describing the ethical life coexist without mutually contradicting one another. It is as if each motif characterising ethics represents a fresh metaphorical construal of the nature of ethics. Such plurality proves extremely

---

[23]   DBW 14, 'Der Wiederaufbau Jerusalems nach Esra und Nehemia', pp. 930–45.

resilient against any approach to biblical hermeneutics using a single category, such as Mosala's historical materialism. A rigorously materialist approach to biblical hermeneutics is not without difficulties; it is not only in Bonhoeffer that liberal reserve runs deep. In notes towards an unfinished section of the *Ethics*, Bonhoeffer writes, '[s]elf assertiveness and an excess of zeal are uncultured'.[24] In the first place, there is always a danger with any theological method dominated by a single defining approach that the prefix overrides theology itself. Thus feminist theology or black theology, liberation theology or narrative theology, Methodist theology or Bonhoefferian theology become so wrapped up in being feminist or black, liberation or narrative, Methodist or Bonhoefferian, that theology is denied to any who approach it without bearing the password of their own particular talismanic shibboleth. And perhaps in the end that is all Bonhoeffer was warning against in inviting us to move beyond any single perspective and viewpoint. The plurality of motifs, or of metaphors for the ethical life in Bonhoeffer's *Ethics*, affords a liberating diversity in ethics and in theology.

Mosala's materialist method entails a number of crucial hermeneutical gains absent in Bonhoeffer's hermeneutics. Yet the plurality of Bonhoeffer's approaches to ethics allows a theological richness that is lacking in Mosala, dominated as he is by the category of struggle. Sure enough, interrogating the relation of a biblical text to the means of production yields important insights, but the variety of biblical genre is not all oriented around this single important category. There is a political dimension to all of the biblical literature, to law and poetry, myth and parable, as well as to history, prophecy, gospel and New Testament letter. But other categories are required to release anything like the full depth and variety of meanings which biblical texts offer. These reflections in no way undermine Gutierrez's judgement that 'The protest movements of the poor … find no place in Bonhoeffer's historical focus.'[25] Mosala writes his theology as a black South African. Bonhoeffer had not the advantage (or the burden) of all the nexus of experiences which that entails. But the plurality of Bonhoeffer's methods and the authenticity of his existential witness, uniquely qualify Bonhoeffer as a bridge builder between his own privileged perspective, and that of those, like Mosala, who truly speak with the experience and zeal of the oppressed.

At the end of E.M. Forster's *A Passage to India*, Fielding, ambivalent representative of the oppressive British Raj, goes on a ride with Dr Aziz, player and victim of the tragic misunderstanding which constitutes the plot of the book. Aziz looks forward to the day when the British shall be driven into the sea, for then the two shall truly be friends. They stretch out their hands, but, as if prevented from becoming one by the history of oppression between them, their horses stumble on the rocky ground and swerve apart. India in its hundred voices say '"no, not yet,"' and the sky says '"no, not there."'[26] There is a huge gap

---

[24]   Dietrich Bonhoeffer, Ethics, ed. E. Bethge, trans. Neville Horton-Smith (London, 1985), p. 160.

[25]   Gustavo Gutierrez, *The Power of the Poor in History* (London, 1983), p. 229.

[26]   E.M. Forster, *A Passage to India* (Middlesex, 1978), p. 316.

between the perspectives from below, and from above. Perhaps, in addition to really hearing the voices from below, we also need theologians like Bonhoeffer to reach out their hands across the rocky ground ahead.

Chapter 8

The Sacrament of Ethical Reality: Dietrich Bonhoeffer on Ethics for Christian Citizens

Reality is the sacrament of the commandment.[1]

(Dietrich Bonhoeffer, July 1932)

In *Torture and Eucharist*[2] and in *Theopolitical Imagination*[3] William T. Cavanaugh presents a rich description of the Eucharist as that true sacrifice to God that makes the Church into Christ's body, thereby constituting (in Augustine's words) the true *res publica*. By this means, Cavanaugh challenges both the 'myth of the state' and the 'myth of civil society as free space' in which the Church is required to act as one player among many according to rules written and umpired by the state. Cavanaugh's positive proposal is therefore not to 'politicise the Eucharist, but to "Eucharistise" the world'.[4]

In this chapter I want to develop a comparison between Cavanaugh's view of the relation between sacrament and public ethics and that suggested by Dietrich Bonhoeffer in his 1932 lecture, 'On the Theological Foundation of the Work of the World Alliance'.[5] In this lecture, Bonhoeffer offers a self-consciously provisional account of the sacramental foundation of the Church's public ethics, an account he sums up in the dense phrase: 'reality is the sacrament of command'. Bonhoeffer's account differs from Cavanaugh's, I suggest, not only in his view that the Church speaks God's ethical command to the world penultimately and with humility, but in his Lutheran conviction that the state, far from being an anti-ecclesial 'public thing' always to be disdained, is one of the means by which God acts to preserve creation. In trying to make sense of what Bonhoeffer meant by stating that 'reality is the sacrament of command', I also propose, as an exegetical 'by-product', to display the coherence in Bonhoeffer's theology against persistent claims that a fundamental reorientation takes place between the theological ethics of *Discipleship* and *Ethics*.[6]

---

[1]   DBWE 11, p. 361; 'Die Wirklichkeit ist das Sakrament des Gebotes', in DBW 11, p. 334.

[2]   William T. Cavanaugh, *Torture and Eucharist* (Oxford, 1998).

[3]   William T. Cavanaugh, *Theopolitical Imagination* (London, 2002).

[4]   Cavanaugh, *Torture*, p. 14.

[5]   The full title of the body on which Bonhoeffer's lecture reflects was 'The World Alliance for Promoting International Friendship through the Churches'.

[6]   The thesis that there are distinct working periods in Bonhoeffer's life and thought is presented most tendentiously by Hanfried Müller in *Von der Kirche zur Welt* (Hamburg, 1961)

'Eucharistising' the World

Cavanaugh's *Torture and Eucharist*[7] is a theological study of the Catholic Church in Chile during the military dictatorship of Augusto Pinochet Ugarte from 1973 to 1990. At the outset Cavanaugh warns that though his book might appear to be an exercise in relating liturgy to ethics, or liturgy to politics, he strongly resists describing his project in this way. For Cavanaugh, conceiving liturgy and ethics, or liturgy and politics, as separate activities that one must work hard to connect is to make a category error with disastrous consequences for the Church's service to the world. This is because the distinction between politics and religion is not one that was discovered by Enlightened thinkers determined to move beyond the wars of religion, but one invented in order to confine the Church to the margins. The Enlightenment creation of a political realm that excluded the body of Christ did not therefore so much solve the conflict of religion and politics as enact it. The problem with the idea that religion and politics are separate spheres of life that need to be connected is that it suggests that to enter the political is to leave the liturgical. Where liturgy must be 'applied' or made relevant to political life and ethics the separation of religion and politics remains intact. Exactly this error lay at the heart, Cavanaugh contends, of the response of the Catholic bishops in the early period of Pinochet's rule. By claiming in the first two-thirds of the Pinochet era that the Church was the 'soul of the nation', the Church acquiesced in its exclusion from the Chilean body politic. Against this view Cavanaugh maintains that the Eucharist is not a sign pointing to a more concrete political reality, but a sign that performs a distinctively Eucharistic political community capable of 'Eucharistising' the world.

The key contrast at the centre of Cavanaugh's argument is between torture and Eucharist. Torture, Cavanaugh sets out to demonstrate, is not merely an assault on individual bodies or an infringement of their rights, but the enactment of a particular conception of society. In a crucial passage Cavanaugh lays out what it might mean to imagine torture as the manifestation of a society formed by an omnipotent state:

---

but is repeated in a diluted form by John Godsey who speaks of three phases of foundation, application and fragmentation, in *The Theology of Dietrich Bonhoeffer* (London, 1960) and by Eberhard Bethge, whose biography is subtitled 'Theologian, Christian, Man for his Times', DB-EB. André Dumas also acquiesces in the thesis, commenting that it is 'on the whole accurate', *Dietrich Bonhoeffer: Theologian of Reality* (London, 1971), p. 70.

[7]   For a helpful study of Cavanaugh's *Torture and Eucharist* and a complementary proposal concerning the role of worship in forming the Church as a moral community, see Samuel Wells, *Improvisation: The Drama of Christian Ethics* (Grand Rapids, 2004) which argues that: 'For Christians the principal practice by which the moral imagination is formed, the principal form of discipleship training, is worship ... Each aspect of worship represents a vital dimension of moral formation' (pp. 81–2).

Torture may be considered a kind of perverse liturgy, for in torture the body of the victim is the ritual site where the state's power is manifested in its most awesome form. Torture is liturgy – or, perhaps better said, 'anti-liturgy' – because it involves bodies and bodily movements in an enacted drama which both makes real the power of the state and constitutes an act of worship of that mysterious power ... The liturgy of the torture room is a *disciplina arcane*,[8] a discipline of the secret, which is yet part of a larger state project which continues outside the torture chamber itself.[9]

It is essential to the 'liturgy of torture', Cavanaugh continues, that the victim takes on the role of enemy of the state. Pinochet's military coup justified itself on the basis that strong military rule was necessary to save Chile from the Communist enemy within. But the coup itself met very little opposition, so enemies had to be created, and the means used was torture. The victims of torture are made to acknowledge their worthlessness and corruption. All that matters – family, friends, causes and values – is betrayed. Torture thus peels away what makes the victim human through the mechanism of pain. The Eucharist, Cavanaugh believes, is the Church's 'counter-politics' to the politics of torture. It is not a *symbol* from which we might draw political insight: it *is* the Church's physical alternative to state terror. At the Eucharist the believer finds forgiveness. All that matters, family, friends, causes and values, are affirmed, strengthened and connected. The Eucharist makes us fully human as the Kingdom interrupts time to confuse the spiritual and the temporal. The Eucharist, Cavanaugh concludes, anticipates the realisation of a new society, a new politics.

The practical outworking of Cavanaugh's view of the political character of liturgy is expressed in an example of how Christians in Chile during the Pinochet era created 'spaces of resistance where bodies belong to God, not to the state'.[10] Cavanaugh recalls the actions of the Sebastián Acevedo Movement, which used public ritual acts of solidarity outside sites of symbolic importance such as torture centres and courts. Banners would be unfurled by groups, often including clergy and members of religious orders, who would sing and recite litanies naming the state's crimes before the police arrived and arrested them. It is significant for Cavanaugh that these activities were termed liturgies, and they involved not simply a 'spiritual' action, but a physical reconfiguration of city space, for example as traffic was disrupted;[11] and it is equally significant that these liturgies were not sacramental, since it is important for Cavanaugh that the sacraments should not be instrumentalised.[12]

---

[8]   The phrase is a striking echo of Bonhoeffer's characterisation of Christian discipleship in the world come of age as an 'Arkandisziplin'.

[9]   Cavanaugh, *Torture*, p. 30.

[10]   Ibid., p. 275.

[11]   Ibid., pp. 273–5.

[12]   In this respect Cavanaugh is similar to Bernd Wannenwetsch whose *Political Worship: Ethics for Christian Citizens* (Oxford, 2004) also maintains that worship has its

Cavanaugh's reflections on the Eucharist as a performance of a true *res publica* are further developed in the provocative essays of *Theopolitical Imagination*. 'The modern state', Cavanaugh claims, 'is best understood ... as an alternative soteriology to that of the Church. Both soteriologies pursue peace and an end to division by the enactment of a social body' but the 'state body is a simulacrum, a false copy, of the Body of Christ'.[13] By 'state', Cavanaugh denotes that modern institution 'in which a centralised and abstract power holds a monopoly over physical coercion within a geographically defined territory'.[14] Within the state, religion 'is no longer a matter of certain bodily practices within the Body of Christ, but is limited to the realm of the "soul", and the body is handed over to the state'.[15] In contrast, Christ's body is an eschatological gathering that is neither an entirely worldly nor an entirely otherworldly event, but one which 'blurs the lines' between the temporal and the eternal, in which the Church interrupts the false politics of the earthly city.

Yet, though Cavanaugh asserts a blurring of some distinctions within the Church (temporal/eternal, earth/heaven) and vigorous resistance to others (public/ private) his argument depends upon the maintenance of other sharp distinctions (state/Church, body of Christ/secular body, secular politics/theopolitics). This is particularly evident in the essay 'The Myth of Civil Society as Free Space', in which he strongly resists attempts to regard civil society as a space that is public without being political, in the sense of being under the direct control of the state. The construct 'civil society' has been regarded by some Christian social ethicists as a rather promising one, allowing the Church to exercise a public role without 'the Constantinian spectre of implication in state coercion'.[16] In contrast, Cavanaugh argues that the distinction of public and private is an instrument by which the state domesticates the Church:

> The great irony, then, is that in trying to arrange for the Church [i.e., by means of its participation in civil society] to influence 'the public', rather than simply be public, the public has reduced the Church to its own terms[17] ... If the Church accedes to the role of a voluntary association of private citizens, however, it

---

own integrity of purpose, since 'the church does not have itself at its own disposal' (p. 2). In other respects Wannenwetsch, who is Lutheran, has more in common with Bonhoeffer, whom he indeed cites as an opponent of the 'triumphant progress of functionalism' (p. 24) in relating worship and ethics. This chapter owes a debt to Wannenwetsch in the phrasing of its title.

13   Cavanaugh, *Theopolitical*, pp. 9–10.
14   Ibid., p. 10.
15   Ibid., p. 35.
16   Ibid., p. 53.
17   Ibid., p. 83.

will lack the disciplinary resources to resist the State's *religare*, its practices of binding.[18]

It is evident from Cavanaugh's immersion in the history of the Catholic Church in Chile that he is well aware that the theological understanding he advances of the Church as the one true *res publica* is not one that is always performed in practice. He is just as aware as was Augustine that '[t]he church is a corpus permixtum, full of both saints and sinners', and elsewhere he expresses matters no more confidently than this, that in spite of its manifold earthly imperfections '[a]s the embodiment of God's politics, the church nevertheless muddles through'.[19] Nevertheless there is, in Cavanaugh, a marked impatience with the provisional and the penultimate, a disdain for the secular and a strong desire to describe the Church in terms of its promised eschatological perfection. Participation in both state and 'civil society' on their terms is regarded with a nearly Donatist distaste for the taint of the secular, and robust engagement with the world is advanced on terms integral to that one true public thing, the Eucharistic community that performs the body of Christ.

How does Bonhoeffer's claim that 'reality is the sacrament of the commandment' stack up against Cavanaugh's aspiration to 'Eucharistise the world'? It is most unlikely that Bonhoeffer's position on the sacrament and politics is either entirely at one or entirely at odds with Cavanaugh's theopolitics, so it is important to be clear about the purpose of such a comparison. It is not my aim to critique Bonhoeffer from a more enlightened contemporary perspective; neither do I want to treat Bonhoeffer as a 'Church Father' whose views may be used to evaluate the orthodoxy of theological epigones. Bonhoeffer is a significant theologian whose life and thought belong to a rapidly receding past and his voice does not carry easily into contemporary theological conversation. The purpose of what follows is to enable a conversation between the living and the dead.

Towards a Theological Basis for the World Alliance (for Promoting International Friendship through the Churches)[20]

In July 1932 the Nazi Party won 230 seats in the Reichstag elections, paving the way six months later for the appointment of Adolf Hitler as Reich Chancellor. In

---

[18]   Ibid., p. 85.

[19]   William T. Cavanaugh, 'Church', in William Cavanaugh and Peter Scott (eds), *The Blackwell Companion to Political Theology* (Oxford, 2004), p. 405.

[20]   The World Alliance existed to promote 'mental and moral disarmament of the people in all countries'. Beginning early in the twentieth century its heyday coincided with the formation of the League of Nations, which it aimed to support. Between 1931 and 1937 the World Alliance worked closely with the Universal Christian Council for Life and Work (in which, with Bishop George Bell, Bonhoeffer also participated) but did not join with that organisation when, from 1938, it shared in the process to form the World

this context, on 26 July 1932, Bonhoeffer (who shared a commitment to peace-building with Cavanaugh) gave a lecture to a youth conference on peace at Ciernohorské, Czechoslovakia, outlining a theological basis for the World Alliance for Promoting International Friendship through the churches. The experience did not prove very satisfying for Bonhoeffer and in a letter to Erwin Sutz following the conference Bonhoeffer remarked: 'I have just returned ... from a very mediocre conference, which once more makes me doubt the value of all this ecumenical work.'[21] Not only did Bonhoeffer's lecture take him well beyond the theme of the conference, his attempt to raise basic questions about the Church's public ethic apparently set him apart from the less critical approach of other conference delegates. Bonhoeffer's lecture began with the stark judgement that 'there is still no theology of the ecumenical movement'. The ecumenical movement, he continued, like its constituent churches, is quite properly in the process of developing a new self-understanding, but the generation of a theology consistent with it lags far behind. Bonhoeffer's concern was that without a coherent theology of the Church's public role the ecumenical movement risked being at the whim of political trends. He seeks to nudge the process on by sketching a theology of the ecumenical movement capable of undergirding its common life and of providing a warrant for its public ethics. At stake for Bonhoeffer was a set of fundamental questions concerning the integrity of the Church's life of reconciliation and the consequences of that for its public action and witness:

> What is this Christianity that we always hear so much about? Is it essentially the content of the Sermon on the Mount, or is it the message of reconciliation in the cross and resurrection of our Lord? What significance does the Sermon on the Mount have for our action? What meaning is there in the message of the cross? What relationship do the forms of our modern lives have to the Christian proclamation? What do the state, the economy, and our social life have to do with being Christian?[22]

Council of Churches. Bonhoeffer's involvement in the World Alliance came through the encouragement of his Superintendent, Max Diestel, who was an enthusiastic supporter. For the history of the World Alliance see R. Rouse and S.C. Neill (eds), *A History of the Ecumenical Movement 1517–1948* (London, 1954), pp. 515ff.

[21]   See DB-EB, pp. 246–8. For Bonhoeffer's letter to Sutz see DBWE 11, p. 136.

[22]   DBWE 11, p. 357; DBW 11, p. 329: 'Was ist das Christentum, von dem wir da immer reden hören? Ist es im wesentlichen der Inhalt der Bergpredigt oder ist es die Botschaft von der Versöhnung in Kreuz und Auferstehung unseres Herrn? Was für eine Bedeutung hat die Bergpredigt für unser Handeln? und was für eine Bedeutung die Botschaft vom Kreuz? Wie verhalten sich die Gestalten unseres neuzeitlichen Lebens zu der christlichen Verkündigung? Was hat der Staat, was hat die Wirtschaft, was hat unser soziales Leben mit dem Christentum zu tun?'

Bonhoeffer's opening response was to assert that the Gospel of Jesus is not a Gospel for the Church or its members alone, but Good News for the world: 'The church as the one church-community of the Lord Jesus Christ, who is Lord of the world, has the task of speaking his word to the entire world. The range of the one church of Christ is the entire world.'[23] The view that there are areas or spheres of life ordained by God and governed by their own laws over which Christ has no authority must vigorously be repudiated. This set of questions was pertinent for two reasons (though Bonhoeffer does not make them explicit). Firstly, in March 1932 Bonhoeffer had 'jumped' within days of its publication, into Emil Brunner's *Das Gebot und das Ordnungen*[24] in which Brunner discussed several themes on which Bonhoeffer's lecture dwells, including the nature of the divine command, of reality, and the orders of creation. Brunner was suspicious of the tendency in Barth's theology to speak as though human reason is entirely overwhelmed by direct revelation, arguing instead that human reason, without direct revelation, had a limited capacity – albeit ultimately subject to Scripture – for knowing God.[25] Bonhoeffer can scarcely have had time properly to digest Brunner's substantial book, but already he seems to be edging away nervously from the view that the orders, including the order of the state, though created by God, may be spoken of as natural spheres of life with autonomous authority. The second reason that Bonhoeffer's lecture was pertinent was that in 1932 the nascent ecumenical movement – then as now – was agonised by the question of what authority the churches have in their common address to the world. Bonhoeffer's response was that the ecumenical Church speaks with the only authority the Church ever speaks with, namely 'the authority of the Christ living and present in it'.[26] In his 1927 doctoral dissertation *Sanctorum Communio*, Bonhoeffer had argued that the holy community of the Church is not simply an aggregation of its members, since it exists in and through Christ, through whom the old Adam is renewed. The Church is not, he therefore concluded, the body of Christ in some representative or metaphorical sense but rather is Christ, present in bodily form in the world today. The Church,

---

[23]   DBWE 11, pp. 358–9.

[24]   English translation: Emil Brunner, *The Divine Imperative*, trans. Olive Wyon (London, 1937). DBWE 11, p. 121. In August 1932, Bonhoeffer wrote to Sutz, who was working at the time under Brunner's supervision, at greater length about his view of *Das Gebot und das Ordnungen*, DBWE 11, pp. 136–8. Brunner's book was to be the focus of Barth's *Nein!* in the latter's polemical exchange with his fellow Swiss in 1934 that effected a theological break between them. Barth returned to discussion of the 'orders of creation' in *Church Dogmatics* III/4 (Edinburgh, 1961), pp. 19–23, where he contrasted Bonhoeffer's version of the orders in the *Mandatsbegriff* favourably with Brunner's, while still detecting in Bonhoeffer 'a suggestion of North German patriarchalism'.

[25]   I am indebted here to John McDowell for an illuminating discussion of Brunner's disagreement with Barth in 'Who Can Hope? Barth, Brunner and the Subject of Christian Hope', a paper given at the Society for the Study of Theology, Dublin, 31 March 2005.

[26]   DBWE 11, p. 359.

in the book's most arresting phrase, is 'Christ existing as church community'[27] and the Word of the Church to the world is the word of Christ spoken with the same authority as words spoken during his earthly life.[28]

Bonhoeffer continues his lecture by asking 'how the church speaks its word?' Realising in practice the authority of the present Christ, he argues, demands rigorous attention to the reality of the one addressed. At the simplest level, attending to reality means addressing the world in the most concrete way possible by resisting the desire to preach timeless principles and by speaking always as if God is God to us today in this specific time, place and situation. Yet, even where facts are expertly grasped and opinions widely canvassed, the question of how concrete a particular ecclesial statement may be is not thereby theologically resolved. Following Luther, Bonhoeffer takes it to be axiomatic that the Word of the Church to the world has two forms: gospel and commandment. The theological problem must therefore be expressed in the following way: can the Church preach the commandment of God with the same certainty with which it preaches the Gospel of Christ? Can the Church speak authoritatively on ethical and political matters – he gives economic justice and war as examples – with the same certainty with which it says 'your sins are forgiven'? For an authentically authoritative proclamation of God's command it is simply not enough to say something like 'ideally there shouldn't be wars, but sometimes they are necessary' or 'ideally it is wrong for someone to be rich while someone else has nothing, but the Church can't make rules about personal property': the Church must say concretely 'fight this war' or 'don't fight this war', or 'give this bread to this man'. Bonhoeffer well understood the danger of assuming a God's-eye view of moral issues, of speaking as if our human word is the Word of God. For this reason he insisted the Church must accept humbly that in proclaiming an ethical command as authoritatively as it proclaims the good news of reconciliation 'it is possible therewith to take the name of God in vain, that the church is in error and is sinful, but it may speak it in faith in the word of the forgiveness of sins that holds true for the church as well'.[29] If this remarkable sentence appeared in Bonhoeffer's *Ethics* or prison papers, where it would not look out of place, it might be supposed to reflect a shift from an apparently 'purist pacifism' of *Discipleship* to an apparent 'pragmatic compromise' implicit in Bonhoeffer's involvement with the Resistance. Its appearance in his 1932 lecture to a peace conference only makes sense if there is considerable consistency in Bonhoeffer's moral view that taking responsibility incurs guilt. The insight is echoed in Bonhoeffer's poem 'Jonah', rich in autobiographical allusion, written in the autumn of 1944 as evidence implicating him in the plot finally came to light:

---

[27]   DBWE 1, p. 141.

[28]   Bonhoeffer reiterates this point in chapter 10 of *Discipleship*, where he again asserts that 'For the first disciples the bodily community with Jesus did not mean anything different or anything more than what we have today', DBWE 4, p. 213.

[29]   DBWE 11, p. 361.

Away with me! The guilt is mine. God's wrath's for me.
The pious shall not perish with the sinner![30]

In his argument so far Bonhoeffer has stated that the Church speaks God's command authoritatively; speaks it concretely (by taking reality seriously); and speaks it in final anticipation of God's forgiveness. Bonhoeffer next begins to put sacramental flesh on the bones of his argument:

> The assurance of the validity of the proclamation of the forgiveness of sins is the sacrament. Here is the universal statement: 'Your sins are forgiven,' bound to water, wine and bread; here it comes to its own peculiar concretion, which is understood by believing listeners as the concrete here and now of the word of God. What the sacrament is for the proclamation of the gospel, the knowledge of concrete reality is for the proclamation of the commandment. *Reality is the sacrament of the commandment.*[31]

Within this short passage Bonhoeffer makes three claims. His first claim takes the form of a theological premise: that the proclamation of forgiveness of sin is made concrete in the sacraments of Baptism and the Lord's Supper, which validate it. His second claim is to state that what the sacrament is for the preaching of the Gospel, knowledge of reality is for the preaching of the command. This leads to the 'concluding' claim that reality is the sacrament of [ethical] commandment. The difficulty with Bonhoeffer's argument in this, its key phase, is that it is not immediately clear how the statement 'What the sacrament is for the proclamation of the gospel, the knowledge of concrete reality is for the proclamation of the commandment' forms a bridge from Bonhoeffer's premise (that the sacraments guarantee the validity of the proclamation of forgiveness) to his conclusion (that reality is the sacrament of the commandment). Why, for Bonhoeffer, do the sacraments 'merely' guarantee the validity of the proclamation of forgiveness? Do not the sacraments (in keeping with Cavanaugh's view of them) *perform* forgiveness, enacting that which they sign? We are led some way towards understanding what Bonhoeffer intends to convey by his ensuing commentary which embeds his central statement concerning the function of knowledge of reality in a theology of creation:

---

[30] DBWE 8, p. 548.

[31] DBWE 11, p. 361; original: 'Die Sicherung der Gültigkeit der Verkündigung der Süundenvergebung ist das Sakrament.Hier ist der allgemeine Satz: "Dir sind deine Sünden vergeben" gebunden an Wasser, Wein und Brot, hier kommt er zu der ihm eigentümlichen Konkretion, die als konkretes Hier und Jetzt des Wortes Gottes allein von dem glaubend Hörenden verstanden wird. Was für die Verkündigung des Evangeliums das Sakrament ist, das ist für die Verkündigung des Gebotes die Kenntnis der konkreten Wirklichkeit. *Die Wirklichkeit ist das Sakrament des Gebotes*' (Bonhoeffer's italics), DBW 11, p. 334.

> Just as the sacraments of baptism and the Lord's Supper are the only forms of the
> first reality of creation in this aeon, and just as they are sacraments for the sake of
> their creative origins, so is the 'ethical sacrament' of reality to be characterized
> as sacrament only so far as this reality itself is completely grounded in its
> relation to the reality of creation. As the fallen world and fallen continue to exist
> only through their relationship to the created world and the created reality, so the
> commandment is based on the forgiveness of sin.[32]

This lapidary formulation, unexpanded in the lecture, becomes the basis for
Bonhoeffer's lectures in the University of Berlin in the winter semester of 1932,
subsequently published as *Creation and Fall*.[33] In these lectures Bonhoeffer
reflected upon God's preservation of His created order after the Fall. Before the
Fall Adam and Eve lived in a state of simple obedience to the divine will. When
they ate of the tree of knowledge of good and evil they became, just as the serpent
had promised, *sicut deus*, able to decide for themselves what is right and wrong.
God's response to Adam and Eve issues as curse and promise: paradise is barred
but God accompanies them on their way into the world. In this new dispensation
'the creator is now the preserver; the created world is now the fallen but preserved
world'.[34] Creation is fallen, but God preserves the original creation within the
fallen in what Bonhoeffer here terms 'orders of preservation' in which the original
unity of reality in humanity's simple obedience to the divine will is preserved.
In such orders, to use phraseology from the *Ethics*, humanity is able to live in
one undivided reality rather than in its fallen state of life in two spheres. The
sacraments of Baptism and the Lord's Supper, Bonhoeffer is saying, constitute a
time when, and a location where, the bifurcation of creation into its original state
and its fallen state is reconciled. They are, as he puts it, only sacraments because
of their relation to creation before the Fall; and fallen reality is only real insofar
as it holds hidden within it the preserved order of original creation. By direct
analogy, the (ethical) word spoken by the Church as God's command is validated
by knowledge of the reality of the fallen world 'only insofar as this reality is itself
wholly grounded in its relationship to the reality of creation'.

In the remainder of his 1932 lecture, Bonhoeffer turned to the practical
question of 'how does the church know what God's commandment is today?'

---

[32]   DBWE 11, pp. 361–2. For the German original see DBW 11, p. 334, 'Wie
die Sakramente der Taufe und des Abendmahls die einzigen Gestalten der ersten
Schöpfungsmäßigen Ursprünglichkeit willen Sakramente sind, so ist das "ethische
Sakrament" die Wirklichkeit nur insofern als Sakrament zu bezeichnen, als diese
Wirklichkeit selbst ganz begründet ist in ihrer Beziehung auf die Schöpfungswirklichkeit.
Wie also die gefallene Welt und die gefallene Wirklichkeit allein durch ihre Beziehung
auf die geschafene Welt und die geschaffene Wirklichkeit Bestand hat, so das Gebot in
der Sündenvergebung.'

[33]   DBWE 3.

[34]   DBWE 3, p. 139.

His two answers constitute a statement of theological intent that will occupy him from 1932 until his arrest in 1943. His first answer is that the Church recognises God's commandment in biblical law, including the Sermon on the Mount. This question would absorb his attention – allowing for digressions into Christology, the life of the Christian community and biblical exegesis – from this point until the publication of *Discipleship* in November 1937. His second answer is that the commandment is recognised in 'the orders of creation'. Expanding this claim was the second part of his agenda and would occupy him immediately in preparing his lectures on *Creation and Fall* and later in his re-narration of Luther's orders of creation and preservation in his theology of the divine mandates, on which he was working at the time of his arrest in April 1943.

The final section of the lecture makes explicit the question: 'to whom does the church speak?' Bonhoeffer gives two answers. On the one hand, the churches come together in the ecumenical movement to speak to Christendom, telling it to hear its Word as the commandment of God because it proceeds from the forgiveness of sins. On the other hand, the Church speaks to the world and tells it to change. Either because of his views concerning the separation of Church and world, or because he is attempting to do what he says by attending to the reality of the Church's situation, Bonhoeffer recognises that neither world nor state pay sufficiently serious attention to the Church's Word. The most he expects in terms of the political consequence of speaking God's command is that the state may recognise in the commandment a boundary to its own rule and authority.[35] The final paragraph of his lecture acknowledges the fact of disunity within the Church concerning what constitutes truth, to which Bonhoeffer offers no solution.[36]

Concerning the Possibility of a Word of the Church to the World

The way Bonhoeffer frames the question of the relationship of the Church's Word to the Church and its word to the world – and of its sacramental life and its public proclamation of command – is one to which Bonhoeffer returned in a manuscript probably written in 1941.[37] In this unfinished document, which resembles a memorandum rather than a section of a book,[38] Bonhoeffer organised his thinking

---

[35] Note that Bonhoeffer's experience of Church–state relations was one largely shaped by the context of the German alliance of 'Throne and Altar'.

[36] In a lecture advocating concentrated attention to reality as the 'sacrament of command', it is striking that Bonhoeffer should nod so casually at the observable fact of ecclesial disunity, or fail to spell out his evident pessimism about the ecumenical movement and the consequences of its weaknesses. It still remains the case that the churches often struggle to agree on anything sufficiently univocally to speak the divine command.

[37] On the likely dating of the essay manuscript see the editors' fn.1, in DBWE 6, p. 352.

[38] The essay was included by Eberhard Bethge in the appendix to the first editions of Bonhoeffer's *Ethics*; it is now included in vol. 6 of DBW and DBWE. However, the editors'

'On the possibility of the Church's Message[39] to the World'. In a clear echo of his 1932 lecture, he begins by stating that '[w]hat is necessary is a concrete directive in the concrete situation'.[40] Answering his own question, Bonhoeffer is now less confident about the Church's public authority than in his 1932 lecture. To be sure, the Church has something to say about worldly things; but the Church simply does not have solutions to every problem the world has. The Word Jesus gives in Scripture is not, for Bonhoeffer, an answer to human questions and problems, it is the divine answer to the divine question addressed to human beings; the Word given in Scripture is not a solution (*Lösung*) but redemption (*Erlösung*) for the world. On this basis Bonhoeffer ruled out a way of relating Church to world which he believes to be characteristically 'Anglo-Saxon' (a term he always used dismissively!), namely a crusading approach to worldly evils for which he uses the anti-slavery movement, Prohibition, and the formation of the League of Nations as examples. It would be wrong, Bonhoeffer continued, to conclude from this that the Church has no political task '[b]ut we will not recognise its [the Church's] legitimate task unless we first find the correct starting point'.[41] The correct starting point for the Word of the Church to the world is the Word of God to the world, which (reiterating his 1932 formulation) is always proclaimed as Law and Gospel. In 1932, Bonhoeffer made commandment dependent on the proclamation of forgiveness, striking a positive note concerning the authority of the Church's Word to the world. But by 1941 (on the basis, it is reasonable to speculate, of his experience of the Church struggle) he now asserts negatively that while the Church may reprehend public policy at variance with Gospel and Law it may only offer its alternative proposal as a word of counsel (not command). He concludes that:

- The Church does not speak to the world on the basis of shared convictions (such as natural law).
- There are not two moral laws – one for the Church, another for the world – since God's entire Word, Gospel and Law, are for all people and all time.

Making reference in a marginal note to 'Rome' and to the 'USA, e.g., Prohibition', he resists attempts to justify any distinction between the autonomy of the state and 'the heteronomy of an ecclesiastical theocracy' because 'before God there is no autonomous realm'.[42]

---

opinion was divided on whether Bonhoeffer intended it for inclusion in his *Ethics*. My own view is that Bonhoeffer did not intend to include this text in his *Ethics*.

[39]   'Über die Möglichkeit des *Wortes* der Kirche and die Welt': the decision to translate 'Wortes' as 'message' somewhat obscures the theological importance the Lutheran Bonhoeffer attaches to the interplay between the Word of God and the ('preached') Word of the Church.

[40]   DBWE 6, p. 353.

[41]   Ibid., p. 356, Bonhoeffer's italics.

[42]   Ibid., p. 362.

The Influence of Luther's Early Sacramental Theology

Reading Bonhoeffer's lecture, and connecting it to similar discussions elsewhere in his writings, has taken us part of the way towards understanding what Bonhoeffer meant by stating that 'reality is the sacrament of the commandment'. It has also allowed me to display the evidence for claiming that the theological foundation of the work of the World Alliance constitutes, one might say, the theological agenda with which Bonhoeffer was occupied from 1932 until 1943. But how far does this take us towards Bonhoeffer's understanding of the relationship between worship and ethics? Are we any the wiser about why, for Bonhoeffer, the sacraments are said to 'guarantee the validity' of the proclamation of forgiveness, rather than performing it? To illuminate Bonhoeffer's views still further it is helpful to turn briefly to the early Lutheran background to Bonhoeffer's understanding of sacrament.

Luther's 95 theses (1517) focused his dispute with Rome on indulgences and papal authority.[43] However, following his meeting in 1518 with Cardinal Cajetan, reformation of the sacraments became more central to his aspirations for ecclesial reform. In three sermons delivered in 1519 Luther developed the view, against Cajetan's Thomistic theology, that the sacraments do not of themselves have any objective salvific effect, but depend rather on the mutual relation between God's Word of promise and the faith of the one who receives it. For Luther there exists a sequential relationship between the absolution spoken by the priest, the words of forgiveness that externalise and express divine grace, and the faith that accepts that which is spoken. 'Everything', Luther says, 'then depends on this faith which alone makes the sacraments accomplish that which they signify, and everything the priest says come true.'[44] Within a sacrament one may distinguish firstly the *sacrament* or sign (he uses the terms interchangeably), secondly its *meaning*, and thirdly, *faith*, which is thereby taken up into a Lutheran understanding of the sacraments. The sacrament is therefore, according to Luther, an external sign of an inner reality. Thus Luther speaks of the form of bread and wine as the sign, of fellowship as its meaning, and of reception of the sign in faith which is a true and personal belief in salvation.[45] In *The Babylonian Captivity of the Church*, Luther concludes that:

> we may learn from this that in every promise of God two things are presented to us, the word and the sign, so that we are to understand the word to be the testament, but the sign to be the sacrament. Thus, in the mass, the word of Christ

---

[43]   For a good overview of Luther's sacramental theology see Bernhard Lohse, *Martin Luther's Theology: Its Historical and Systematic Development* (Edinburgh, 1999), particularly chapters 13, 31 and 32.

[44]   'The Sacrament of Penance', in *Luther's Works: The Word and Sacrament*, American edn 35, ed. E. Theodore Bachman (Philadelphia, 1960), p. 11.

[45]   *Luther's Works*, 35, pp. 50–51. Bonhoeffer cites this sermon in DBWE 1, p. 179.

is the testament, and the bread and wine are the sacrament. And as there is greater power in the word than in the sign, so there is greater power in the testament than in the sacrament; for a man can have and use the word or testament apart from the sign or sacrament. 'Believe' says Augustine, 'and you have eaten'.[46]

What is crucial here, for the purpose of understanding Bonhoeffer's sacramental theology, is his firm confessional adherence to a distinction between the word of Christ, the external sacrament that signs, and the emphasis placed on the role of faith in receiving the promises of God signed in the sacraments. In Lutheran theology, the sacraments in and of themselves are not instruments of divine action, whether on persons or in public, *unless accompanied by faith*. The sacraments depend for their effect on the gift of the Word of God that they sign and the reception of that Word by faith, which is itself a gift from God. This proves to be the basis of Bonhoeffer's premise that the sacraments of Baptism and the Lord's Supper guarantee the validity of signed forgiveness, rather than directly enacting or performing it. This, in turn, helps us to grasp his conclusion that just as the sacraments guarantee the validity of the proclamation of the Gospel (which is apprehended only where there is faith), knowledge of reality guarantees the validity of the Church's proclamation of Law (which is apprehended only where there is obedience). In the same way that Gospel and Law are not, in Lutheran theology, identified or conflated, for Bonhoeffer sacraments and command are to be understood as distinct aspects of the one proclamation of God's Word. And as the proclamation of the Law is based or founded on the Gospel, the ethical command is based or founded on the proclamation of forgiveness, validated in the celebration of the sacraments.[47] Our discussion of Bonhoeffer may be summarised in five points:

- Bonhoeffer's view concerning the possibility of a Word of the Church to the world, condensed in the statement that 'reality is the sacrament of [the ethical] commandment', was one he held with remarkable consistency from 1932 until at least 1943.
- Bonhoeffer's assertion that 'reality is the sacrament of [the ethical] commandment' depends for its intelligibility on Lutheran distinctions between Law and Gospel; between word, sign and faith; between Church and state and on Luther's doctrine of the orders of creation and preservation.
- For Bonhoeffer the Word of the Church to the world is the Word of God to the world.

---

[46] *Luther's Works*, American edn 36, ed. A.R. Wentz, trans. A.T.W. Steinhäuser et al. (Philadelphia, 1959), p. 45.

[47] Bonhoeffer's account in 1932 anticipates in certain respects the distinction made in the *Ethics* between the penultimate and the ultimate, in which the penultimate is dependent on the ultimate.

- For Bonhoeffer the Church's Word to the world arises only from its proclamation of the Gospel of forgiveness – with which it is, nonetheless, not to be confused.
- Because it depends on God's ultimate Word of forgiveness, the Church's penultimate word to the world is spoken with a degree of humility (one that varies in degree between Bonhoeffer's accounts of 1932 and 1941).

Conclusions

It is time to 'listen in' to how a conversation between Cavanaugh and Bonhoeffer on the sacraments and politics might unfold. Both theologians are concerned to explicate that ancient confession of the Church that 'Jesus is Lord' and to do so in ways that realise Jesus' authority concretely and politically. Both theologians understand the Church to be 'Christ's body' in more than a representative or merely 'metaphorical' sense; and for both theologians, these insights are worked through in creative exploration of the political dimension of the Church's sacraments. These are substantial points of agreement, but here their theological paths diverge on at least two further matters.

The first divergence concerns eschatology. Cavanaugh's eschatology is essentially realised, while Bonhoeffer's is more in keeping with the Pauline tension between the now and the not yet. Cavanaugh, who knows the imperfections of the Church, prefers to describe the Church not as it is but as it theologically should be: a 'theopolitical' body clearly distinguishable from the secular body politic. Bonhoeffer is more inclined to operate with penultimate and the ultimate categories. Jesus Christ is certainly *pro me* in the Church, but it speaks God's Word penultimately, only in the promise of God's ultimate Word of forgiveness. The second divergence flows directly from the first. Bonhoeffer, following Luther, recognises in social bodies other than the Church – his mandates name family and state as examples – other bodies in which a space is kept open for human community. Cavanaugh, on the other hand, proposes a kind of 'liturgical supercessionism', in which the liturgically perfected body of Christ renders invalid now all other kinds of body, making it axiomatic that the Church as the only genuinely true and good public thing and showing up all other '*res publica*' as mere forgeries.

Returning to my summary of the discussion, the first point – concerning the consistency of Bonhoeffer's theological ethics – is largely 'domestic' to Bonhoeffer scholarship and need not detain us here. The second point – that Bonhoeffer's view of the ethical sacrament of reality is intelligible only in the context of Luther's theology – raises the question of the extent to which a confessional understanding of the sacraments is likely to shape the view one takes of the relationship between worship and ethics. Certainly, some of the issues concerning how worship shapes ethics are as likely to be disputed intra-confessionally as much as inter-confessionally. Yet, if virtue-ethics is right to insist that particular traditions form individuals and communities in particular ways – a conviction Cavanaugh applauds and which, for what it is worth, I share – it would be strange if Cavanaugh's Catholic tradition and Bonhoeffer's Lutheran tradition had done nothing to shape them distinctively. Working within the parameters set by Lutheran theology Bonhoeffer distinguishes between sign and meaning in sacrament and emphasises the role of faith in receiving the promise signed in the sacraments. If what matters is belief then the sacraments themselves assume a secondary role: they confirm but they do not effect that which is signed. In contrast, for Cavanaugh, the 'Eucharist makes real the presence of Christ both in the elements and in the body of believers'.[48] For this reason he is able boldly to assert that 'the Eucharist effects the body of Christ'[49] while Bonhoeffer holds that the performance of the divine commandment rests on the forgiveness of sins guaranteed by the sacraments. The third and fourth points in my summary of the early discussion in this chapter – that the Word of the Church to the world is God's Word, which arises from its proclamation of forgiveness – constitute points of agreement between Bonhoeffer and Cavanaugh. But the final point – that the Church's Word to the world is a penultimate Word that may be spoken authoritatively only where the Church acknowledges that its ethical command to the world 'blasphemes the name of God' – once more pinpoints a confessional dimension to the debate. Cardinal Ratzinger, long before his election as Benedict XVI, made clear that for Catholics the Church is a 'superhuman reality' whose 'fundamental structures are willed by God himself and are thus untouchable'. The liberal historian Felipe Fernàndez-Armesto predicted in 1995 that '[t]he effect [of Christian fundamentalism] will be mitigated if the Catholic Church – the world's biggest and most widespread communion – keeps up what may become a unique commitment to moral absolutism in defence of human dignity, individual freedom, social justice and the sanctity of life'.[50] Set against a Catholic confidence in universal moral absolutes, Luther (and Bonhoeffer) set out in their ethics from the conviction that they are members of a church in which each individual is *simul iustus et peccator*. Is this the reason that Bonhoeffer is so sanguine about the fact of ecclesial disunity? Is this the reason that he cannot escape the paradox implicit in his dual assertion that though the Church does speak God's Word to the world through the 'ethical sacrament of reality', it errs and sins as it speaks it? Bonhoeffer's last word on the relation between worship and public action is informed by the politics of human frailty:

> Our church has been fighting during these years only for its self-preservation, as if that were an end in itself. It has become incapable of bringing the word

---

48   Cavanaugh, *Torture*, p. 205.

49   Ibid., p. 206.

50   Felipe Fernàndez-Armesto, *Millennium* (London, 1995), p. 701.

of reconciliation and redemption to humankind and the world. So the words we used before must lose their power, be silenced, and we can be Christians today in only two ways: through prayer and in doing justice among human beings.[51]

---

[51] DBWE 8, p. 389.

Chapter 9
Bonhoeffer's Interfaith Encounters

In March 1963 Bishop J.A.T. Robinson sprang his controversial work *Honest to God* on the British public. So much debated was the material within it that by September of the same year it had run into its ninth impression. To the professional theologians the ideas in the book seemed old hat, yet the book's importance did not lie in originality, but in provoking a widespread public debate about theological issues. The book set itself the apologetic task understood as 'at radical questioning of the established "religious frame"' in which Christianity had hitherto been offered.[1] It is a task of overwhelming importance in increasingly multi faith British society. In no small part of this task it sought assistance from the thought of a Lutheran theologian from Germany. Whilst in a Nazi prison cell and shortly to be executed in 1945, this thinker had coined the phrase 'Religionless Christianity' to express something of his vision for the future of the Christian Church. The theologian's name was Dietrich Bonhoeffer, and, but for his involvement in the July bomb plot to assassinate Hitler, we might never have heard of him as a theologian at all. Where the notion of 'Religionless Christianity' originated is the theme of this chapter, for it is my suggestion that one avenue of exploration into the meaning of Bonhoeffer's legacy could begin with the tantalising hints we receive of what he had learnt from his encounter with people of other faiths, and especially in his perception of the unity within them of religious and secular aspects of human existence.

What, then, was the extent of Bonhoeffer's contacts with the world's living faiths? Bonhoeffer was in many ways a pure product of the German Philosophical tradition. Yet because Bonhoeffer's father was a psychologist of international renown, it was both financially possible, and expected within the Bonhoeffer family that the young Dietrich would travel as a part of his education. At the age of 17, he therefore set out for Italy. This journey was hugely significant in the formation of his theological priorities. The interest he developed in Rome concerning the form of the Church determined the subject of his doctoral thesis, a biographical point that is widely known and accepted. Much less well known however, is that during this time he visited North Africa for 10 days, though without first asking his parents' permission. In Tripoli he briefly came into contact with Islam, regretting the linguistic and cultural difficulties that prevented any deeper encounter. What engaged his attention most in Islam was the absolute unity in it of the secular and the religious. In what must have been an eyebrow-raising letter to his parents in April 1924 he wrote:

---

[1]   John A.T. Robinson, *Honest to God* (London, 1963), p. 9.

In Islam, everyday life and religion are not separated at all. Even in the Catholic church they are separated, for the most part. At home, one just goes to church. When one returns a completely different life begins … It would be really be interesting to study Islam on its own soil.[2]

Thus, even at this early point in his life, Bonhoeffer appears uncomfortable with what he knew of 'Western Christianity'. He discerned the dangers of the kind of religious devotion that gets in the way of responsible living in the world. This dishonesty, this dualism, was something that did not seem to pervade the lives of the Muslims he met briefly in North Africa.

This experience of travel outside Europe must have left a deep impression in Bonhoeffer's mind, for by 1928 he had begun talking about the possibility of making an extended visit to India, a visit that became an unrealised project that would fascinate him for several years. Though to some extent limited by his youth, Bonhoeffer in the early 1930s had come to the fore within what was known as the Confessing Church in Germany, a group of Christians who refused to acknowledge any authority but Christ within the life of the Church. This meant deciding how best to conduct their opposition to the interference of the State within the life of the Church. Bonhoeffer's ecumenical contacts, made at an international level, convinced him both of the need for peace, and of the need to conduct effective passive resistance to the bigotry of National Socialism. In this India and the 'East' became for him symbols, both of what he felt to be lacking in 'Western Christianity', and of the best model of religious opposition to the state. But for Bonhoeffer, 'India' was still fairly ill defined. Its symbolic meaning did not allow for an effective distinction between the differing religious traditions within the subcontinent. However, from all that he knew the appeal was once more the apparent unity of the religious and the secular in Indian life. Here, the fact that Gandhi exercised both spiritual and political leadership was especially appealing. But there was also in Bonhoeffer an unadulterated thirst for new horizons of knowledge, new perspectives on how to do the will of God. In May 1932 he wrote to his friend Erwin Sutz about his proposed journey to India:

I can hardly think of it [his visit to Mexico] without yearning like crazy to travel again, this time to the East. I don't know yet when. But it must not be too long. There must be other people in the world, ones who know more and can do more than we can know or do. And it is simply irresponsible not to go there and learn.[3]

And again in the May of 1934 he was writing to his Grandmother:

Before I tie myself down for good, I'm thinking of going to India. I've given a good deal of thought lately to the issues there and believe that there could be

---

[2] DBWE 9, p. 118.
[3] DBWE 11, p. 121.

important things to be learned. In any case it sometimes seems to me there's more Christianity in their 'heathenism' than in the whole of our Reich Church. Christianity did in fact come from the East originally, but it has become so westernised and so permeated by civilized thought that, as we can now see, it is almost lost to us.[4]

A good example of what he admired lay in the disciplined lifestyle of those involved in the *Ashram* movement. Simple living, combined with a strong sense of community, were elements which his own Lutheran tradition had largely thrown out with the bath water of sixteenth-century monasticism. Bonhoeffer yearned to experience them in India. Throughout 1934 he made quite concrete plans for his proposed visit, even borrowing tropical suits to have them altered to fit him. He received a personal invitation from Gandhi to join him at his *Ashram*; but the visit never happened. Bonhoeffer's colleagues in the Church struggle, and in particular Karl Barth included, were loath to lose him at such a crucial time. Instead, Bonhoeffer accepted the responsibility of setting up and running a community of his own, a preachers' seminary to train pastors for service within the Confessing Church. Bonhoeffer prepared for this by visiting a number of religious communities in England. There, he was able to learn something of what he had hoped to learn in India. Yet it must be true to say that without the conviction of the inadequacy concerning 'Western Christianity' which he had gained from his knowledge of the East, these preparations would probably not have occurred. The community which he was able to found as a result, first at Zingst and later at Finkenwalde, and the spiritual life he encouraged there, prompted what are probably his two best known books, *Life Together* and *Discipleship*.

The most significant interfaith encounter which Bonhoeffer had was very much closer to hand and was much more pressing in Nazi Germany. In a letter in 1967 thanking Eberhard Bethge for a complimentary copy of his biography of Bonhoeffer, Karl Barth commented:

New to me ... was the fact that Bonhoeffer in 1933 viewed the Jewish question as the first and decisive question, even as the only one, and took it on so energetically. I have long felt guilty myself that I did not make this problem central, in any case not public, for instance in the two Barmen declarations of 1934 which I had composed. Certainly, a text in which I inserted a word to that effect would not have found agreement in 1934 – neither in the Reformed Synod of January, 1934; nor in the General Synod of May at Barmen. But there is no excuse that I did not fight properly for this cause, just because I was caught up in my affairs somewhere else.

Within this interfaith encounter there were at least three strands in Bonhoeffer's thinking. Firstly, Bonhoeffer was keen to emphasise that in the Church there is

---

[4] DBWE 13, p. 152.

neither Jew nor German. Yet secondly for Bonhoeffer, the responsibility of the Church towards the 'Jewish Question' included the need to speak out against the persecution of all Jews. Thus in 1935 he vehemently criticised the Augsburg Synod for making a pronouncement only on the issue of Jewish Baptism, for, as Bethge puts it, 'such a pronouncement on Jewish Baptism would be an embarrassment if it was not accompanied by a clear statement condemning the general persecution of the Jews'.[5] This was not simply for humanitarian reasons; Bonhoeffer, with St Paul, understood the Jews to be included within God's plan of election. In his *Ethics* Bonhoeffer wrote: 'The Jew keeps open the question of Christ ... [d]riving out the Jew(s) from the West must result in driving out Christ with them.'[6]

Thirdly, Bonhoeffer's understanding of the Bible was directly related to his respectful encounter with Judaism. In *The Old Testament as a Book of Christ*,[7] Martin Kuske shows the importance of the Old Testament within Bonhoeffer's thinking. At a time in German theology when the Old Testament was either being removed altogether as Scripture (by the German Christians), or regarded as having merely secondary value (e.g., Bultmann), Bonhoeffer affirmed the Old Testament as of equal weight with the New as Christian Scripture.

What, then, was the contribution of these encounters to his understanding of 'Religionless Christianity'? The phrase itself comes from two letters written to Eberhard Bethge on 30 April and 5 May 1944, and it is as well to look there for some idea of its meaning. By 'Religious people' Bonhoeffer means those who 'speak of God at a point where human knowledge is at an end (or sometimes when they're too lazy to think further), or when human strength fails'.[8] These are people who place God out at the boundaries of life instead of at its centre. To 'interpret religiously' means 'to speak metaphysically, on the one hand, and on the other hand individualistically'.[9] Neither of these ways is, for Bonhoeffer, appropriate or indeed biblical. Thus for him, 'Religious' speech, in this pejorative sense, means conceiving God as somehow 'out there', as a divine 'pie in the sky'; it means to speak in a way that focuses selfishly on the 'me' at the expense of the 'other' and of the *community*.

Bonhoeffer's argument is constructed here along historical grounds that concern only the Western world. In this he acknowledges that secularisation is a problem that had hit the West harder than the East. But is he not also acknowledging that in the East, the dependence of religious faith on a religious a priori had always been less significant? Might the implication that this critique of 'religious interpretation' is, as it were, a critique not of 'religion' generally, but of *Western* religion from the perspective of Eastern understandings and practices of religion in which God, the world, and the life of faith are *not* metaphysical and individualistic? Martin Kuske

---

[5]   DB-EB, p. 488.

[6]   DBWE 6, p. 105.

[7]   Martin Kuske, *The Old Testament as the Book of Christ* (Philadelphia, 1976).

[8]   DBWE 8, p. 366.

[9]   Ibid., p. 372.

suggests something similar when he writes in relation to the Hebrew Scriptures that, for Bonhoeffer, 'What "nonreligious" and "worldly" mean is determined by the Old Testament'.[10]

It is to Bonhoeffer that we turn for the final word, again from his letter of April 1944: 'I often wonder why my "Christian instinct" frequently draws me more toward non-religious people than towards the religious, and I am sure it is not with missionary intent; instead I'd almost call it a "brotherly" instinct.'[11]

Exactly whom does Bonhoeffer mean here by 'religionless people'? Is it only the secular members of Western society? Surely it must also be the 'religionless peoples' of the world, all of those who live out their lives in ways which God and the 'Man come of age' really do meet at the centre of the world, of whatever culture and to whatever tradition of faith or ideology they belong.

---

[10]   Kuske, *Old Testament*, p. 138.
[11]   DBWE 8, p. 366.

Chapter 10
'In the Sphere of the Familiar':
Heidegger and Bonhoeffer

Context and Text

In an unusually expansive moment towards the end of his 'Letter on "Humanism"', Martin Heidegger retails an anecdote concerning Heraclitus, a pre-Socratic philosopher he held in particularly high esteem. In a story reported by Aristotle, a group of foreigners make a surprise visit to Heraclitus's house and find him warming himself at a stove. Expecting to find the philosopher deep in thought, the visitors are put out to discover him in an everyday activity they could have observed at home without the rigours of their long journey. Observing their discomfort Heraclitus welcomed them with the words: 'εἶναι γὰρ καί ἐνταῦθα θεούς' ('here too the gods are present').[1] This phrase, Heidegger interprets:

> places the abode (ἦθος) of the thinker and his deed in another light ... 'even here,' at the stove, in that ordinary place where every thing and every circumstance, each deed and thought is intimate and commonplace, that is, familiar [geheuer], 'even there' in the sphere of the familiar, εἶναι θεούς, it is the case that 'the gods come to presence.' Heraclitus himself says, ἦθος ἀνθρώπῳ δαίμων, 'The (familiar) abode for humans is the open region for the presencing of god (the unfamiliar one)'.[2]

The anecdote is vintage Heidegger. It encapsulates one of his main contributions to philosophical thought – the insight that the human condition is embedded (or 'thrown' in his distinctive vocabulary) in the everyday world of simple things. In Heidegger's 'hands' everyday objects – a pair of worn shoes, a hammer, a lectern, a stove – become occasions of philosophical revelation. 'Vintage' Heidegger too, in that with the anecdote Heidegger sums up the counter-intuitive view, articulated in the *Letter*, that the world needs *less* philosophy, and more thinking that 'gathers language into simple saying'.[3] Yet unwittingly the anecdote also puts before us one of the most immediate questions to arise from Heidegger's legacy: what is the relationship between the everyday life of the philosopher and the philosophy that arises from it? If thinking is an everyday activity, what are we to make of the way

---

[1] Martin Heidegger, *Pathmarks*, ed. William McNeill (Cambridge, 1998), pp. 269–70.
[2] Ibid., pp. 270–71.
[3] Ibid., p. 276.

a thinker's life interprets – or obfuscates – the meaning of his thought? How, if at all, are readers to make connections between context and text, life and thought; between a philosopher's bio*graphy* and the *graffiti* he leaves scratched upon the history of ideas?

Few writers in the twentieth century raise these questions more vexingly than Martin Heidegger. Yet he is hard pressed by the presence of similar questions arising from reflection on the life and writings of Dietrich Bonhoeffer. Heidegger was a Nazi; Bonhoeffer expended his life opposing Nazism: how do these biographical data help or hinder our apprehension of their writings? Is it possible, or even desirable, to insulate a comparison between their writings from the sphere of these familiar facts? In a chapter that sets out to examine the influence of one man on the other, how can we handle their respective attitudes to Nazism in ways that are not prejudicial to the outcome? 'What needs careful sifting', George Steiner advises wisely, 'is the distinction to be drawn – if it can be drawn – between the singularity of the person, with all its pathological markers, and the autonomous weight of the work.' And if Steiner is right to judge that 'generations will pass before any confident delineation can be proposed in our sense of Martin Heidegger'[4] may not the same be said of Bonhoeffer? These questions never quite drop below the horizon in what follows, but my aim in the body of this chapter is to place 'the autonomous weight' of their work in the scales and see which way the balance tilts.

Comparing Heidegger's thought with Bonhoeffer's is a formidable task for any individual, and is certainly impossible within the compass of a single chapter. Bonhoeffer's writings extend through 17 volumes; the publication of Heidegger's *Gesamtausgabe* is ongoing but is scheduled for publication in 102 volumes.[5] The question therefore is not whether to be selective, but how to be selective. An obvious means by which to limit the scope of the present chapter is to concentrate attention upon those passages in Bonhoeffer's writings in which Heidegger is explicitly discussed; and this is indeed where I propose to begin. But I want to suggest that the most lasting and most significant impact that Heidegger's thinking had on Bonhoeffer's is not to be found in the most obvious place – namely the influence of Heidegger's *Being and Time* on Bonhoeffer's *Act and Being* – but lies tucked away in the methodology of a text which does not once mention Heidegger's name: Bonhoeffer's formative lecture series on *Christology*. In what

---

[4] George Steiner, *No Passion Spent: Essays 1978–1996* (London, 1996), p. 178. The *Letter on 'Humanism'* provides a striking example of the difficulty of bracketing knowledge of Heidegger's life off from what he writes. The *Letter* was Heidegger's first published essay after the end of the war, and it is hard to read statements such as the following and forget he was undergoing de-Nazification: 'Because we are speaking against "humanism" people fear a defense of the inhuman and a glorification of barbaric brutality', Heidegger, *Pathmarks*, p. 263.

[5] For details and updates of the publication of the various volumes see the publisher's website: http://www.klostermann.de/ Accessed 23 October 2013.

follows I trace the origins of Heidegger's *Being and Time*, before turning to its central themes and arguments; next I turn to Bonhoeffer's reading of Heidegger, and thence to the reasons for believing that it is in his theological method, displayed in the *Christology* lectures, that Heidegger's thinking may be most influential on Bonhoeffer's.

The Origins of Heidegger's Being and Time

Being and Time made Heidegger's name, but his journey towards philosophical fame and fortune had been far from easy.[6] Born in 1889 in Messkirch, a small town between the Swabian Alps and Lake Constance in South West Germany, Heidegger grew up in the house that came with his father's job as sexton of the town's Roman Catholic Church. In his maturity Heidegger often dwelt on his small-town upbringing, comparing himself to a plant with roots in the earth, and at the end of his life he naturally chose to reunite his body with the soil of the Messkirch graveyard for which his father had been responsible. Though not especially poor, the family lacked the funds for the best education money could buy and Heidegger learned the Latin he needed to enter the *Gymnasium* (high school) from the parish priest, who also helped obtain a Church grant to pay his fees, beginning a period of 13 years during which Heidegger was financially dependent on the Catholic Church.[7] He lodged in Constance in a Catholic boarding house and in 1906 entered the archiepiscopal seminary in Freiburg where he began training for the priesthood. Essays written by Heidegger in his early years in Freiburg are models of Catholic anti-modernism and in 1909 he entered the Society of Jesus as a novice. After two weeks, however, the Jesuits let him go on account of heart pains. Yet even in what would prove to be the final years of his training, Heidegger's attention was turning increasingly to formal and mathematical logic that became 'a kind of worship' to him.[8] Though at this stage he considered the objectivity of strict logic as a complement to the authority of faith, on the recurrence of heart trouble two years later he discontinued his training for the priesthood (he abandoned Catholicism altogether in 1919). It was in these years, in 1911–12, that a decisive intellectual discovery directed Heidegger finally on the path that would lead him to *Being and Time:* he began reading the writings of Edmund Husserl, and in particular Husserl's *Logical Investigations*. Fifty years later the smell of that book was still in his nostrils: 'I remained so fascinated by Husserl's work', remarked Heidegger looking back, 'that I read in it again and again in the years to follow ... The

---

[6] Far the fullest intellectual biography of Heidegger is Rüdiger Safranski's *Ein Meister aus Deutschland: Heidegger und seine Zeit* (Munich, 1994); English translation, *Martin Heidegger: Between Good and Evil* (Cambridge, MA, 1998).

[7] Ibid., pp. 9–19.

[8] Ibid., p. 24.

spell emanating from the work extended to the outer appearance of the sentence structure and the title-page.'[9]

Husserl's spell on Heidegger lay in a distinctive philosophical method that Husserl deployed with such verve that he re-branded it as his own: the phenomenological method. Husserl had started out academic life as a scientist, and came to philosophy via psychological investigation of how subjects arrive at concepts such as number. Initially, he tried to reduce logic and arithmetic to psychological functions. But in the two volumes of the *Logical Investigations* (1900–1901) he argued that a distinction is to be drawn, key to phenomenology, between the *objects* of consciousness and our *consciousness* of such objects. Because Heidegger at once adopts, adapts and ultimately remoulds the phenomenological method in *Being and Time* it is important to get to grips with what is at stake in it.

'Phenomenology' is etymologically derived from two Greek words. τὸ φαινόμενον is derived from the Greek verb φαίνεσθαι, meaning 'to make appear' or 'to show'. τὸ φαινόμενον thus suggests 'that which shows itself' or the 'self-showing' of things. Thus, 'phenomenology describes giving an account of the self-showing of things'.[10] In *Being and Time* Heidegger describes phenomenology as a going 'back to the things themselves' (*Zu den Sachen selbst!*). Husserl thought that most philosophers before him had failed adequately to consider the role that the act of cognition made by a perceiving subject plays in her encounter with things. Even before I *sense* the world, Husserl thought, my experience of it is already organising itself in my mind. I don't hear a series of noises made by catgut echoing over a chamber of wood, and then, as a next step think 'aha … that's music!' When I hear the sounds my mind presents them to me instantly as a Bach cello sonata. Husserl called this process in the mind the structure of *intentionality*. The world is to be thought of as a network of meaning (intentionality) that is the horizon in which we come across phenomena. It was not Husserl's intention to oppose appearance and essence – as if all that the mind encounters along this horizon is the *appearance* of things and never their *essence*. Rather, Husserl asserted that *essences appear*. His own illustration was to picture himself seeing a table while walking around it: though his perspective on the table changes with each step, his consciousness of the table existing 'in person' remains unchanged: what the mind perceives is always a table, which it 'organises' in the mind into a single continuous impression. In a subsequent book Husserl developed the phenomenological approach by means of another methodological innovation that would be employed and reshaped by Heidegger with startling effect: the coining of a new philosophical vocabulary in order to draw the eye to the newness of the insights and ideas that the philosopher is attempting to convey. In *Ideas Pertaining to a Pure Phenomenology and to a*

---

[9]   Ibid., p. 25.

[10]   For the etymology of the notion of 'phenomenology', Heidegger's own account is illuminating; cf. Martin Heidegger, *Being and Time*, trans. J. Macquarrie and Edward Robinson (Oxford, 1962), pp. 49–63.

Phenomenological Philosophy,[11] Husserl ceases to speak of intentional conscious acts and their contents – appearances and essences – and speaks of *noesis* and *noema* to help take philosophy beyond the old distinction between subject and object in which he thought it had stagnated. The point of all this was to say that what should really matter to philosophy is not the perceiving subject or the object perceived: rather the object as meant (*noema*) and the intentional act (*noesis*) that presents the object as meant are inextricably bound up in one another. One simple consequence is that a phenomenologist, according to Husserl, must suspend judgement about the actual existence of things and pay exclusive attention to the way those things present themselves within the structures of consciousness (an insight we shall return to in relation to Bonhoeffer's Christology).

To begin with, Heidegger was a good and loyal servant of Husserl's phenomenological method. In his doctoral dissertation 'The Doctrine of the Judgement in Psychologism' (1914), Heidegger expressly echoed Husserl's argument that logic is not reducible to psychology, and he is again phenomenological in the approach taken in his *Habilitation* thesis[12] and in his inaugural lecture of 1916, exploring the way time 'shapes up' in the human consciousness. But then Heidegger fell into a long reflective silence. From 1916 to 1927 (years 'interrupted' by war service, marriage and children) Heidegger busied himself reading – Paul, Augustine and Luther from the Christian tradition; classical Greek thought, and in particular the pre-Socratic philosophers in whose fragmentary writings ontology (the 'science' of being) is an important emphasis. But he published nothing and in consequence, though his teaching began to earn him a reputation as an independent thinker, he struggled to win the professorial chair that would guarantee him status and financial security. He served as Husserl's assistant in Freiburg from 1918 to 1923 when he took a post as an *extraordinarius* professor – not yet a full and secure chair – in Marburg, which he disdained rather as an academic backwater. As Husserl drew closer to retirement, he attempted to engineer a smooth succession for Heidegger to a philosophical chair. Heidegger was nominated to the chair of philosophy at Marburg but the Minister of Culture in Berlin, who was responsible for ratifying appointments to full professorial rank, while recognising Heidegger's success as a teacher, wrote that 'it does not seem appropriate to me to entrust him with an established full professorship ... until major literary achievements have earned that special

---

[11] E. Husserl, *Ideas Pertaining to a Pure Phenomenology and to a Phenomenological Philosophy*, trans. F. Kersten (The Hague, 1982).

[12] The thesis was written to qualify him as a university lecturer. It was titled: 'Duns Scotus's Doctrine of Categories and Meaning', and is a study of a treatise subsequently re-attributed to Thomas of Erfurt. The terms of Heidegger's funding determined that he should concern himself with Catholic metaphysics, but he may already be seen finding his own 'voice' by means of the phenomenological method.

recognition from his colleagues in the field which such an appointment calls for'.[13] It was in order, therefore, to make Heidegger eligible for a full professorship that Husserl encouraged the publication of *Being and Time* in a relatively obscure volume of phenomenological research. As he published it, Heidegger intended the volume to be most of the first part of a two-part book. In Part II he planned to stand on the foundations of the ontology, built in Part I, and from this vantage point to lob grenades into the representative ontologies of philosophers such as Aristotle, Descartes and Kant.[14] Though, in the event, the project was never completed, it continued to be published for some time as if the rest of Part II would soon appear.

From Husserl's point of view as Heidegger's mentor, it seemed natural to ensure that his phenomenological legacy would be left in the hands of his supposed *protégé*. Husserl had it in mind that his erstwhile assistant would follow faithfully in his footsteps and as he turned to the dedication page of Heidegger's book (two years after it had been published!)[15] he would have felt his hopes had been fulfilled.[16] But as he read on, it dawned on Husserl that his pupil had not only moved beyond phenomenology as Husserl envisaged it; he had blown it apart. In George Steiner's words, 'dedicated to Edmund Husserl, *Sein und Zeit* is that rarest of paradoxes: a monument which would destroy'.[17] From theologian to Catholic philosopher, from Catholic philosopher to phenomenologist, from phenomenologist to … what? What was the innovation that would lead Hannah Arendt to say that Heidegger had gained for philosophy 'a thinking that expresses gratitude that the "naked That" had been given at all?'[18]

Being and Time

Like many pupils who go beyond the premises of their teachers, Heidegger *seems*[19] to have thought that Husserl had not gone far enough to make the break with

---

[13]   Since professors were employed essentially as senior civil servants, see Safranski, *Heidegger*, p. 143.

[14]   Ibid., p. 171.

[15]   Thomas Sheehan, 'Reading a Life: Heidegger and Hard Times', in Charles B. Guignon (ed.), *The Cambridge Companion to Heidegger* (Cambridge, 1993), p. 84.

[16]   Heidegger dedicated the volume to 'Edmund Husserl in friendship and admiration', a dedication removed from editions during the Nazi period – on Heidegger's account of events – because his publisher advised him that censors would not countenance the reissue of a book dedicated to a Jew.

[17]   Steiner, *Passion*, p. 182.

[18]   Hannah Arendt, *The Life of the Mind: Thinking – Willing – Judging* (San Diego, 1981), vol. 1, p. 185 (cited in Safranski, *Heidegger*, p. 427).

[19]   Readers are left to draw their own conclusions about Heidegger's view of Husserl's legacy since he hardly mentions him in *Being and Time*.

traditional philosophy. The argument that explains why, according to Heidegger, all modern philosophy – Husserl included – had been travelling up a blind alley when it came to epistemology, extends through the whole 500 pages (including notes) of *Being and Time* in the English translation. But to aid navigation through this complex text we may say at this point that the gist of Heidegger's argument may be glimpsed in the image of Heraclitus warming his backside at a stove. For Heidegger, traditional philosophers were like Heraclitus' visitors: they expected philosophical insights to arise from deep reflection on the world they live in when, in the event, the 'gods' are revealed in the everyday and the familiar. Heidegger's basic idea is that, in fact, the philosopher is not one who *reflects on* the world but one who *is in* the world. The world is not a thing that I understand by thinking about it because the world is not something separate from myself at all. Philosophy had taken epistemology to be the *primary* problem; that is, the question of how we may know anything so it may be trusted is the question that philosophy has to get right before it can ask any other question. From Heidegger's point of view, this was also true of Husserl who, for all that he was concerned with appearance of essences, was nonetheless concerned with recasting the subject/object relation. Husserl's sort of phenomenology showed too much of its origins in psychologism; it was constantly treading over the eggshells of its origins in science. Heidegger's departure was to say that epistemology is in fact a secondary problem, one *derived* from the problem of ontology – the question of the meaning of being. The real starting point for philosophical enquiry is to learn to ask the right questions, and the right questions are not 'how' questions, such as '*how* may I know a thing in the world?'; the right question is the 'is' question: '*the question of the meaning of Being*'.[20] All other forms of human enquiry, all sciences, natural or human, interesting as they are, beg the truly fundamental question, of what being means. Heidegger wants in *Being and Time* to push back to this fundamental question, and it is here where the slogan, already cited above, bears reiteration: Heidegger urges enquirers after knowledge to go: '*zu den Sachen selbst!*' – 'back to the things themselves'.[21]

It is useful to recall that the immediate historical context for *Being and Time* – as for Karl Barth's similarly iconoclastic *Römerbrief* – was the aftermath of the Great War of 1914–18, which devastated that fundament of the Enlightenment: belief in human progress. Enlightenment philosophy had typically been characterised by a quest for a transcendent truth that would steer humanity towards its fulfilment. After the trenches, humankind seemed more to be at the whim of history than at

---

[20] The translation used here is Martin Heidegger, *Being and Time*, trans. J. Macquarrie and Edward Robinson (Oxford, 1962). For an alternative translation see *Being and Time*, trans. J. Stambaugh (New York, 1996). For a German edition see *Sein und Zeit* in the Martin Heidegger *Gesamtausgabe Band 2* (Frankfurt-am-Main, 1977). See Heidegger, *Being*, p. 19, where he makes this question the starting point of his investigation.

[21] Heidegger, *Being*, p. 50.

its helm, and 'the philosophical issue of the day was the relation between truth and history'.[22] In reflecting upon being and time Heidegger's intention was to show that the apparent conflict between truth and history disappears where human beings are located where they truly are: 'thrown' in the everyday.

Heidegger opens *Being and Time* with a gnomic citation from Plato's *The Sophist*: 'For manifestly you have long been aware of what you mean when you use the expression "*being*." We, however, who used to think we understood it, have now become perplexed.'[23] For Heidegger, in his perplexity concerning the meaning of being, Socrates was at least one stage in advance of modern people, for at least he recognised that the question mattered. 'This question has' however, 'today been forgotten' and a dogma has developed that sanctions the complete neglect of the question.[24] Heidegger gives three apparently contradictory reasons to explain this state of affairs: 'being' has been regarded as the most universal concept; it has been maintained that 'being' is indefinable; and it has been claimed that the meaning of 'being' is obvious. Yet Heidegger does not despair. He finds in the word 'being an important clue pointing to a way forward in his investigation: the language of being is in everyday use. People use phrases like 'I am', 'we are' and 'she is' and do so in ways that suggest that they have a basic understanding of what the verb 'to be' means. Heidegger believes – and here he displays his indebtedness to the phenomenological method of Husserl – that investigations such as the one he is embarking upon have a familiar structure. Every investigation is, in the first place, a seeking (*Suchen*). It involves something that is asked about (*sein Gefragtes*) and – which is subtly different – something that is interrogated (*ein Befragtes*). Finally, an investigation also seeks something that is found out by asking (*das Erfragte*). Already in the first pages of his long book – Heidegger may be seen using language in a distinctive way, a way that is unfortunately not always obvious when his terms are translated into English. On the one hand he uses words that are familiar in everyday speech and reshapes them into a special philosophically serviceable language. And on the other hand, he uses etymological relationships between the words he is using beguilingly to draw the eye of his reader to the intimate philosophical relationships between the words he uses.

Armed with this description of philosophical enquiry, Heidegger turns to the question of the meaning of Being. The 'seeking' in this particular investigation is the question of Being; the 'that which is asked about' is 'Being' as it is given to us in the distinction between 'Being' and the 'beings' that exist; the 'that which is interrogated' is beings and the 'that which is to be found out by asking' is the meaning of Being. In suggesting that in this enquiry beings are 'that which is interrogated' Heidegger does not intend to reduce his enquiry to the scientific investigation of things that exist in the world (for example through anthropology,

22   Jonathan Rée, 'Heidegger: History and Truth in Being and Time,' in R. Monk and F. Raphael (eds), *The Great Philosophers* (London, 2000), pp. 293–330.

23   Plato, *Sophistes*, 244a; Heidegger, *Being*, p. 19.

24   Heidegger, *Being*, p. 21.

through astrophysics or through biology); in fact he distinguishes enquiry into human beings, the planets and the stars, and the beings in the animal kingdom from his more fundamental investigation calling the former sorts of enquiry *ontic* questions, and only the latter sort of enquiry *ontological* questions. Particle physics is an ontic science; philosophy is ontological. Of course, even for philosophy, one sort of being – human being – takes ontical priority, since human beings are distinguishable from other sorts of being precisely because they – and they alone – ask ontological questions. To denote this unique characteristic Heidegger uses a special term to describe human being, *Dasein*: 'Dasein is an entity which does not just occur among other entities. Rather it is ontically distinguished by the fact that, in its very Being, that Being is an *issue* for it.'[25] Dasein alone, that is, grasps at the question of the meaning of existence, which is not merely a question of Da-sein (literally 'being there') – but as a self-understanding of human possibilities. Once more, to nuance what he means, Heidegger makes a subtle distinction between *existentiell* questions – questions concerned with the meaning of existence that we either face up to, or ignore; and *existential* questions that are concerned with the structure of existence. 'Being' is thus not an epistemological question, because what is at stake is not the knowledge of objects that arises from the study of them by investigating subjects: *we* are the 'ontological analytic of Dasein', i.e., the description of Dasein's existence. It is this that brings Heidegger to *time*, for time, he asserts, is the horizon in which both the meaning of 'our' Dasein will be laid bare, and also that on which the meaning of 'Being' appears. He calls this laying bear of the meaning of time 'historicity' to distinguish it from the mere sequence of events and historical facts.

Dasein's existence for Heidegger may not be understood as the mere presence of a thing in the world, but is to be understood in terms of its possibility. This does not mean, however, that all beings understand themselves in this way: many, perhaps most, do not, and this fact means that there are in practice two ways in which Dasein is in the world: inauthentic and authentic. This is a tempting distinction for theology, and indeed Rudolf Bultmann, Heidegger's colleague in Marburg, seized on it in order to describe the life of Christian faith as authentic life and the life of sin as inauthentic life. Heidegger, however, does not make value judgements about authenticity and inauthenticity, but sees them as ways of being – the former way, a way in which I can see that who I am is a choice, the latter as a way in which I am unreflective about who I am. We may return at this point to the question of how, if at all, Heidegger distinguishes his own philosophy from that of Husserl. Husserl, Heidegger believed, thought that the primary problem was the problem of how subjects may truthfully know the world in which they dwell. But, in fact Heidegger continued, such knowing is 'founded' on another question, because before it can know anything, Dasein has to exist! In this sense the question of the world is an ontological question, and not an ontic one; the sciences, therefore, because they are concerned with ontic questions, can

---

[25] Ibid., p. 32.

tell us nothing truly interesting about the world. The really riveting question is what Heidegger terms the 'worldhood' – *die Weltheit* – of the world.

It is to get at the *worldhood* of the world that Heidegger takes up the relation of Dasein to the world as it is instructively displayed in beings' use of tools. Think for a moment about how the world appears to us: you have in your hands a book, but, until I draw your attention to the fact that you are holding a book, you are not really conscious of it. You are not holding a book for the fun of it but in order for this piece of equipment, this tool, to function as it was made to function – in the case of a book to convey to you what I am trying to say. Heidegger's own example is a hammer: when I pick up a hammer to bang in a nail it is something present-at-hand; I'm not conscious of it as it is made up of a metal head and a wooden handle; I'm not conscious of it at all ... unless it breaks; I use it in order to do something, and in this everyday function, it is transparent. Just so, in the everyday, lots of things remain invisible to my perception as I just get on with life. But it only *makes sense* as it has this function along the horizon of Dasein.

So far, Heidegger has been speaking chiefly about being in the world – Da sein. In chapter 4 of *Being and Time*[26] he turns his attention to questions of being in the world as a being-with (others) in the world, and to the question of how to be oneself. As with authentic and inauthentic existence, it is not Heidegger's aim to make moral judgements, but to *describe* Dasein's being. Dasein has two means by which to concern itself with others, with the 'they' it may dominate and control, or, it may liberate itself by means of liberating the other. What it may not do, and still be authentic, is to remain indifferent. Unfortunately, this is what Heidegger thinks most people are, most of the time. A majority are swept along by social forces and fashions they barely understand. The 'they' (*das Man*) rules existence:

> We take pleasure and enjoy ourselves as *they* (*man*) take pleasure; we read, see, and judge about literature and art as *they* see and judge; likewise we shrink back from the 'great mass' as *they* shrink back; we find 'shocking' what *they* find shocking. The 'they,' which is nothing definite, and which all are, though not as the sum, prescribes the kind of Being of everydayness.[27]

This 'public' life is the common form Dasein's existence takes, but Heidegger thinks he sees a way to be free of it, and that way is the possibility afforded by existential analysis. Before existential analysis can get to work, however, Dasein has to come to a sense that something is awry, it has to become *anxious*.

Heidegger was not the first philosopher to notice that anxiety was a part of the human condition – Søren Kierkegaard (or more precisely his persona, Anti-Climacus) had anatomised despair in *The Sickness unto Death*. Kierkegaard thought that '*before God*', it was a sin '*in despair not wanting to be oneself,* or

---

26 Ibid., p. 149ff.
27 Ibid., p. 164.

wanting in despair to be oneself.[28] Now, as we have seen, Heidegger was not interested in making moral judgements in *Being and Time*; his interest is the meaning of being. And anxiety, he thinks, has an important role in alerting Dasein to its place in the world. He is not, of course, talking here of the location of Dasein on planet earth (the fact I live in Cambridge does not illuminate the meaning of being). Moods perform an important role in waking us from our indifference to our Da-sein – our being there in the world. I can bumble along for weeks without really being conscious of myself; but if I receive a knock – a job interview goes the wrong way, a friend dies, or my back develops an agonising pain – I may become anxious and begin to reflect on the 'there' of Dasein. 'The basic state-of-mind of anxiety' as Heidegger puts it, is therefore 'a distinctive way in which Dasein is disclosed'.[29] Not that anxiety discloses anxiety as a matter of course:

> when something threatening brings itself close, anxiety does not 'see' any definite 'here' or 'yonder' from which it comes. That in the face of which one has anxiety is characterised by the fact that what threatens is *nowhere*. Anxiety 'does not know' what that in the face of which it is anxious is.[30]

What in fact anxiety directs us to is the 'nowhere', and Heidegger draws the dramatic conclusion that this 'nowhere' turns out to be Dasein's being: 'this means that *Being-in-the-world itself is that in the face of which anxiety is anxious*'.[31] We are afraid of (the disclosure of) our own shadow. As in a nightmare, life feels like falling; the task of Heidegger's project is to make Dasein turn back towards that it instinctively flees from in its anxiety, which is the 'nothing' (*das Nichts*) of the world. He wants Dasein to stop filling the world with shallow pleasures, with the din of TVs and MP3 players, of ceaseless business and traffic, and come face to face with the being of Dasein: 'in anxiety there lies the possibility of a disclosure which is quite distinctive; for anxiety individualizes. This individualization brings Dasein back from its falling, and makes manifest to it that authenticity and inauthenticity are possibilities of its *Being*.'[32] Anxiety, in short, can put life into perspective.

Thus far, everything we have discussed falls in Part I of *Being and Time*. Heidegger now shifts gear, and we move into the incomplete Part II of his argument, and to that which is signalled in the title of the book, as he begins to explore the theme of 'Dasein and Temporality'.[33] Yet though this is a new phase of his argument, Heidegger is at pains to reiterate that the basic question he is

---

[28] Søren Kierkegaard, *The Sickness unto Death* (Harmondsworth, 1989), p. 109; italics in original.

[29] Heidegger, *Being*, p. 228.

[30] Ibid., p. 231.

[31] Ibid., p. 232.

[32] Ibid., p. 235.

[33] Ibid., p. 274ff.

investigating remains the same: the meaning of being.[34] The preceding phase of the argument has clarified what the question is, but what it has succeeded in revealing is that 'in Dasein's very state of Being, there are important reasons which seem to speak against the possibility of having it presented (*Vorgabe*) in the manner required' for it to be accessible in its being-a-Whole.[35] To sort out these and other questions posed in Part I, in Part II Heidegger has 'the task of characterizing ontologically Dasein's Being-at-an-end and of achieving an existential conception of death'.[36] At first glance, it may seem odd to look for the meaning of being in death – in which my being would appear to be extinguished. But Heidegger thinks that, though we cannot *per definitionem* experience our own ceasing to be, we may see what is involved in our death through a meaningful encounter with the death of others:

> When Dasein reaches its wholeness in death, it simultaneously loses the Being of its 'there.' By its transition to no-longer-Dasein [*Nichtmehrdasein*], it gets lifted right out of the possibility of experiencing this transition and of understanding it as something experienced. Surely this sort of thing is denied to any particular Dasein in relation to itself. But this makes the death of Others more impressive. In this way a termination [*Beendigung*] of Dasein becomes 'Objectively' accessible. Dasein can thus gain an experience of death, all the more so because Dasein is essentially Being with Others.[37]

It is not the case, for Heidegger, that I can experience my *own* death through the death of others; what the death of others *does* do, however, is to awaken me to the *possibility* of my own death, to bring me to an existential realisation that I am going to die. This Being-towards-death becomes a way of relating to my own mortality. 'Death is a way to be',[38] and what this Being-towards-death reveals is not only that the human condition is indelibly uncertain, but that the proper way to orient oneself to Dasein is to embrace uncertainty, accept the possibility of death, and thereby turn back from flight and discover the meaning of Dasein in the sphere of the familiar. So what did Bonhoeffer make of it all?

Direct Evidence of Bonhoeffer's Reading of Heidegger

In spite of the relatively obscure location of its publication, *Being and Time* fell with a great splash into the waters of German intellectual life, a phenomenon we find evidenced in Bonhoeffer's own flurry of interest in Heidegger. In

---

[34]   Ibid., p. 274.
[35]   Ibid., p. 279.
[36]   Ibid., pp. 280–81.
[37]   Ibid., p. 281.
[38]   Ibid., p. 289.

the first place, the book had its desired effect: published in April 1927, by the autumn of that year Heidegger could finally settle his behind into the chair in philosophy at Marburg University; a year later he was appointed to the position he most coveted when he succeeded Husserl as professor of philosophy at the University of Freiburg. Heidegger was not the only German academic to write a foundational text in 1927. In Berlin a scarce-bearded Bonhoeffer submitted his doctoral dissertation to the university authorities, eventually published in 1930 as *Sanctorum Communio*. Unsurprisingly, since *Being and Time* was Heidegger's first significant publication and his first of any kind for several years, Bonhoeffer does not mention him in this or indeed in any of his student writings. Yet it was probably in 1927 that Bonhoeffer first became aware of Heidegger's growing reputation, since Hans-Christoph von Hase, a theologian and Bonhoeffer's cousin, was a student in Marburg and the two were regular correspondents.[39] Though there is no direct evidence, Hans-Richard Reuter is most likely right to suggest that 'presumably Bonhoeffer first familiarised himself with *Sein und Zeit* while he was in Barcelona, at the insistence of his cousin'[40] sometime between February 1928 and February 1929, though Bonhoeffer gave no indication of having done so when he outlined the likely subject of his thesis to Reinhold Seeberg in July, 1928.[41] If Bonhoeffer owned a copy of Heidegger's book, it does not survive and we are therefore deprived of any possible insights to be gleaned from his marginal notes. And if Bonhoeffer was blown away by his first impressions, he kept quiet about it and does not rave about Heidegger in his letters as he did, for example, on discovering Karl Barth.[42] So the first impression we have of Bonhoeffer's reading of Heidegger is in the published text of *Akt und Sein*, Bonhoeffer's *Habilitation* thesis, which he completed in February 1930, and which he successfully defended in an oral examination at Berlin University later in the same year. Even before the outcome of his defence was known, Bonhoeffer must have been working on his inaugural lecture on 'The Anthropological Question in Contemporary Philosophy and Theology', which deepened his discussion of Heidegger and which he delivered on 31 July 1930. Whatever Bonhoeffer's views of the matter, Professor Wilhelm Lütgert, to whom Bonhoeffer acted as a teaching assistant in 1929 and 1930, thought of Bonhoeffer as a follower of Heidegger, a fact still lodged in his mind when in 1933 he felt it important enough to mention in a reference

---

[39]   According to Eberhard Bethge, DB-EB, pp. 82–3, 'Hans-Christoph von Hase, who was a student in Marburg' kept Bonhoeffer 'supplied with news of Heidegger and Bultmann who were working there'. Bonhoeffer sometimes shared lecture notes with students in other universities, and it is possible he had access to notes of some of Heidegger's Marburg lectures.

[40]   See the Editor's Afterword in Dietrich Bonhoeffer, DBWE 2, p. 167.

[41]   Cf. DBWE 10, pp. 119–23.

[42]   The closest we get to such discussion is hinted at in a memoir of Hans-Christoph von Hase, who recalls after dinner conversation with Bonhoeffer revolving around several thinkers including Heidegger: see DBWE 10, p. 596.

for Bonhoeffer.[43] Lütgert was suspicious of Heidegger's philosophy for what he took to be its neo-Thomism, and told Hans-Christoph von Hase, who succeeded Bonhoeffer as his assistant, that he had only taken Bonhoeffer on as a favour to Seeberg, his predecessor and Bonhoeffer's *Doktorvater*. No amount of protest from Hase could persuade Lütgert that Bonhoeffer may not have been a Heideggerian.[44] In fact, after his inaugural lecture, Bonhoeffer became largely silent on the subject of Heidegger's philosophy. He mentioned Heidegger in a seminar presentation at Union Seminary in 1930–31 as part of the background to 'The Theology of Crisis'.[45] 'Phenomenology/Heidegger' are mentioned in lectures given during the winter semester 1932–33 on recent publications in systematic theology as one of three important streams of philosophical thought shaping theology (the others are Grisebach and the *völkische* movement). Bonhoeffer again referred to Heidegger in 1932 in an essay on Karl Heim;[46] and in the same semester he may have tied Heidegger into a discussion of '*das Nichts*' (i.e., nothingness/non-being) in lectures on Genesis 1–3.[47] Certainly, Bonhoeffer's vocabulary in the lectures echoed Heideggerian themes,[48] and there may be at least one similar echo in *Discipleship*[49] (1937). In 1938 Bonhoeffer contrasted the Christian experience of temptation with an existentialist ethic, since 'the sentence that every moment of life is a time of decision does not make sense as an abstraction to the Christian', a view that Bonhoeffer may have thought was exemplified by Heidegger's existentialism.[50]

Perhaps strangely – given the different paths their political views had taken them in – it was during the war years that Bonhoeffer's interest in Heidegger appears to have revived. In his essay on 'Natural Life', intended as part of the *Ethics*, Bonhoeffer describes the distinctively human capacity for suicide with a phrase lifted from Heidegger when he writes that 'human beings have freedom toward death'.[51] Similarly, in the first draft of 'History and Good' Bonhoeffer recalls Heidegger in describing the inevitable failure of human ethics that follows from the 'historicity' (*Geschichtlichkeit*) of human existence.[52] A reference to Heidegger is unmistakeable in the second draft of 'History and Good' in a discussion of conscience as the call of (authentic)

---

[43] DBWE 12, p. 154.

[44] Cf. DB-EB, pp. 129–30.

[45] DBWE 10, p. 472.

[46] DBWE 12, p. 245.

[47] Some students taking notes during the lectures record such a link, but it is not explicit in the published version of the lectures, see DBWE 3, p. 33, fn.28.

[48] DBWE 3, p. 65, fn.24.

[49] DBWE 4, p. 58, fn.3.

[50] DBWE 15, p. 388.

[51] DBWE 6, p. 197, fn.93.

[52] See DBWE 6, p. 220, fn.6 in which the editors draw a parallel with para. 75 of Heidegger, *Being*, pp. 439–44 on 'Dasein's Historicality'.

human existence.[53] Heidegger may also lie behind Bonhoeffer's thoughts about the essence of truth in the essay 'What does it mean to tell the truth?'[54] However, the editor's footnote on this essay misleadingly reports that 'from a letter from his father, Karl Bonhoeffer, dated 11 July 1943 ... we know that Bonhoeffer had wrestled with Heidegger while in Tegel prison'.[55] In fact, as a closer reading of Karl Bonhoeffer's letter, and as Eberhard Bethge's list of books Bonhoeffer read in prison make clear,[56] the book that Bonhoeffer read in his cell in June 1943 was *Phänomenologie des Zeitbewusstseins* which was written by Husserl, in a series 'merely' edited by Heidegger.

In the face of this summary of the evidence concerning Bonhoeffer's reading of Heidegger, it is clear that after Bonhoeffer engaged the philosopher in *Act and Being* and in his inaugural lecture – that is between 1928 and 1930 – Heidegger's *Being and Time* dropped off the theologian's radar screen. In order to find references to Heidegger in Bonhoeffer's writings from 1930, editors of the critical editions of Bonhoeffer's writings are, in the absence of similarly substantive discussions of Heidegger, left reading the runes of Bonhoeffer's books, essays and papers, in order to speculate in footnotes about possible echoes of Heideggerian themes. We may say with more certainty that after *Being and Time* Bonhoeffer did not bother to read any of Heidegger's subsequent writings – which one might have expected if he had thought Heidegger was genuinely significant. Yet it would be a mistake to conclude from the virtual absence of direct references to Heidegger in Bonhoeffer's writings after 1930 that Bonhoeffer was not either consciously or unconsciously bearing him in mind. Following Bonhoeffer's two academic dissertations in 1927 and 1930, the style of Bonhoeffer's theological writings changes dramatically, and he abandons many of the conventions of academic writing, such as extensive footnotes and discussion of primary and secondary sources. From this point, Bonhoeffer very rarely discusses the thinking of other theologians and philosophers, even where there is compelling evidence that they influenced him. There are two sorts of evidence for this assertion: textual evidence, and the evidence of content. Two examples suffice to make this point. In notes written during the drafting of the *Ethics* Bonhoeffer frequently named sources that he had read – including scriptural sources – that are *not* mentioned explicitly in the essays arising from his notes.[57] The second example is related to content: in Switzerland in May 1942 Bonhoeffer got hold of proofs of volume II/2 of Karl Barth's *Church Dogmatics* in which, especially in paragraphs 36–9, Barth discusses ethics in terms of 'the command of God'. Immediately thereafter,

---

[53] DBWE 6, p. 276, fn.112; see paras 56 and 57 of Heidegger, *Being*, 317–25.

[54] DBWE 16, p. 604.

[55] Ibid., p. 604, fn.9.

[56] DB-EB, p. 944.

[57] See Dietrich Bonhoeffer, *Zettelnotizen für eine 'Ethik'*, ed. Ilse Tödt (Gütersloh, 1993) and compare notes with parallel sections in DBWE 6.

Bonhoeffer began work on 'The "ethical" and the "Christian" as a Topic' and on 'The concrete commandment and the Divine Mandates'. In both texts ethics is characterised – for the first time in the *Ethics* – in terms of divine command/ commandment. The influence of Barth is unmistakeable; yet one searches in vain for a direct reference to Barth within the text. This is not a case of plagiarism; Bonhoeffer simply chose, by and large, not to discuss the work of others directly unless he was engaged explicitly in biblical exegesis or in decidedly historical theology (as when he discusses Luther's understanding of law and gospel in the 1943 essay on the '*Primus Usus Legis*'). I have laboured this point because it is important for the purposes of what follows in my argument to keep an open mind about the possibility that the writings of an important source may lie behind a text or texts written by Bonhoeffer that he does not explicitly cite or discuss. We shall return to this possibility when we take up Bonhoeffer's *Christology* lectures, but for now, we turn to the two texts in which Heidegger *is* discussed at length.

A Monument That Would Destroy? Bonhoeffer's Theological Reading of Heidegger's Philosophy

If commentators must speculate about Heidegger's significance in Bonhoeffer's later writings, the evidence for Heidegger's importance in *Act and Being* is plain. Most immediately there is what *must* be Bonhoeffer's admiring nod in the direction of *Sein und Zeit* in his choice of title for *Akt und Sein*. More concretely, as Eberhard Bethge for example has pointed out, there are more references in *Act and Being* to Heidegger than to any other thinker, bar Luther, 'even before Barth'.[58] To get at quite *how* Heidegger's thinking functions in Bonhoeffer's *Act and Being* we shall need now to read that text with bi-focal lenses that allow us to keep one eye on Bonhoeffer's discussion of *Being and Time* and the other focused on how that discussion fits into the argument of the book as a whole.

   In reading *Act and Being* there is a seductive possibility that – taking its lead from the dialectic implicit in the title – we may come to think that Bonhoeffer is saying something like this: 'some philosophies/theologies (e.g., Kant) approach the problem of revelation primarily through the *act* of reason; other philosophies/ theologies approach the problem of revelation primarily through *being* (e.g., Heidegger). But the proper method is one that approaches the problem of revelation through the categories of act *and* being (i.e., Bonhoeffer).' It is important, if we are to make sense of Heidegger's role in Bonhoeffer's argument, straightway to disabuse ourselves of thinking that this is in fact what Bonhoeffer is doing. To be sure, Bonhoeffer's theological 'answer' to the problem he takes on in the book will result in his concluding that Heidegger has not got matters quite right; Bonhoeffer is in this sense offering a critique of Heidegger. But he is decidedly *not* saying that Heidegger has got it all wrong. And this takes us immediately into one of *Act*

---

[58]   DB-EB, p. 133.

and Being's most significant features: Dietrich Bonhoeffer believed that theology, without slavishly taking its lead from philosophy, can nonetheless learn from it.

Like *Being and Time*, *Act and Being* begins by outlining the problem that it sets out to resolve. 'The most recent developments in theology', Bonhoeffer writes, 'appear to me to be an attempt to come to an agreement about the problem of act and being.'[59] At stake is:

> the issue of determining the relationship between 'the being of God' and the mental act which grasps that being. In other words, the meaning of 'the being of God in revelation' must be interpreted theologically, including how it is known, how faith as act, and revelation as being, are related to one another and, correspondingly, *how human beings stand in light of revelation.*[60]

At the outset, Bonhoeffer is clear that 'the concept of revelation must, therefore, yield an epistemology of its own' and he undertakes to show, building on his doctoral dissertation on the Church, that 'the dialectic of act and being is understood theologically as the dialectic of faith and the congregation of Christ'.[61]

It is perhaps striking, given what he had read in *Being and Time* about the erroneousness of making epistemology the *primary* question of philosophy, that Bonhoeffer concedes that the act/being problem arises from 'the question that Kant and idealism have posed for theology'[62] which is 'the attempt of the I to understand itself'.[63] Having outlined the problem, Bonhoeffer turns to a more detailed analysis of how act and being have been treated in recent philosophy. First, he outlines the approaches of Kant, of neo-Kantians, and of Hegelian Idealism, each of which he sees as caught in the snare of the "I" turned in on itself, of, in Luther's words, the *'ratio in se ipsam incurvato'* [reason turned in upon itself]. Here, Bonhoeffer turns to 'the ontological attempt.' Summarising these 'failed attempts' Bonhoeffer writes: 'Transcendental philosophy regards thinking to be "in reference to" transcendence; idealism takes transcendent being into thinking; and finally, ontology leaves being fully independent of thinking and accords being priority over thinking',[64] that is, being over the *act* of thinking.

It is important to note here that Bonhoeffer lumps 'the ontology of the Husserlian school' in with idealism, and equally important (for the purposes of this chapter) to ask what is the substance of his suspicion of Husserl. Bonhoeffer's worry is that in Husserl 'the "noetic-noematic parallel structure" remains immanent in consciousness';[65] the consequence of this is that the a priori belongs not on the

---

[59] DBWE 2, p. 25.

[60] Ibid., pp. 27–8, Bonhoeffer's italics.

[61] Ibid., p. 31.

[62] Ibid., p. 27.

[63] Ibid., p. 33.

[64] Ibid., p. 60.

[65] Ibid., p. 62.

side of the object but on that of consciousness. Two things are at stake here, and for both of them Bonhoeffer may be indebted to Heidegger. Let us recall what it was that was at issue in Heidegger's departure from Husserlian thinking. In so far as we can tell, Heidegger believed, that in spite of identifying problems in traditional epistemologies, in the end Husserl had been incapable of leaving behind a world-view based on the subject/object divide. Bonhoeffer simply takes over this view in asserting that 'phenomenology poses no questions of being, only of essence'.[66] Husserl's is *not*, for either Heidegger or Bonhoeffer, a *genuinely* ontological philosophy; indeed it actually 'passes over' being altogether.[67] The second problem with Husserl is what becomes of Dasein's relation to the 'Other', i.e., to the possibility of transcendence. Heidegger identified that being with others was a condition for the existential analysis of Dasein. In *Sanctorum Communio* Bonhoeffer had similarly established sociality as an essential aspect of being human. If the question of existence is 'bracketed out' from the outset, as Husserl has it, 'others' become simply pieces of furniture within consciousness, blunting a sense of obligation towards them.

Now, with the drama of the arrival of the Commendatore at Don Giovanni's dinner table, Heidegger rises up into the centre of the stage in Bonhoeffer's discussion: 'precisely where Husserl "brackets," Heidegger discloses being itself'.[68] This introduces a summary of the key points in *Being and Time*, which Bonhoeffer offers without critical comment. He concludes that, for Heidegger: 'being understands itself in Dasein, in spirit. But Dasein is the existence of human beings in their historicity, in the momentariness of the decisions that they, in every instance, have already taken.'[69] This leads Bonhoeffer to the apparently affirmative provisional conclusion that: 'From the perspective of the problem of act and being, it would seem that here a genuine coordination of the two has been reached.'[70] Unlike Hegel, continues Bonhoeffer, Heidegger successfully makes being temporal; and unlike Husserl, he does not allow consciousness to dominate. Moreover, Heidegger, unlike earlier transcendentalist, idealist and phenomenological philosophies, is awake to the limitations of Dasein: being is limited not only by the 'other' but by its being-towards-death, i.e., the realisation of the finitude of Dasein.

But there is a problem: 'no room has been left for the concept of revelation'.[71] For a start, Heidegger has not, thinks Bonhoeffer, allowed scope for the being of God, who in Heidegger's account would have to exist in time since all beings, *per definitionem*, exist temporally. Revelation teaches that God is eternal. Now,

---

[66]   Ibid., p. 64.

[67]   Ibid., p. 67, the translator's use of the wording 'has done violence to' for '*vergangen*' here is misleading.

[68]   Ibid., p. 67.

[69]   Ibid., p. 71.

[70]   Ibid., p. 71.

[71]   Ibid., pp. 72–3.

Bonhoeffer continues, there might be a way to open up ontology to the question of revelation, through the Thomist idea of an *analogia entis* between God's 'Dasein' and human Dasein – a way sign-posted in the ontology of the Catholic Thomist Erich Przywara.[72] In the event, however, for Bonhoeffer even this Christianly oriented philosophy remains 'merely' philosophy, and *'per se*, a philosophy can concede no room for revelation unless it knows revelation and confesses itself to be a Christian philosophy in full recognition that the place it wanted to usurp *is* already occupied by another – namely, by Christ'.[73]

The offence of philosophy – Heidegger's included – turns out to be the attempt to achieve self-understanding autonomously, since such thinking is 'as little able as good works to deliver the *cor corvum in se* [the heart turned in upon itself] from itself',[74] an insight that concludes the first part of *Act and Being*, and with it the discussion of philosophical contributions to the problem under investigation.

We may discuss Part B of *Act and Being* much more briefly. From the point of view of revelation 'only those who have been placed into the truth can understand themselves in truth'.[75] But what are the consequences for knowledge of this theological claim? Just what sort of thinking does God permit human beings to undertake if philosophy is so peremptorily swept aside? This question leads Bonhoeffer to what are among the most penetrating and precise sentences of the book:

> In revelation it is not so much a question of the freedom of God – eternally remaining within the divine self, aseity – on the other side of revelation, as it is of God's coming out of God's own self in revelation. It is a matter of God's *given* Word, the covenant in which God is bound by God's own action ... God is free not from human beings but for them. Christ is the word of God's freedom. God *is* present [and here is a lasting imprint of Bonhoeffer's dialogue with Heidegger's ontological enquiry], that is, not in eternal nonobjectivity but – to put it quite provisionally for now – 'haveable', graspable in the Word within the church.[76]

What room does this leave for Heidegger? The answer is 'none', and Bonhoeffer spells this out in dialogue with the Heideggerian existential theology of Rudolf Bultmann, who portrays the Christian as 'the person of decision'.[77] Being in Christ calls for a certain kind of continuity. Heidegger's Dasein calls for continuity, too, but it is a continuity of perpetual crises in which decisions are called for, a continuity of 'always-being-already-in-guilt', which means – in Bonhoeffer's

---

72 Ibid., p. 74.
73 Ibid., pp. 76–8.
74 Ibid., p. 80.
75 Ibid., p. 81.
76 Ibid., pp. 90–1.
77 Ibid., pp. 96–103.

devastating judgement – that 'Heidegger's concept of existence is of no use for the elucidation of being in faith'.[78]

Part C of *Act and Being* – the shortest of the three parts that make up the book – elucidates the difference between always-being-already-in-guilt (being in Adam) and being in faith (being in Christ). Here too, though Heidegger is not discussed as he has been earlier in the book, he plays an important cameo role in a contrast Bonhoeffer draws between being-towards-death and being in Christ as a being-towards-the future. Being-towards-death is still to exist in sin. Being in Christ alone opens up the future since 'the human being "is" in the future of Christ – that is, never in being without act, and never in act without being'.[79]

Bonhoeffer's inaugural lecture on 'The Anthropological Question in Contemporary Philosophy and Theology'[80] recasts the problem of *Act and Being* – the question of revelation – as the question 'what does it mean to be human?' Once more, Bonhoeffer uses Heidegger as a key dialogue partner. But both his approach and his conclusions are substantively the same as they had been in *Act and Being*. Heidegger's analysis of Dasein takes thinking beyond previous philosophies to the heart of the question: but '[u]ltimately the person himself answers the question about the human being'.[81] Heidegger helps sharpen the question, but revelation alone can answer it.

Secondary Discussion of Heidegger's Influence on Bonhoeffer

For reasons that are perhaps plain in the light of our earlier remarks concerning a lack of explicit discussion of Heidegger in Bonhoeffer's writings after 1930, the standard compendia of Bonhoeffer's theology which mapped out the first stages of Bonhoeffer interpretation, are by and large silent on the question of if and how Heidegger influenced Bonhoeffer's thought.[82] In one leading text on Bonhoeffer's theology – Ernst Feil's *Die Theologie Dietrich Bonhoeffers*[83] – Heidegger is generally conspicuous by his absence: Feil mentions Heidegger

---

[78]   Ibid., p. 98.

[79]   Ibid., p. 159.

[80]   DBWE 10, pp. 389–408.

[81]   Ibid., p. 396.

[82]   For example, John Godsey simply mentions Heidegger as one of several dialogue partners in *Act and Being* in his *The Theology of Dietrich Bonhoeffer* (London, 1960); André Dumas briefly discusses Heidegger, again in relation to *Act and Being* in *Dietrich Bonhoeffer: Theologian of Reality* (London, 1971), pp. 101–103, and in passing as an influence on Bultmann's existentialist theology.

[83]   Ernst Feil, *Die Theologie Dietrich Bonhoeffers: Hermeneutik, Christologie, Weltverständnis* (München/Mainz, 1971); *The Theology of Dietrich Bonhoeffer*, trans. Martin Rumscheidt (Philadelphia, 1985), is a slightly abridged version of the German original.

only seven times, mostly in footnotes, and mostly in connection with Rudolf Bultmann rather than Bonhoeffer. This may reflect the tendency in the early stages in the reception and interpretation of Bonhoeffer's writings, to read his theology backwards, i.e. beginning with the drama of the prison correspondence, interpreting earlier material in the light of the later. The academic dissertations *Sanctorum Communio* and *Act and Being* did not sit easily with attempts to harness Bonhoeffer to radical or liberal theological agendas.[84] More recently, however, several commentators have begun to show interest in Heidegger's influence on Bonhoeffer, leading to a number of very fruitful discussions. Charles Marsh seeks to bring theological clarity to Bonhoeffer's reading of Heidegger particularly with respect to the influence of the latter's 'notions of potentiality-for-being, authenticity, and being with others' on Bonhoeffer's thinking about 'human selfhood and sociality'.[85] Robert P. Scharlemann considers Bonhoeffer to be the only one among Heidegger's theological interpreters to have taken the significance of time seriously.[86] Craig J. Slane uses Heidegger's notion that the structure of *Dasein* is disclosed as *Sein zum Tode* (being-towards-death) to take him 'towards a hermeneutic of Martyrdom'.[87] 'I want', Slane writes, 'to illuminate the *passageway* between belief and behaviour with the use of martyrdom.'[88] Joel Lawrence asks, however, whether Slane's treatment neglects Bonhoeffer's sharp critique of Heidegger concerning Being-towards-death.[89] Collectively, these studies are suggestive of a much deeper relationship between Heidegger and Bonhoeffer than was previously thought.

Bonhoeffer's *Christology* Lectures as 'Phenomenological Theology'?

I turn now to the *denouement* of the present study: my suggestion that Heidegger's most lasting legacy in the writings of Bonhoeffer may lie in the methodology of

---

[84]   For discussion of the reception of Bonhoeffer, see Stephen R. Haynes, *The Bonhoeffer Phenomenon* (Minneapolis, 2004) and Ralf K. Wüstenberg (ed.), *Dietrich Bonhoeffer lesen im Internationalen Kontext* (Frankfurt, 2007).

[85]   Charles Marsh, *Reclaiming Dietrich Bonhoeffer* (New York, 1994), pp. 111–34, citation from p. 112.

[86]   Robert P. Scharlemann, 'Authenticity and Encounter: Bonhoeffer's Appropriation of Ontology,' in Wayne W. Floyd and Charles Marsh (eds), *Theology and the Practice of Responsibility* (Valley Forge, PA, 1994), pp. 353–65.

[87]   Craig J. Slane, *Bonhoeffer as Martyr* (Grand Rapids, 2004), pp. 119–36.

[88]   Slane, *Martyr*, p. 119.

[89]   'Bonhoeffer's freedom is freedom that is grounded not in his future death but in his past death ... the freedom that Bonhoeffer has towards death exists because he knows he has already died in Christ', Joel D. Lawrence, 'Death Together: Thanatology and Sanctification in the Theology of Dietrich Bonhoeffer', unpublished dissertation, Cambridge University, 2007.

the *Christology* lectures. In making this suggestion it is important explicitly and openly to acknowledge that I am engaged in conjecture. Earlier in this chapter I laboured the point that tracing the origins of Bonhoeffer's thinking to sources is by no means a simple matter of reckoning on the basis of explicit references: Bonhoeffer was not – at least after 1930 – the sort of writer to disclose each and every occasion when he had a source in mind. The most that my speculation can hope for is to enumerate a number of points of *resemblance* between Heidegger's reworking of Husserl's phenomenological philosophy and what Bonhoeffer may be seen to be doing in the *Christology* lectures. And as if this were not already to rely uncomfortably on guesswork, we must also reckon with the fact that in *Christology* we are working, since Bonhoeffer's manuscript is lost, with a text assembled from student notes, with the added textual problems that brings.[90]

The first resemblance that I want to point out is a relatively cosmetic one: Bonhoeffer, like Heidegger, draws his reader's eye by coining a distinctive vocabulary around which he structures his argument. In Heidegger, we see this most plainly in the deployment of a group of words – some in common use and others neologisms created by him for the purpose – concerned with 'Being'. Some of these words take on different meanings in different contexts and pose considerable problems for his translators (which is why key terms are often followed in translation by their German original). The group includes *Dasein* (which Macquarrie and Robinson leave untranslated); *Da-sein* (being there); *daseinsmässig* (of the character of *Dasein*, etc.,); *seiend* (being); *Seiendes* (entity); *sein* (be); *Sein* (Being); *Sein-bei* (being alongside); *Sein zu* (being towards), and so on.[91] For Bonhoeffer's part, the primary term in the lectures with which he engages in 'word-play' (pun intended) is 'Logos', taken ultimately, of course, from the prologue to John's Gospel. There is *Christologie* (Christology); *Logologie* (logo-logy – the study of the Logos); *Gott-Logos* (Logos of God); *menschlicher Logos* (human logos) and *Gegen-Logos* (counter-logos). As with Heidegger, Bonhoeffer finds some of these terms in use already; others are his own neologisms. And as with Heidegger, Bonhoeffer claims to begin his investigation by attending to clues in everyday conversation: 'In our everyday speech, the question, "Who are you?" does exist' writes Bonhoeffer, 'but it can always be dissolved into the "how question." Tell me *how* you exist, tell me *how* you think, and I'll tell you who you are.'[92]

Beyond these superficial stylistic resemblances is anything more *methodological* going on? To begin to explore this it may be helpful to recall Heidegger's summary, sketched above, of the phenomenological method, which he describes as an attempt to go *Zu den Sachen selbst!* – back to the things themselves. Partly, this is perhaps simply to express the desire to do what all philosophers think

---

[90]   The textual status of the Christology lectures is detailed in DBWE 12, p. 299, fn.1.

[91]   See Heidegger, *Being*, 'Glossary of German expressions', pp. 505–23.

[92]   DBWE 12, p. 303.

they are doing, namely to ask fundamental questions. But Heidegger thought that modern philosophy, in its preoccupation with epistemology, had in fact been pursuing *secondary questions* derived, on close inspection, from the true primary question, which is the meaning of being. In *Being and Time* Heidegger presses *zu den Sachen selbst* in at least three ways that, I want to suggest, are paralleled in three key ideas in Bonhoeffer's *Christology* lectures.

The first is Heidegger's appropriation of Husserl's 'discovery' that the object as meant (*noema*) and the intentional act (*noesis*) that presents the object as meant are inextricably bound up in one another. Subjects do not, as traditional epistemologies had conceived, observe things and think about them: Dasein is thrown in the world. For a phenomenologist, we may recall, the stuff philosophy has to work on is already being organised in the mind before we reflect upon it. A phenomenologist, therefore, cannot press beyond appearances to essences. The significance of this for Bonhoeffer's Christological method occurs in his discussion of the Chalcedonian definition. At Chalcedon the Fathers had attempted, Bonhoeffer thought, to preserve the mystery of the incarnation. In doing so, they recognised that human beings simply *cannot* press beyond the God-Man, Jesus Christ. Theology cannot get behind the formulation of Chalcedon to work out *how* divine stuff and human stuff are able to cohere in the one God-Man, Jesus Christ: all that we may say is that they do. One must – and here is the phenomenological echo – suspend judgement about the nature/s and will/s of the incarnate Son of God and pay exclusive attention to the way those things present themselves within the structures of faith. All the Church has to go on is the appearance of his essence in its appearing.

From this, there follows a second methodological similarity between Heidegger's philosophical method and Bonhoeffer's Christological method; this concerns Heidegger's distinction between *ontic* questions and *ontological* questions. Ontic questions, we may recall, are for Heidegger questions about beings (about planets and stars, about biology, about geology, etc.). These are interesting questions, to be sure, but they are not basic questions; investigating beings does not take us to the meaning of Being. Now look at what Bonhoeffer says about 'how' questions and about 'who' questions. 'All scholarly questions' Bonhoeffer teaches (and by '*wissenschaftliche Fragen*' he means, of course, not only questions in natural science but in the human sciences) 'can be reduced to two fundamental questions: First, what is the cause of X? Second, what is the meaning of X? The first question covers the realm of the natural sciences; the second, that of the arts and humanities.'[93] These questions are basically questions of classification. But what happens, Bonhoeffer continues:

> what happens if the counter-logos suddenly presents its demand in a wholly new form, so that it is no longer an idea or a word that is turned against the autonomy of the [human] logos, but rather the counter Logos appears, somewhere and

---

[93]   Ibid., p. 301.

at some time in history, as a human being, and as a human being sets itself up as judge over the human logos and says, 'I am the truth,' I am the death of the human logos, I am the life of God's Logos … .[94]

Of course there is an insight here that is *not* present in Heidegger – the theological claim that attempts by the human logos to classify the world by means of how questions are radically called themselves into question by the Logos of God. Nonetheless, the distinction with which Bonhoeffer is working here between questions about classification and *the* basic question addressed by the Logos to the human logos, resembles closely Heidegger's distinction between ontic and ontological questions.

The conclusion to this phase of his lectures brings Bonhoeffer's text to what, I want to suggest, is a third resemblance with Heidegger: the question of the meaning of Being. Let us try a thought experiment: imagine for a moment that what Bonhoeffer does in his lectures is essentially to replace ontology with Christology as *the* fundamental human question. What would Bonhoeffer's enquiry look like? If we return to the description of his investigation that Heidegger outlines in the opening pages of *Being and Time* we may recall that what Heidegger seeks is the meaning of Being, whereas Bonhoeffer seeks the meaning of Christ. Heidegger's 'that which is asked about' is 'Being' as it is given to us in the distinction between 'Being' and the 'beings' that exist; Bonhoeffer's 'that which is asked about' is 'Christ' as he is given in his self-revelation. Heidegger's 'that which is interrogated' is beings; Bonhoeffer's 'that which is investigated' is the human logos, which is 'interrogated' by the counter-logos. And finally, Heidegger's 'that which is to be found out by asking' is the meaning of Being; while Bonhoeffer's 'that which is to be found out by asking' is the answer to the question 'who is Jesus Christ?' The 'authenticity' that would follow would then be being-towards-death, but a being-towards-death to sin and birth to new life in Jesus Christ. True life would be found in conformation to the form of Jesus Christ, who alone can teach us what it means to be truly human. The connections click home so sweetly that it is difficult for me to imagine that Bonhoeffer was *not* influenced – wittingly or unwittingly – by Heidegger in the formation of his Christology, such that it may not be entirely fanciful to characterise Bonhoeffer's Christology as a *phenomenological Christology*.

Towards a Conclusion

I began this chapter by making explicit the difficulty of delineating the distinction between Heidegger's life and his writings; I conclude it in the place where I

---

[94] Ibid., pp. 301–302. It is unclear whether Bonhoeffer would have determined that Heidegger's *suchen* into the meaning of being belongs or does not belong to the second sort of question.

began. Does it matter to our interpretation of his philosophy that he was a Nazi? Heidegger himself gives mixed signals about that question. On the one hand, his philosophical method is *par excellence* one that asserts the significance of Dasein's 'throwness' in the world. On the other hand, he also suggests in *Being and Time* that it is possible to achieve, through existential analysis that moves beyond the anxiety typical of Dasein to an authentic, 'disinterested' answer to the question of the meaning of Being. Several of Heidegger's interpreters have attempted to say that his was a short-lived flirtation with Nazism, later corrected, that left little mark on his thought. John Macquarrie, for example – the theologian who co-translated the English edition of *Being and Time* I have been using – writes that although Heidegger 'was a firm supporter of the party, he did not share in its fanatical excesses. In any case, he very soon became disillusioned', which leads Macquarrie to deride as 'quite unscrupulous' attempts to 'discredit' Heidegger on account of his Nazi connections.[95] To my mind this is wholly inadequate; it neglects both the *extent* and the *duration* of Heidegger's Nazism.[96] More troublingly, it fails adequately to grasp the historical contingency of ideas and the consequent blurriness of the edges between life and thought. Of course it matters that Heidegger was a Nazi because Heidegger's life was the 'sphere of the familiar' in which his ideas came to presence. But that is no reason to dismiss him, and in this Macquarrie is right: one must weigh the texts.

In this study I have attempted to weigh Heidegger's and Bonhoeffer's work in the scales and found both differences and resemblances – perhaps more of the latter than previous readings may have led us to expect. In my view, Bonhoeffer is right to think it axiomatic that theology does not take its lead from any philosophy. But that is no reason for theologians not to read philosophy with interest and with profit, especially where, as is the case with Heidegger, so much of his thinking is in dialogue with theology: as Fergus Kerr observes, 'almost every philosophical innovation in *Sein und Zeit* may easily be traced to a theological source'.[97] I have suggested that in the end, Heidegger's legacy in Bonhoeffer's theology may not lie so much in his 'close reading' of *Being and Time* in the early 1930s, but in certain stylistic and methodological features of the *Christology* lectures. It is difficult to demonstrate conclusively whether this suggestion arises from exegesis or eisegesis. Yet the possibility alone conjures the thought that in May 1933, the month that Martin Heidegger was installed as Rector of Freiburg University and,

---

[95]   John Macquarrie, *Martin Heidegger* (London, 1968). See also Walter Biemel, *Martin Heidegger: An Illustrated Study* (London, 1973), p. 150: 'the political error was of short duration ... it is superficial to pounce on it in order to discredit Heidegger'. For a lucid short study, see Jeff Collins, *Heidegger and the Nazis* (Cambridge, 2000).

[96]   This is painfully clear in the interview Heidegger gave to *Der Spiegel* on 23 September 1966 and which was published on 31 May 1976. During the interview Heidegger is unedifyingly defensive, evasive and dissimulating with regard to his earlier support for Nazism.

[97]   Fergus Kerr, *Immortal Longings* (London, 1997), p. 47.

amidst swastikas and a loud chorus of '*Sieg Heil*', was delivering the infamous Rectorial address that lent intellectual credence to the Nazi revolution, a junior *Privatdozent* in Berlin University may have been sublimating the great professor's phenomenological method in order, against the *Verführer*, to proclaim 'Jesus is Lord.'

PART IV
Taking Stock

Chapter 11
Reading Bonhoeffer in Britain

Und so darf man jetzt noch weniger nach England gehen? Was in aller Welt sollen und wollen Sie dort drüben? ... ich kann Ihnen schon nicht ausdrücklich und eindringlich genug aussprechen, daß Sie nach Berlin und nicht nach London gehören.

(Karl Barth to Bonhoeffer, 20 November 1933)[1]

One of the most famous exchanges in British crime fiction occurs in Sir Arthur Conan Doyle's story 'The Silver Blaze'. In the final denouement Sherlock Holmes is interrogated about the clues that led him to solve the crime:

> 'Is there any point to which you would wish to draw my attention?'
> 'To the curious incident of the dog in the night time.'
> 'The dog did nothing in the night-time.'
> 'That was the curious incident', remarked Holmes.[2]

The story of reading Bonhoeffer in Britain resembles the curious incident of a dog that didn't bark. Relative to the United States, to East and West Germany, or even to South Africa, the resonance of Bonhoeffer's life and thought with British theology and Church life has been muted. No leading British theologian stands out as an interpreter of Bonhoeffer and attempts by Bonhoeffer enthusiasts to draw him to the attention of academy and Church have sometimes felt like uphill struggles. Karl Barth's judgement seems characteristically acute: Bonhoeffer belongs to Berlin and not in London. That this should be so is in one respect surprising. Bonhoeffer was a committed Anglophile.[3] He lived in Britain during a formative period in his career and made several other significant visits. Some of the key relationships of his life were with Britons. His last known earthly message, as he was being led off to Flossenbürg concentration camp for trial and execution, was passed via an Englishman to an Englishman.[4] But in another respect the relative lack of impact made by Bonhoeffer in Britain is perhaps predictable because the British – or more accurately the English – have a history of being bad at doctrinal

---

[1]   DBW 13, p. 33; Eng. tr: 'So it is even less the time to go to England! What in the world are you supposed to be doing or hoping to do there? ... I cannot tell you explicitly and urgently enough that you belong to Berlin and not in London', DBWE 13, p. 41.

[2]   Arthur Conan Doyle, 'Adventure 1: The Silver Blaze', *The Memoirs of Sherlock Holmes*.

[3]   On this see Keith Clements, *Bonhoeffer and Britain* (London, 2006).

[4]   See DB-EB, p. 927.

theology. To explain this last remark, and by means of this explanation to begin to give an account of receptions of Bonhoeffer in Britain, it will help to sketch out some of the factors shaping British ecclesial life which, in turn, have made departments of theology and religious studies in Britain what they are.

Why Are the English Bad at Theology?

The most important fact to take note of is that the United Kingdom is not one nation but several. All of the nations that make up the United Kingdom – England, Northern Ireland, Scotland and Wales – have distinct histories, which include distinct Church histories that have led to contrasting national patterns of Church life and tradition. This might seem too obvious a point to mention, were it not for the fact that many outside the United Kingdom seem unaware of it.[5] Getting some sense of this complexity matters for the purposes of this chapter because it accounts for differences between the ways the English and the Welsh on the one hand, and the Scottish on the other, have regarded dogmatic (or systematic) theology in general and continental dogmatic (or systematic) theology in particular.

Until quite recently Scottish religious and political life has been characterised by endemic religious sectarianism. The conflict between Roman Catholic and Reformed traditions in Scotland extends from the Reformation almost to the present day.[6] The bitterness of this religious conflict was the decisive factor in Scottish political life until well after the upheavals of the mid-seventeenth century usually and erroneously called the English Civil War. The consequences for Scottish theology are several. The Presbyterian Church of Scotland is the result of centuries of polemical exchange in which religious views made a decisive difference. In such circumstances theological study is taken very seriously. Today, Scottish theology retains a strong confessional identity. It is perhaps to guard this identity, that the imposing figure of John Knox, one of Calvin's most ardent followers, stands watch in the entrance to New College, the Divinity Faculty

---

[5] The habit, in both the United States and Germany, of using the name of one nation (England) to designate the whole of the United Kingdom, is one indicator of this lack of attention to the complexity of cultural and religious life in the United Kingdom.

[6] Religious sectarianism has been one of Scotland's most successful exports: the migration in the 16th and 17th centuries of Scottish Presbyterians to Ulster lies at the root of religious conflict in Northern Ireland. The depth of this sectarianism is still evident in the divide between Glasgow Celtic football club (Catholic) and Glasgow Rangers (Presbyterian), which, until very recently, frequently led to violence in both Glasgow and Northern Ireland whenever the sides met. This is a conflict in which I have a modest interest. My paternal ancestry is Glaswegian and one of my Scottish forbears, a Presbyterian, was one of the many Scots who fought on the English side against the largely Catholic feudal levies of Prince Charles Stuart at the Battle of Culloden in 1746, which ended the Jacobite revolt.

of the University of Edinburgh. The strongly confessional character of Scottish theology also accounts for the links that Scottish theologians have maintained with continental theology. It was entirely of a piece with this history that Scottish theologians took the lead in translating Karl Barth's *Church Dogmatics* and it is no accident that one of the the leading journals of systematic theology in the English-speaking world is the *Scottish Journal of Theology*.

In England and Wales the Reformation took a very different course. English Protestantism was from the outset a unique and complex fusion of Lutheran, Reformed and Catholic traditions within the Church of England, a national Church established by law, in which the English monarch was (and is) Supreme Governor of the Church of England and Defender of the Faith. The history of the Church of England is one in which these respective theological traditions ebb and flow. In the nineteenth century, for example, the Oxford Movement, led inter alia by John Henry Newman, attempted to re-form the Anglican Church by calling it back to its Catholic roots. One view of the English Reformation, still widely retailed, is that it was chiefly a practical political affair led by Henry VIII's desire for male heir. In fact, the Reformation in England was heatedly theological. In 1553 when the Roman Catholic Queen Mary came to the English throne, Thomas Cranmer (Archbishop of Canterbury), Nicholas Ridley (Bishop of London) and Hugh Latimer (Bishop of Worcester) were tried in Oxford for disbelieving the doctrine of Transubstantiation. Found guilty, Ridley and Latimer were burnt at the stake in October 1555. Several months later Archbishop Cranmer, who originally recanted, followed them to their dreadful fate. Well into the nineteenth century such convinced Protestantism was essential to the project of forging a united British identity.[7]

The mix of English and Welsh Christianity was added to in the seventeenth century by the rise of dissenting Protestant traditions, and in the eighteenth century by the evangelical revival whose most lasting product was the Methodist Church. In contrast to most of continental Europe, these dissenting traditions were numerically and culturally significant; and consequently the Anglican Church held no monopoly on English or Welsh religious life. Until the late nineteenth century, the Anglican Church did, however, monopolise theology in the only English/ Welsh Universities of Oxford and Cambridge. Until the late nineteenth century (with the foundation of the universities of Durham and London) and the beginning of the twentieth century (with the creation of several new universities) English and Welsh theology was therefore Anglican. When this stranglehold was broken, the new departments of theology self-consciously reflected the denominational diversity of English and Welsh religious life by being non-confessional, and this has continued to be the case. The rise of the social sciences swept across Britain in the 1960s and led to the formation of a number of departments of religious studies in contrast to existing departments of theology. For several decades these two

---

[7] See, on this, Linda Colley, *Britons: Forging the Nation 1707–1837* (New Haven, 1992).

approaches to religion – social scientific and theological– coexisted in an uneasy tension. Increasingly, however, the disciplines have united to form departments of theology and religious studies in which confessional theology, social scientific study of religion, and the study of other faiths, are carried out in one department or faculty.

What are the consequences of these colourful theological and ecclesiastical tapestries for the receptions of Bonhoeffer in England and Wales? The exclusion of (male) members (women were of course excluded until the late nineteenth century on account of their gender) of the 'Free Churches'[8] from the English universities created a theological skill deficit from which, at least in terms of doctrinal theology,[9] they have perhaps never fully recovered. But the most significant consequence, for our purposes, has been, as a leading Anglican theologian, Bishop Stephen Sykes has put it, that 'Anglicans are not supposed to know about, or to be interested in, systematic theology'.[10] In making a case for the theological integrity of Anglicanism, Sykes nonetheless concedes that there are three reasons why Anglicans have traditionally neglected doctrine. Firstly, Anglicans have tended to justify 'the position of the Anglican church more on practical than on theoretical grounds'. Secondly, 'the circumstances of the establishment of theological faculties in the universities of England have led to the neglect of systematic theology especially ecclesiology, compared with the development of historical and philosophical theology'. Finally, tensions between Anglo-Catholic and evangelical traditions in Anglicanism in the nineteenth century tended to keep Anglicans away from controversial doctrinal matters such as ecclesiology in order to keep the communion intact.[11] In English and Welsh departments and faculties of theology in the second half of the twentieth century, therefore, academic theology has been concerned with a non-denominational approach to theology in which doctrine has primarily been studied on the basis of pre-Reformation sources common to all participating traditions. The influence of the British empirical tradition helped to underwrite this approach by focusing on textual and philosophical study.

To sum up: a distinction needs to be made between theology as it has been conducted in Scotland and theology as it has been conducted in England and Wales. The former context has been marked by a strong confessional identity and by a healthy tradition of doctrinal thought that has been receptive to influences from continental theology. The latter context is more confessionally mixed and has tended to be less receptive to doctrinal influences from continental Europe.

---

[8]   The usual, if debilitating, euphemism used to denote churches such as the Methodist Church, the Baptist Church and the English Presbyterian churches.

[9]   The *free churches* have had, nonetheless, a strong record of producing leading historical theologians and biblical scholars.

[10]   Stephen Sykes, *The Integrity of Anglicanism* (London, 1978), p. ix. See also Peter Sedgwick, 'Anglicanism', pp. 178–93, in David F. Ford with R. Muers (eds), *The Modern Theologians* (Oxford, 2005).

[11]   Sykes, *Anglicanism*, pp. 76ff.

Bonhoeffer and the British[12]

Bonhoeffer's own inclinations were almost entirely towards English Anglicanism. Somewhat in awe of the Anglican establishment, he tended to overestimate the influence of the Church of England on British political life, inflating the significance of the presence in the second parliamentary chamber, the House of Lords, of the *Lords Spiritual*, the senior Church of England bishops. Bonhoeffer first visited England in 1931 as a youth delegate to meetings of the World Alliance for Promoting International Friendship through the Churches. Following preliminary meetings for youth and student delegations on the south coast, Bonhoeffer travelled to Cambridge, where he stayed in one of the two Anglican seminaries in the town, Ridley Hall (named after one of the three Oxford Protestant martyrs). This was not his first encounter with British theology: at Union Seminary in New York Bonhoeffer had been taught by John Moffatt and by the Scottish theologian John Baillie (who may have been the first Briton to employ a citation from Bonhoeffer's *Act and Being* in a book published in 1939).[13]

In October 1933 Bonhoeffer accepted a position as pastor to St George's United German congregation in Sydenham and St Paul's German Reformed Church in Aldgate. He embraced London, finding out quickly the best restaurants to eat in and making the most of London's galleries, museums and theatres. With a colleague, Julius Rieger, Bonhoeffer also familiarised himself with patterns of English social and pastoral work, for example by visiting Dr Barnardo's 'children's village' at Barkingside.[14] Perhaps fortuitously, Bonhoeffer's letter to Barth informing him of his decision to go to England was delayed in the post. Barth's reply,[15] when it arrived, was so stinging that Bonhoeffer showed it to his father for a professional psychiatric opinion. The 18 months during which Bonhoeffer served in London were the most significant in the Church struggle and Barth instructed Bonhoeffer to stop playing Elijah under the juniper tree or Jonah under the gourd and to return to the battle front. To an extent, Bonhoeffer was able to carry the Church struggle with him to England. He was instrumental in forming a very nearly united alliance of the German congregations in England in support of the nascent Confessing Church. By exercising influence through his ecumenical contacts, he also scored a meaningful publicity goal when the Archbishop of Canterbury, Cosmo Gordon Lang, declined to meet Joachim Hossenfelder, leader of the German Christians, while on a trip to woo Anglican support in 1933 (Bonhoeffer, however, was himself invited to Lambeth Palace to meet the Archbishop).

Towards the end of Bonhoeffer's London pastorate, when he had been appointed to direct one of the new Confessing Church seminaries, Bonhoeffer made a number

---

[12]   In this section I am indebted to Clements, *Britain*.
[13]   Clements, *Britain*, p. 9.
[14]   Ibid., p. 25.
[15]   DBWE 13, pp. 39–41.

of visits to religious communities and theological colleges in England,[16] including Woodbrooke, a Quaker house at Selly Oak in Birmingham, Richmond Methodist Theological College in south London, and the Anglican communities of the Society of St John the Evangelist at Cuddesdon near Oxford, and the Community of the Resurrection at Mirfield. These visits left deep impressions on Bonhoeffer and did much to shape his thinking about life together.

Among the relationships formed or deepened by Bonhoeffer during his London pastorate, two stand out. The first of these was with the Scottish lay theologian and ecumenist J.H.Oldham (1874–1969).[17] A year before he met him, Oldham had read Bonhoeffer's dissertation *Akt und Sein*. They met on several occasions and Oldham helped Bonhoeffer find resources to support German refugees who, from 1933, began arriving in England and he pumped Bonhoeffer for information and insight in relation to the German situation. Bonhoeffer's leading friend in England was, however, undoubtedly George Bell, Bishop of Chichester (1883–1958).[18] A month after his arrival in London Bonhoeffer (after enquiring whether he would need to bring a dinner jacket!)[19] travelled to Chichester to spend a couple of days in the Bishop's Palace in Chichester. Bell, who came to refer affectionately to Bonhoeffer and his friend Franz Hildebrandt as 'my boys', famously relied on them as his main points of access to German politics and to the Church struggle. These and other relationships with Britons continued to play a significant role for Bonhoeffer even after his return to Germany, not least in easing the emigration to England of his twin Sabine, her husband Gerhard Leibholz and their daughters in 1938. Bonhoeffer's last visit to England, on his return from America in 1939, included meetings with Sabine and with George Bell. Clements's judgement on the importance of Bonhoeffer's sojourn amongst the English is a just one: 'the engagement of Bonhoeffer with the British scene and with British people was of central significance to him throughout the last fourteen years of his life … Yet it has not generally been highlighted as fully as it deserves'.[20]

British Reception of Bonhoeffer

Any division into periods or phases of the reception of Bonhoeffer's legacy in Britain is bound to be arbitrary. In identifying four phases in the British reception of Bonhoeffer I am imposing a tidy filing system on a complex process in which

---

[16] See Clements, *Britain*, pp.77–87, where these visits are narrated in more detail than in Bethge's biography.

[17] For a biography of this leading figure in the ecumenical movement see Keith Clements, *Faith of the Frontier: A Life of J.H. Oldham* (Edinburgh and Geneva, 1999).

[18] For an accessible study of Bell's role see Edwin Robertson, *Unshakeable Friend: George Bell and the German Churches* (London, 1995).

[19] Clements, *Britain*, p. 31.

[20] Ibid., p. ix.

there have often been exceptions that buck the trends I am sketching. But as a heuristic device, the following divisions may serve to give some impression of the ways British readings of Bonhoeffer have developed from 1945 until this, the centenary year of Bonhoeffer's birth.

Bonhoeffer as Spiritual Writer: 1945–1963

In the immediate post-war period, Bonhoeffer's role was twofold. On the one hand, the dramatic story of his involvement in the anti-Nazi resistance was used by those most interested in reconciliation between Germany and Britain to make Britons aware of another Germany to that they had encountered in six years of war-time propaganda. Bonhoeffer fitted the bill perfectly: young, courageous, good and humane, he was from the outset the perfect posthumous ambassador for the rehabilitation of Germany in Britain. Though led by some of his closest friends in Britain – George Bell, Julius Rieger and Franz Hildebrandt – there is a whiff of this need for ambassadors for reconciliation about the memorial service for Bonhoeffer held in London and broadcast on the BBC World Service on 27 July 1945, which proved to be the medium through which Bonhoeffer's parents learned for sure that he and his brother Klaus were dead. That the first post-war appearance of Bonhoeffer in Britain was in a liturgical (not an academic) context set the tone for the years that were to follow. For a decade Bonhoeffer's impact was primarily as a *spiritual* writer. The clue to where interest in Bonhoeffer was initially focused lies in the order in which his writings were translated into English. The first book to appear was an abridged translation of *Nachfolge* translated into English as *The Cost of Discipleship* (a title it retained until the publication of the critical edition of the Dietrich Bonhoeffer Works appeared in 2001). A complete edition did not appear until 1959. Next to arrive was an abridged edition, in 1953, of *Letters and Papers from Prison*[21] whose English title, once more, differed from the German original. A year later, *Life Together* was published. In 1955 an English translation of the first edition of the *Ethics* came into print.

It took 16 years from his death for the first of Bonhoeffer's more academic books to be translated. *Act and Being* was published in 1961, followed in 1963 by *Sanctorum Communio*. The individual responsible for many of these translations was a Scottish Presbyterian, Ronald Gregor Smith, who was editor of the SCM press from 1950 until his appointment as Professor of Divinity at Glasgow University in 1956.

---

[21] Because this text is so well known by this original title, the decision was taken to retain it in the Dietrich Bonhoeffer Works in English, vol. 8.

Bonhoeffer as Sexy Sixties Icon: 1963–1970

The great tsunami in British readings of Bonhoeffer, and indeed in British post-war theology, took place in 1963 with the publication of J.A.T. Robinson's *Honest to God*.[22] Even before the publication of this volume, John Robinson (1919–1983) enjoyed a certain notoriety. In 1960 he appeared in a groundbreaking court case to defend the publication of an unexpurgated version of D.H. Lawrence's controversial novel *Lady Chatterley's Lover*, describing the sexual relations between Lady Chatterley and her husband's gamekeeper as akin to holy communion, thereby earning himself archiepiscopal censure. A competent if idiosyncratic New Testament scholar, Robinson was Dean of Clare College, Cambridge, before his appointment in 1959 as Anglican Bishop of Woolwich. He wrote *Honest to God* while laid out by a painful back problem, intending it as little more than a theological clearing of the throat. But when an article summarising the book's argument was published in *The Observer* newspaper under the headline 'Our Image of God must Go', controversy erupted. It had undergone 12 reprints within 3 years – over a million copies. Robinson received over 4,000 letters about it; he never lived it down.

Honest to God is a short book – less than 150 pages. It called for a radical recasting of Christian faith 'in the process of which the most fundamental categories of theology – of God, of the supernatural, and of religion itself– must go into the melting'.[23] The means by which Robinson began this recasting was a dialogue with three German theologians: Rudolf Bultmann, Paul Tillich and Dietrich Bonhoeffer. His use of Bonhoeffer's writings was limited to the prison letters, with no attempt to place Bonhoeffer's characterisation of Jesus as 'the man for others' or of post-war Christianity in terms of 'worldly holiness' in the context of Bonhoeffer's earlier writings. Most professional theologians disliked the book, seeing in it a clumsy conflation of three quite distinct theologians into a shallow populist project. Writing to his old friend Rudolf Bultmann in the year of the book's publication, Karl Barth represented the views of many when he rejected it as 'a document of the scandal of our times' and compared its origin to the act of a man who went and drew off the froth from three full glasses of beer (with the inscriptions R.B., P.T. and D.B.), and made out that the resultant mixture was the finally discovered theological elixir, as which it was consumed by thousands and thousands of buyers.[24]

The judgement was true, but harsh. Robinson was certainly premature and possibly hubristic, even in the interrogative mood, to hail his insights as *The New Reformation?*,[25] but he had done more than any individual for decades to get lay

---

[22]   John A.T. Robinson, *Honest to God* (London, 1963).

[23]   Ibid., p.7.

[24]   *Karl Barth ~ Rudolf Bultmann Letters 1922–1966*, ed. Bernd Jaspert (Grand Rapids, 1981), letter of 28 December 1963, p. 111.

[25]   John A.T. Robinson, *The New Reformation?* (London, 1965).

people in Britain talking about theology. The book was received as if it were a permit to question and to explore. Today, one still meets people for whom *Honest to God* was the book that kept them from leaving the Church.

The impact on the reception of Bonhoeffer in Britain was both immediate and lasting. Bonhoeffer swept across the landscape of the British churches and British theology. By associating him with an ill-defined project of radical Christianity, Robinson created an impression of Bonhoeffer as a prophet of a cultural and theological sixties revolution. For Bonhoeffer studies, there have been two lasting effects. On the one hand, Robinson helped make Bonhoeffer popular in radically inclined sections of the British Churches. On the other hand, he helped to turn serious scholars off Bonhoeffer for good. For some, the effect of *Honest to God* was to link Bonhoeffer with a particular moment (the early sixties) and a particular theological fashion (radical liberalism): when the moment passed reading Bonhoeffer felt outmoded. For many more, Robinson helped create a trend for reading Bonhoeffer's legacy through the lens of his prison letters resulting in some troubling distortions.

To capitalise on Bonhoeffer's popularity and to correct some of the most egregious misappropriations of his life and thought a number of translations began to make available in English advances in German Bonhoeffer scholarship. In 1967 Ronald Gregor Smith published a volume of essays containing translations of key essays from the four volume collection *Die Mündige Welt* (published between 1955 and 1963), as well as from other sources, expressly to open his thinking up to readers 'innocent of theological nuances, but open to the realities with which theology is concerned'.[26]

Other essay collections and monographs concerned with Bonhoeffer of course appeared, but these were typically English versions of texts that had appeared elsewhere in the English-speaking world. An even more important contribution was made by Edwin Robertson, who began to edit and translate three volumes containing extracts, with short contextualising introductions, from Bonhoeffer's *Gesammelte Schriften*.[27] The end of this phase of reading Bonhoeffer was marked by the translation (again under the indefatigable direction of Robertson) of a slightly abridged edition of Eberhard Bethge's *Dietrich Bonhoeffer: A Biography*. Bethge's volume made an incalculable contribution to Bonhoeffer scholarship throughout the world. In Britain, it provided a solid foundation for any reader who wished to set Bonhoeffer in his historical, cultural and theological context.

---

[26] *World Come of Age*, ed. Ronald Gregor Smith (London, 1967), p. 9.

[27] *No Rusty Swords*, ed. E. Robertson (London, 1965); *The Way to Freedom*, ed. E. Robertson (London, 1966) and *True Patriotism*, ed. E. Robertson (London, 1973).

Bonhoeffer Lost: 1970–1998

In spite of the arrival in English of Bethge's biography – the single most significant secondary volume on Bonhoeffer – after the burst of energy that had followed Robinson's *Honest to God*, with some notable exceptions, serious attention to Bonhoeffer slipped from 1970. Bonhoeffer continued to appear somewhere on the curricula of most departments of theology in Britain, but there was no duplication of the prominence he was being given in some courses on the other side of the Atlantic. Bonhoeffer was accepted into the pantheon of leading twentieth-century theologians: for example, David F. Ford's widely used textbook *The Modern Theologians*[28] included Bonhoeffer with Barth, T.F. Torrance and Jüngel in a section headed 'corresponding to revelation'. But by and large theological fashions had moved on – for example to theologies of liberation.

A personal recollection may serve to illustrate the British lack of interest in Bonhoeffer in this period. In June 1988, as I was about to begin doctoral research on Bonhoeffer in the University of Cambridge, my supervisor (Stephen Sykes) sent me off to the fifth International Bonhoeffer Conference in Amsterdam where he hoped I might meet other British researchers working on Bonhoeffer. In the event, of the 126 participants, only 8 attended from Britain, of whom, including myself, 3 were graduate students; one of these, the late Jörg Rades, was German.[29]

Keith Clements, a Baptist theologian, provides an exception to the rule. In 1984 Clements published *A Patriotism for Today: Love of Country in Dialogue with the Witness of Dietrich Bonhoeffer*.[30] In 1982 the Falklands War released a burst of patriotism in Britain. In the middle of the war John Paul II made his first papal visit to Britain, where he prayed with Archbishop Robert Runcie at Canterbury Cathedral and lit candles in memory of several modern martyrs, including Bonhoeffer. Clements's book reflected on 'true patriotism' in dialogue with Bonhoeffer. Clements wore his considerable scholarly skills lightly and, though pitched at Church and world more than at the academy, it is an important book that is still worth reading.[31]

---

[28]   *The Modern Theologians*, ed. David F. Ford, 1st edn in 2 vols (Oxford: Blackwell, 1989). The latest edition, the 3rd, is: *The Modern Theologians*, in one vol., ed. David F. Ford with R. Muers (Oxford: Blackwell, 2005).

[29]   Following that meeting, an attempt was made to revive a British section of the *International Bonhoeffer Society*, but this too 'enjoyed' limited success before it too fell into abeyance.

[30]   First published by Bristol Baptist College (Bristol, 1984) and reissued by Collins (London, 1986).

[31]   In a similar vein see the collected essays in Keith Clements, *What Freedom? The Persistent Challenge of Dietrich Bonhoeffer* (Bristol, 1990).

Bonhoeffer Regained? 1998–

In 1995, as an extensive programme of renovation at Westminster Abbey concluded, a decision was taken to fill a number of niches intended for statues of saints that had remained unoccupied since the building of the West Front in the fifteenth century. Ten of these plinths, those immediately above the West door, were filled by statues of twentieth-century martyrs representing all who have died as a result of persecution and oppression in that most bloody century. The statues were unveiled in 1998; one was of Dietrich Bonhoeffer. The statue visibly signalled a revival of interest in Bonhoeffer in the lead-up to the centenary of his birth.

At the same time as Bonhoeffer's statue was being unveiled in the heart of the English ecclesiastical establishment, there were several indicators that his theological legacy was being explored with renewed energy. In part, this (modest) renewal of interest was the natural consequence of the slow absorption by British theologians of the new critical edition of the *Dietrich Bonhoeffer Werke* that had begun to appear in German in 1986. This was perhaps boosted when, in 1996, the first volumes of an English critical edition began to appear. The publication of *The Cambridge Companion* to *Dietrich Bonhoeffer*[32] was further indicative of renewed academic interest. Though it was edited by a South African and only 2 of its 14 essays were written by Britons, by including Bonhoeffer in a major international series dealing with only the most significant thinkers and movements, the volume represented recognition of Bonhoeffer by a leading British academic publisher.

Also in 1999, the same publisher issued David F. Ford's *Self and Salvation*[33] which includes a study of Bonhoeffer by one of the country's most prominent dogmatic theologians. In *Self and Salvation* Ford seeks to gain access to the 'range of salvation' which is as 'broad as creation' primarily by discussing 'the self in transformation'.[34] In 'Polyphonic living: Dietrich Bonhoeffer' Ford identifies in Bonhoeffer an exemplar of the book's main themes. The essay sets out from the 'crosslights' cast by a comparison between Bonhoeffer and Thérèse of Lisieux. In both, Ford concludes:

> there is an intrinsic connection between the abundance (of God's generosity and love) and their reserve. Anything so rich, so full of love, joy, pain, and responsibility cannot simply be laid out for immediate inspection and comprehension. Above all, God cannot be shared directly or comprehensively. In both Bonhoeffer and Thérèse we find disciplines which serve the secret of the

---

[32]   ed. John de Gruchy (Cambridge, 1999).
[33]   David F. Ford, *Self and Salvation: Being Transformed* (Cambridge, 1999).
[34]   Ibid., p. 3.

crucified and risen Jesus Christ in his relationship to the whole reality, which Christians believe to be the mystery of God and of humanity together.[35]

The essay itself, richly suggestive as it is, is not perhaps so significant for the purpose of this chapter; what is significant is the way that Ford's thinking about Bonhoeffer has arisen from and shaped conversations with a new generation of systematic theologians who have devoted all or part of their doctoral research to Bonhoeffer. Several of those influenced by Ford have subsequently published significant studies of Bonhoeffer including Paul Janz, Rachel Muers and Ann Nickson; with further students currently working on Bonhoeffer in Cambridge, academic attention to Bonhoeffer is as lively now in England as it has ever been.[36] These are very diverse studies, but what they have in common is that they seek not to offer some new interpretive key to reading Bonhoeffer, but rather, that they attempt to bring Bonhoeffer's theology into dialogue with pressing theological themes, such as holiness, the nature of reason or freedom. A similar approach characterised a major academic conference in January 2006 hosted by Harris Manchester College, Oxford, on 'Bonhoeffer through the lens of his poetry'. Bonhoeffer's centenary was further marked by a number of public lectures[37] and publications,[38] further suggesting that Bonhoeffer is being treated with greater theological attention than for some years.

Reading Bonhoeffer Today: Challenges and Opportunities

In the last sections of this chapter I want briefly and from my own perspective to point towards one of several challenges (or opportunities) for reading Bonhoeffer in Britain now and in the immediate future. These are interesting times for the disciplines of theology and religious studies in Britain. The Anglican Communion was until recently led by Rowan Williams (who stood down as Archbishop of Canterbury in January, 2013), one of Britain's most original and wide-ranging theologians; he marked the anniversary of Bonhoeffer's birth by preaching the opening sermon at the International Bonhoeffer Congress in the

---

[35]   Ibid., p. 264. One theme in the essay, holiness, is further amplified in David F. Ford, 'Bonhoeffer, Holiness and Ethics', in Stephen Barton (ed.), *Holiness Past and Present* (London, 2003), pp. 361–80.

[36]   For published work, see e.g. Paul Janz, *God, the Mind's Desire: Reference, Reason and Christian Thinking* (Cambridge, 2004); Rachel Muers, *Keeping God's Silence* (Oxford, 2005); Ann Nickson, *Bonhoeffer on Freedom: Courageously Grasping Reality* (Aldershot, 2002).

[37]   e.g., the Hugh Price Hughes lectures at the West London Mission, February–June 2006.

[38]   e.g., *Studies in Christian Ethics* was one of a number of journals that devoted an issue to the centenary (December 2005, Vol. 18), SAGE publications.

University of Wrocław.[39] Well over half of all pupils now sit one of their GCSE examinations in Religious Studies and, in 2005, for the second consecutive year the largest rise in 'Advanced Level' entries was for Religious Studies – up by 16.9 per cent on 2004: the study of religion in Britain seems to be in good shape.[40] This ought to be good news not only for academic theology, but also for the churches. In practice, however, Britain may be witnessing a widening gap between religious communities and the academic departments that study religion and theology. Most school pupils who opt to sit for examinations in Religious Studies are not actively involved in a religious community, and many are unreceptive to the complex orthodoxies of institutional religion. Moreover, as pressures on universities to compete for funding have increased in recent years, partly as a result of a substantial reduction in the proportion of student fees paid by the local or national government, many departments of theology and religious studies fight for their survival by prioritising research. In contrast, in church institutions that train students for ordained ministry (many now train part-time), teaching loads are comparatively heavy and research leave comparatively infrequent so staff involved with training for ordained ministry risk falling out of touch with the latest developments in theology. The average time ordinands spend in theological education has also dropped significantly as the average age of ordinands has risen. All of this contributes to the creation of a growing gap between Church and academy in which the more technical research undertaken by university theologians is increasingly inaccessible to most in the churches, and the theological questions vexing typical churchgoers are increasingly remote from theologians in the university. Among twentieth-century theologians, Dietrich Bonhoeffer's theology has as much potential as any to assist in bridging this gap. Richly and profoundly theological, Bonhoeffer was also rooted to an unparalleled degree in the life of the Church and the world. Bonhoeffer's 'this worldly' theology is one in which one lives 'fully in the midst of life's tasks, questions, successes and failures, experiences and perplexities – then one takes seriously no longer one's own sufferings but rather the suffering of God in the world. Then one stays awake with Christ in Gethsemane.'[41] Such theology is capable of integrating life in academy, church and world: it is desperately needed.

---

[39]   For the text of his address, see: http://www.archbishopofcanterbury.org/sermons_speeches/060203.htm/ Accessed 15 July 2006.

[40]   That this should be the case – given trends of declining attendance in British churches – cannot simply be explained by heightened awareness of the geopolitical and psychological importance of religion following the events of 11 September 2001 and the London bombings of 7 July 2005, since the rising numbers of those studying religion predate those events. One possible explanation lies in interest among the young in deep philosophical and personal questions and a decline in the number of contexts in which they can explore them.

[41]   DBWE 8, p. 486.

Index